Praise for

THE MAN WHO BROKE CAPITALISM

"One of the most profound and impactful books that I've read in a very, very long time."

—Raj Sisodia,
founder of Conscious Capitalism

"[A] sharp, provocative book."

—*Financial Times*

"A vigorous argument for a more humane capitalism."

—*Kirkus Reviews*

"Full of color and vitriol, this is an incisive, eye-popping history."

—*Publishers Weekly*

"An indispensable history of how we wound up with a business culture that believed employees were owed nothing more than yesterday's paycheck. But David Gelles does not just sound the alarm. He contrasts this warped world view with a new emerging reality—accelerated by the pandemic—that puts the employee experience and well-being at the center of business priorities. A must-read for anyone who wants to say good-bye forever to a toxic chapter of American capitalism."

—Arianna Huffington,
founder and CEO, Thrive Global

"In vivid prose and reporting that lights up each page, Gelles probes how Jack Welch influenced a generation of business leaders to ignore the feelings of employees and the malign impact of corporate mergers, and how decisions made today might strangle a company's long-term health. This powerful book shows why GE and so many companies run by Welch's disciples have badly stumbled, along with Welch's reputation."

—Ken Auletta,
author of *Hollywood Ending*

"A compelling indictment of short-termism that offers an urgent call for business leaders at all levels to be responsible and care. Gelles clearly makes the case that business is more than for profit and that it is by doing good that you can do well, and provides us a roadmap for the way forward. An indispensable read for our time."

—Hubert Joly, former chairman and CEO,
Best Buy, and author of *The Heart of Business*

"Jack Welch is one of the more important political and business leaders in modern American history. His strategies destroyed a once-great company, and more broadly, he helped pave the way for the destruction of the American middle class and the erosion of American democracy. For years, the business press has lauded Welch's visionary spirit, but few reporters have ever asked what that vision was. With *The Man Who Broke Capitalism*, David Gelles has delivered a book that explains what we can learn from a man like Welch, as we try to restore the shattered society he left behind."

—Matt Stoller, author of *Goliath: The 100-Year
War Between Monopoly Power and Democracy*

"A robust and necessary portrait of a complex figure. A lesson in shareholder value vs. stakeholder value that will only become more relevant in the coming years."

—Scott Galloway, *New York Times*
bestselling author and serial entrepreneur

"A provocative page-turner that exposes the dark truths about Jack Welch, America's first celebrity CEO. After [his] building a sprawling global empire through unmanageable mergers, shady accounting, and heartless downsizing, with undue veneration and countless imitators, it's good to see Welch finally cut down to size."

—Jennifer Taub,
author of *Big Dirty Money*

THE MAN WHO BROKE CAPITALISM

How Jack Welch Gutted the Heartland
and Crushed the Soul of Corporate America—
and How to Undo His Legacy

DAVID GELLES

SIMON & SCHUSTER PAPERBACKS

New York   London   Toronto   Sydney   New Delhi

Simon & Schuster Paperbacks
An Imprint of Simon & Schuster, Inc.
1230 Avenue of the Americas
New York, NY 10020

First Simon & Schuster trade paperback edition May 2023

SIMON & SCHUSTER PAPERBACKS and colophon are registered trademarks of Simon & Schuster, Inc.

For information about special discounts for bulk purchases, please contact Simon & Schuster Special Sales at 1-866-506-1949 or business@simonandschuster.com.

The Simon & Schuster Speakers Bureau can bring authors to your live event. For more information or to book an event, contact the Simon & Schuster Speakers Bureau at 1-866-248-3049 or visit our website at www.simonspeakers.com.

Interior design by Joy O'Meara @ Creative Joy Designs

Manufactured in the United States of America

1 3 5 7 9 10 8 6 4 2

Library of Congress Control Number: 2022932424

ISBN 978-1-9821-7644-0
ISBN 978-1-9821-7642-6 (pbk)
ISBN 978-1-9821-7643-3 (ebook)

For my family,
with thanks for all they provide

CONTENTS

THE MAN WHO BROKE CAPITALISM

INTRODUCTION

To understand a civilization, consider its heroes. Ancient Egyptians glorified the pharaohs, intermediaries between gods and men. Romans celebrated their generals, who expanded the empire through conquests abroad. The Greeks had their philosophers, searching for the truth. Other great societies were defined by their poets, their painters, their sculptors, and composers. More recently, explorers, scientists, and civil rights leaders have emerged as the iconic figures of their eras. Our heroes reflect our collective aspirations, offering clues to our deepest desires, idealized behaviors, and societal priorities. They bend the arc of history, defining their times and influencing events long after they are gone. Generations from now, when future anthropologists try to make sense of this moment in the American experiment, looking to our idols for clues about our priorities, they will need to contend with a perplexing but undeniable fact: in America, we worship our bosses.

We put our chief executives up on pedestals, granting them wide latitude to influence our national discourse and endowing them with vast wealth while absolving them of accountability. We herald entrepreneurs and venture capitalists as our most brilliant minds, lionizing their achievements and celebrating increased shareholder value as if it were a major medical breakthrough. We elevate the richest among us to positions of moral authority, letting CEOs, not religious leaders or philosophers, shape our views on the fraught political and social issues of the day. We elect billionaires as mayors and private equity barons as senators, and have would-be monopolists for our most prominent philanthropists. Surveys routinely show that the public has more faith in CEOs than it does in politicians or priests, more confidence in corporations than in the government. Our faith in bosses is so absolute that we even elected a failed businessman who played a successful one on television as president of the United States.

Yet even when the results are disastrous, even when our heroes turn out to be crooks, we can't help but want for more. How could we not? In a nation made powerful by its staggering industriousness and titanic economy, captains of industry are the very embodiment of American success. CEOs as much as presidents have ushered us from one epoch to the next. Railroad tycoons and robber barons gave way to industrialists, who gave way to media moguls, who gave way to financiers, who gave way to technologists. And still, even in a society obsessed with successful businessmen, there is one CEO above all others who was revered as a cultural and economic hero in his own time, who radically transformed the world around him and continues to hold sway even after his demise, who seized on changes in the zeitgeist and used them to rewrite the rules of our economy: Jack Welch.

As chairman and chief executive of General Electric from 1981 to 2001, two decades that shaped the world we inhabit today, Welch exerted unmatched influence on American capitalism. In his heyday, as head of one of the country's most powerful companies, he was lauded as a visionary. He identified the promises of globalization and rapidly reshaped GE to compete on the world stage. He could see around corners and pushed GE into the media and finance industries at just the right time. Above all, he understood the power of the stock market, and used GE's might and complexity to reward those lucky enough to own the company's shares. The financial results he delivered were undeniably great. During his tenure, GE posted annualized share price growth of about 21 percent a year, far outpacing the S&P 500 even during a historic bull market. When Welch took over, GE was worth $14 billion. Two decades later, the company was worth $600 billion—the most valuable company in the world.

All that material success obscured darker truths. Welch was not, as he would have liked us to believe, a patrician steward of sound business judgment and good character. Nor was he just another skilled manager with a knack for dealmaking and a good golf game. Rather, he was hungry for power and thirsty for money, an ideological revolutionary who focused on maximizing profits at the expense of all else. The changes he unleashed at GE transformed the company founded by Thomas Edison from an admired industrial behemoth known for quality engineering and laudable business practices into a sprawling multinational conglomerate that paid little regard to its employees and was addicted to short-term profits. And we all went along for the ride.

For the fifty years before Welch took over, corporations, workers, and the government enjoyed a relatively harmonious equilibrium. Most companies paid decent wages, employees put in their time, just about everyone paid their taxes, regulations were accepted as necessary safeguards, and the government invested in things like education and infrastructure. It wasn't perfect, and there were certainly inequities, but it worked well for much of the twentieth century, giving rise to a diverse, thriving economy and a prosperous middle class.

Then in the 1970s, the established order came under attack. A cadre of economists including Milton Friedman reimagined the purpose of the corporation and its role in society, laying the philosophical groundwork for an upending of the economic order. In their view, companies ought to maximize profits for shareholders at any cost, markets should be free, governments should stay out of the way, and the rest of society ought to take care of itself. Their views were anathema to the postwar balance that seemed to be working so well, and at first they failed to gain traction. Indeed, the dream of unrestrained markets and a world where profits came first was so drastic that for a decade it remained almost entirely theoretical. There were policy papers, academic treatises, and speeches, and some of its chief proponents began ascending to positions of power. Yet by 1981, no one had truly put this philosophy to work. No one, that is, until Welch.

Some disruption was inevitable when Welch took over. All CEOs want to put their own mark on a company, and the world was rapidly changing in ways that would force GE to adapt, whoever was in charge. American corporations had grown complacent. Overseas competition was on the rise. Technology was upending everything from plastics to banking. Yet in responding to these challenges, Welch decided to take GE—the epitome of the benevolent postwar employer—in a sharp new direction. He embraced the strategies promulgated by the economic revolutionaries on the right, devised his own mercenary twists, and refashioned GE from the inside out.

Welch employed three main tools in his crusade: downsizing, dealmaking, and financialization. He is best known for the first of these. Upon taking over, he instituted a series of mass layoffs that destabilized the American working class. For generations, it was generally true that once you got a job at a company like GE, you could keep it until you retired. This was blasphemy to Welch. He found the notion that a company should be loyal to employees to be laughable, and he undertook a crusade to disabuse workers of the belief that GE owed them anything more than yesterday's wages. He fired workers by the thousands, convinced that a smaller head count was a desirable end in its own right. After all, he reckoned, a leaner workforce meant lower labor costs, which meant juicer profits, which meant a higher stock price. To codify this new, transactional relationship between employer and employee, Welch developed a new policy, colloquially known as "rank and yank." Each year, managers rated their employees. Those who were in the bottom 10 percent were let go.

When he couldn't fire workers outright, Welch devised other

ways to wash GE's hands of the responsibilities that come with being an employer. Welch championed offshoring and sent thousands of union jobs overseas to countries like Mexico, where labor was cheap. And he reveled in outsourcing, turning to other companies to provide back-office functions like accounting and printing. It was enough to earn him the nickname "Neutron Jack," a reference to the neutron bomb, which purportedly kills people while leaving buildings intact. Welch's affinity for downsizing, which his own employees called the "campaign against loyalty," fundamentally altered GE. No longer was it a model employer, the kind of company where successive genera-tions of machinists could prosper. Instead, it became the kind of place where even a long-tenured employee might find themselves suddenly out of a job just before retirement, a company where what mattered most was not the quality of its people, but the quantity of its profits.

The second main weapon Welch employed in his quest to make GE the world's most valuable company was dealmaking. Through compulsive mergers and acquisitions, he transformed GE from a proud domestic manufacturer to a cash-spewing collection of unre-lated businesses, unleashing an M&A boom that would extend well beyond GE and lead industries from media to finance to become more concentrated and less competitive. GE made nearly 1,000 acqui-sitions during Welch's tenure, spending some $130 billion buying up companies. At the same time, GE sold some 408 businesses for about $10.6 billion. No company had ever done so many deals so quickly. The biggest of these took GE far from its industrial roots. Often, the deals were disasters. Sometimes, Welch quickly sliced up the compa nies he bought, then sold them off for parts. Yet even when the results were less than optimal, dealmaking served several of Welch's greater goals. Welch wanted every business GE operated to be number one or number two in its respective category. If it couldn't achieve that, it would be jettisoned. "Fix it, close it, or sell it," he would say. By selling companies—even ones that were regarded as central to GE's identity—Welch was able to retain only what he believed were the most profitable businesses, even if they had little to do with GE's leg-acy manufacturing operations. And with his relentless acquisitions, he took out competitors and consolidated industries, gaining market share while pushing GE to expand in every direction imaginable.

The third dark art that Welch mastered was financialization. GE was an industrial company when Welch took over. By the time he retired, the company derived much of its profits from GE Capital, which was essentially a giant unregulated bank. Welch got the company into all manner of risky debt instruments, insurance products, and credit cards. The finance division became GE's center of gravity, ultimately accounting for 40 percent of revenues and 60 percent of profits. To Welch, it seemed easier—and cheaper—to make money through financial wizardry than by producing quality products. With so much money coursing through the finance division, Welch used it to his advantage, shifting zeros throughout a sprawling international web of subsidiaries, and extracting whatever he needed to meet or beat analysts' estimates for nearly eighty quarters in a row, an unprecedented run. Earnings targets were achieved using dubious accounting methods. Black box financial models and limited public disclosures afforded the public with little understanding of GE's inner workings. Yet quarter after quarter, the profits flowed, and Welch used them to reward shareholders with a gusher of buybacks and dividends.

All three of these tactics—downsizing, dealmaking, and financialization—served the same aim for Welch, aiding his endless quest to enrich his investors. If that meant cutting hundreds of thousands of jobs, so be it. If that meant companies were acquired and then sold for parts, c'est la vie. If it meant playing fast and loose with accounting rules, what was the harm? Welch had a lust for money, yes. He wanted GE to be as profitable as possible. But simply reducing what motivated Welch to greed is insufficient. He was possessed with a world-beating ambition, a drive to make his GE a company for the ages. He believed he had the skills, the means, and the divine right to make General Electric the greatest generator of profits in history, and he harbored extreme prejudice against anyone who doubted him, stood in his way, or couldn't contribute to his relentless pursuit of financial glory. Welch was the embodiment of the shareholder primacy dogma hatched by Milton Friedman, and for twenty years just about everything he did worked. GE did become the most valuable company on earth. GE shareholders were showered with riches. Welch was revered as the greatest CEO of all time.

Along the way, he elevated the role of the chief executive from that of a people manager to something closer to a pop star, chasing the limelight and mastering the art of self-promotion. The business press adored him, splashing his piercing eyes on magazine covers and chronicling GE's every move. Business schools treated Welch like an oracle, turning his strategies into case studies and curricula. Wall Street analysts marveled at his seemingly magical ability to hit the numbers, quarter after quarter. And though Welch didn't start a company or invent a breakthrough new product, he earned millions of dollars, then tens of millions of dollars, then hundreds of millions of dollars, his net worth finally topping out at nearly $1 billion, landing him on *Forbes*'s list of the 400 richest Americans. In retirement, GE picked up the tab for his apartment in the Trump International Hotel and Tower, his meals at Michelin starred restaurants, his floor seats to Knicks games, and more. Welch was the personification of American, alpha-male capitalism, a pin-striped conquistador with the spoils to prove it. His exploits were so over-the-top, his personal wealth so enormous, it was impossible for other executives not to try and emulate him. At the end of his illustrious career, *Fortune* magazine dubbed him "Manager of the Century."

That kind of success, over that long a run, made Welch singularly influential in the corridors of economic power. Most CEOs make a splash for a few years, then either retire or are pushed aside. Welch never went away. His reign atop GE spanned three decades and four U.S. presidents. A tenure that began during the uneven economy of the Reagan administration endured through Clinton-era globalization and the bursting of the dot-com bubble, ending just days before the terrorist attacks of September 11, 2001. He was the first celebrity CEO. Welch golfed with presidents and mingled with movie stars. His love life was tabloid fodder, and his gargantuan pay packages were glorified at a moment when conspicuous consumption was in vogue. His roaring success inspired countless imitators, as an entire generation of managers sought to emulate his techniques, his growth strategies, and his values. Without anyone quite realizing it was happening, Welch redefined how corporations measured success, setting the standard for a generation of business titans.

But while Welch made GE the most valuable company on earth, his strategies ultimately destroyed what he loved so dearly. Not long after he retired, GE fell into a spiral of decline set in motion by Welch's short-term decision-making. Within months of his departure, it became clear that GE was deeply troubled, and in a matter of years, the corporation was falling apart. His handpicked successor tried to replicate Welch's success by following the same playbook, but it was a losing strategy. Welch's underinvestment in research and development caught up with the company as it failed to introduce new, innovative products. A habit of incessant dealmaking resulted in a series of bad trades that burdened the company with money-losing divisions when it could least afford the losses. And the quest for ceaseless growth in the finance division led GE to become a major holder of subprime mortgages just in time for the financial crisis of 2008. At its nadir, GE needed a $139 billion rescue from the Obama administration and an eleventh-hour investment from Warren Buffett to stave off collapse. GE stock fell 80 percent in the years after Welch retired, becoming the worst performer in the Dow Jones Industrial Average. Finally, in 2021, executives announced a plan to break up GE, separating what was left of the company into three distinct corporations, and abandoning Welch's world-conquering aspirations once and for all.

Although Welch's legacy was tarnished by the collapse of GE, his worldview continues to shape much of corporate America to this day. The methods he devised nearly a half century ago are still in use, the priorities he established still shape decision-making in boardrooms across the country, and some of his disciples are still in charge of major multinational corporations. This enduring influence is a testament to the power of the man himself, but also to what he stood for, which we might call Welchism. The prevailing power dynamic of our economic age, Welchism has at its heart the conviction that companies must prioritize profits for shareholders above all else, that executives are entitled to enormous wealth and minimal accountability, and that everyday employees deserve nothing more than their last paycheck. Welchism ascribes moral worth to material success, bestowing millionaire CEOs with the veneer of virtue, almost entirely irrespective of their actions. It thrives on downsizing, dealmaking, and financialization. And the Welchist worldview adopts a Darwinian attitude toward the labor market, a smug conviction that those who don't make it are to blame for their own misfortune, that the poorest among us ultimately deserve their fate. The closest historical analog to Welchism is probably imperialism. The empires of yore had a comparable multinational reach to today's biggest corporations, a similar willingness to confer absolute power upon their rulers, and the same tendency to exploit their subjects. Yet unlike imperialism, which has largely faded into history, Welchism still thrives today. Forty years after Welch took power, his warped worldview is still shaping our economy in ways large and small.

In GE, Welch had the perfect apparatus to disseminate his new ideology. For much of the twentieth century, the company was a pioneer of organizational design and executive training. That continued under Welch. Not only did his underlings study his ways, parroting his mannerisms and internalizing his maxims, but they also went to what was known as GE University, a leafy campus where budding titans were sent to learn the ropes, and where Welch infected a new generation of business leaders with his values. In time, those executives went on to lead dozens of other major companies—including Boeing, 3M, Honeywell, Chrysler, Home Depot, Albertsons, and many more—where they seeded new clusters, spreading Welchism across the whole of corporate America. At the time of Welch's retirement, sixteen public companies were run by men who had studied at his knee. Several more would appoint his pupils in the years that followed. At each of these corporations, the arrival of a CEO from GE was met with great fanfare, investors believing the board had appointed a leader who possessed the Midas touch. Sometimes, the executives were able to engineer short-term gains. Yet inevitably, whether in months or years, many of them failed.

There is capitalism in America before Jack Welch, and after him. His career serves as a line of demarcation, a split between the past and the present. Look at the trend lines for any number of key economic indicators—wages, mergers and acquisitions, manufacturing jobs, union representation, executive compensation, corporate tax rates—and it's clear that right around 1981, the year Welch took over, things started to go off the rails.

American manufacturing jobs peaked at nearly 20 million just as Welch came to power, accounting for nearly a quarter of full-time employment in the country. Once he began his merciless campaign of cost cutting and outsourcing, that figure began to decline, and has never recovered. Today, there are roughly half as many manufacturing jobs in the United States as there were in 1980.

Mergers and acquisitions were relative rarities when Welch took over, acts of unusual corporate ambition or desperation. In 1980, the value of all the corporate deals in the United States amounted to a few tens of billions of dollars. Welch changed all that. Thanks in part to GE's own uptick in dealmaking, that figure doubled and doubled again during the early years of Welch's reign. By the end of his tenure, the value of mergers and acquisitions topped $1.5 trillion annually for three years in a row.

As Welch's lawyers did their best to pay the Internal Revenue Service the absolute minimum necessary under the law, the share of taxes U.S. corporations paid to the government steadily fell. When Welch became CEO, the effective tax rate on capital income was 46 percent. Twenty years later, it was down to 35 percent, and would continue to fall. Today it is just 21 percent.

Wealth grew more concentrated during his reign. Before Welch, corporate profits were largely reinvested in the company or paid out to workers rather than sent back to stock owners. In 1980, American companies spent less than $50 billion on buybacks and dividends. By the time of Welch's retirement, a much greater share of corporate profits was going to investors and management, with American companies spending $350 billion on buybacks and dividends in 2000.

And Welch's outsize pay packages helped usher in an era of run-away executive compensation that has steadily taken wealth out of the hands of workers and placed it in the accounts of managers. In 1980 the average pay for a CEO of one of the top American companies was $1.85 million. In 2000, it was $21.5 million. Whereas CEOs made less than 50 times the annual worker salary when Welch took over, they were making 368 times as much by the end of his term. Put another way, CEO compensation has grown by 940 percent since 1978. During the same time, the average worker's wage has increased by 12 percent. Slashing jobs, rampant dealmaking, outsourcing, financialization, and supersized executive compensation—all these trends became widespread only after Welch implemented them at GE and continued to evangelize for them as an elder statesman.

Welch, who died in 2020, was able to witness this great unraveling. He fretted as GE fell apart and lamented the misdeeds perpetrated by other corporate bad actors. Never the most self-reflective type, he brushed aside any suggestions that he might bear some responsibility for this national catastrophe. Instead, in retirement, he transformed himself into a management guru, offering inspiration to a new generation of capitalists and doing everything he could to enshrine his ideals as gospel. He penned columns for *Businessweek*, Reuters, and *Fortune*. He sat for interviews with the *Harvard Business Review*. He created a $50,000 online MBA offered by the Jack Welch Management Institute. And he wrote books, made speeches, and appeared on cable news, praising the executives he had groomed while continuing his assault on taxation and regulation.

The bluster of a former CEO might seem insignificant. But Welch's star remained largely undimmed after he left GE, and his opinion continued to hold great sway. During panel discussions, he disparaged organized labor. On CNBC, he extolled mass layoffs. In all, it amounted to a twenty-year campaign to make his warped vision of capitalism the norm. And for the most part, it worked. His extreme practices became commonplace. The myth that Welch's way of doing business was a winning strategy lived on. Over the years, his influence reshaped the economy, eroding this country's middle class, sowing distrust in once revered institutions, chipping away at the tax base, and exacerbating inequality.

The empty factories, hollowed-out cities, and unemployed workers—all lorded over by a wealthy ruling class—have contributed to the broad sense of disenfranchisement afflicting so much of the country, a combustible mix that helped lay the groundwork for the political rise of Welch's friend, Donald J. Trump. Welch and Trump orbited each other for decades. GE Capital partnered with Trump while Welch was CEO. In retirement, Welch trafficked in conspiracy theories about the Obama administration and the Clinton Foundation. When Trump ran for president, Welch put wind in his sails. And when Trump won, Welch celebrated him as an exemplar leader and traveled to the White House to advise the president on economic issues.

In recent years, some business leaders have come to realize the damage that Welchism has wrought. Instead of pursuing profits at any cost, a new generation of executives is beginning to express a renewed commitment to serve not just shareholders, but all stakeholders, including workers, communities, and the environment. They recognize that if they don't pay wages that create a strong middle class, the economy will ultimately grow weak. They understand that companies that leave their communities polluted and impoverished will wither before long. And by gently downplaying the importance of the stock market, they are even questioning the very measure of success that was so sacrosanct to Welch.

There are tentative signs of progress. Companies that for years promoted policies that exacerbated income inequality and gutted labor unions are suddenly expressing concern about the plight of everyday workers. After decades of lobbying for environmental deregulation, big business is now beginning to tackle climate change. And there are new standards, certifications, and even stock exchanges emerging to support this work. No longer is the purpose of a corporation to maximize shareholder value, according to this new cohort of enlightened captains of industry. Instead, CEOs are talking about themselves as part of an interconnected whole—just as they had done a half century ago, before Welch came on the scene.

Stamping out Welchism will be a formidable challenge. The great hero of late-twentieth-century American capitalism, Welch occupies an exalted place in the business world's collective imagination. Even today, with the ruinousness of his methods clear to see, he is revered as a master strategist, peerless in the art of maximizing shareholder value and empire building. Tactics he pioneered are still commonplace, values he embodied are still championed, and in many instances, disciples he groomed are still in charge. Twenty years after he surrendered his office to one of his loyal acolytes, we are all still very much living in Jack Welch's world.

ONE

The Most Valuable Company in the World

"I plan to blow up the *Queen Mary*"

It was 1980 and the country was languishing. Culturally, politically, and economically, the previous decade had offered up a series of indignities that seemed to question the premise of American exceptionalism. The Vietnam War raged and Richard Nixon resigned. The stock market was flat and inflation was on the rise. Across the country, there was a sense of pervasive dissatisfaction, and an accompanying conviction that something had to change dramatically. In November, Ronald Reagan—who worked as a pitch man for GE before entering politics—beat Jimmy Carter in a landslide, becoming the fortieth president of the United States with the slogan "Let's Make America Great Again." The new president's economic policy, known as Reaganomics, prioritized lower taxes, decreased regulation, and a favorable posture toward Wall Street, a combination that would benefit corporations while marginalizing workers.

In the boardrooms of corporate America, a revolution was also stirring. A month after Reagan was elected, GE announced that John Francis Welch Jr. would become its next chairman and chief executive. The young, tempestuous, ambitious son of a train conductor and a homemaker, Welch would be just the eighth man to lead GE since the company was founded by Thomas Edison nearly a hundred years earlier, at the dawn of the Electric Age.

As CEO of GE, Welch assumed responsibilities that went far beyond those of a typical manager. To preside over the General Electric Company required, back then, something closer to statesmanship. The company's enormity and financial might made it an economic, political, and cultural force. Its output accounted for a full percentage point of gross domestic product. Its CEO commanded a loyal workforce of 400,000 men and women—greater than the entire population of Cincinnati. Its televisions, refrigerators, and toasters were in countless American homes. Its jet engines hung on the wings of planes flying coast to coast. Its nuclear reactors lit up cities around the globe.

The great diversity of GE's holdings provided its CEO with what seemed like an almost omniscient view of the economy. And thanks to GE's century of success, the company was considered a pioneer in management philosophy, setting the standard by which legions of executives were trained, organized, and evaluated. More than anything else though, GE was a role model. Other executives—inside GE, and at companies large and small around the country—looked to its leader for guidance on how to comport themselves, and what kind of balance their companies should strike with employees, the government, and investors. GE's previous CEOs had counseled presidents, reshaped business school curriculums, and redefined how Americans worked. It was the most important job in the corporate world, and wherever Welch took the company, other corporations would inevitably follow.

Given the job's expansive responsibilities, the process by which GE selected its next CEO was extensive and intense. The vetting took years and had all the theatrics of cardinals choosing a new pope. The outgoing CEO pitted candidates against one another, demanded memos articulating their vision, and asked each the same question: If they died in a plane crash, who besides them should run the company? Outside observers expected GE to pick a seasoned in-house executive with a conservative approach, a man steeped in "the GE Way" who would continue with the current strategy. But inside GE, the sense that something needed to change dramatically was acute. When the figurative white smoke finally rose from the company's Fairfield, Connecticut, headquarters, Welch was the winner.

Welch succeeded a genteel Englishman named Reginald Jones who had run the company for the previous decade. Jones, with an Ivy League education and a deliberating, cerebral aura, was highly regarded for his poise, judgment, and discretion. President Carter twice asked Jones to join his cabinet. Tall and lean, Jones wore tailored suits, and his office at GE headquarters was a hushed enclave, where he and his lieutenants pondered strategy far from the factory floor. Jones had spent his career at GE, distinguishing himself as a financial whiz and rising to become chief financial officer before taking over, and he ran a hierarchical, bureaucratic company. Yet for all his élan, Jones was modest. He lived in a simple colonial brick home in Greenwich, not far from GE headquarters. He once asked his wife if she wanted anything more, and her reply reflected the family's abiding humility. "Why would we want anything more?" she said. Though Jones was regarded as the most accomplished CEO in America, he drew a salary that would today be considered a pittance for an executive of his stature, earning $200,000, just twelve or thirteen times what new management recruits to the company took home. GE did not grow at breakneck speed while Jones was CEO. Nonetheless, during the decade he was in charge, GE managed to preserve its standing as a model corporate citizen, a company held in high regard by its workers and by society at large.

Welch was Jones's opposite in every way. He grew up poor and went to state school. He was impatient, impulsive, and crass. Short, quick-witted, and coiled with energy, Welch wore jeans and rolled-up shirtsleeves whenever he could get away with it. He spoke with a thick Boston accent, and when he grew angry, a boyhood stutter flared up. Welch had a PhD in chemical engineering, but preferred chatting up machinists to sitting in a boardroom and deliberating with directors. He loathed hierarchy and bureaucracy and didn't give a damn what people thought of him, so long as he was making money for the company. Over twenty years, he had risen through the ranks at GE by growing sales and slashing costs, and what time Welch did spend in the office was often marked by shouting matches. He was a cursing, kinetic tornado of a man, arguing his way from one decision to the next. GE had "replaced a legend with a live wire," the *Wall Street Journal* quipped upon the news that Welch was taking over from Jones.

But while Welch could not have been more different from Jones, GE had a way of choosing CEOs who were prepared to meet the moment, and American industry was on the cusp of profound change. Four decades of postwar prosperity had made America the greatest economic force in history, and much of the country's population enjoyed substantial improvements in their quality of life. Incomes rose, productivity skyrocketed, unemployment remained relatively low, and a great middle class flourished. Corporations like GE, Exxon, General Motors, Ford, Westinghouse, U.S. Steel, IBM, and Xerox fueled much of this growth, mass-producing products that the world desperately wanted, and paying their workers well. Yet by the start of the 1980s, the status quo was no longer working. Productivity had stagnated and inflation was growing, a distressing new combination known as "stagflation." Complacency had also taken root in corporate America. Decades of success and a dearth of credible rivals had made many big companies less eager to invest, innovate, and pursue growth. And new competition was finally emerging around the globe. Germany and Japan had rebuilt and modernized their economies after World War II, and were suddenly churning out sophisticated, high-quality, competitively priced goods.

Welch was keenly aware of the threat posed by globalization. In the mid-1970s, he had toured a GE joint venture with Yokogawa

Medical Systems in Japan, where ultrasound machines were being produced, and was stunned by what he saw. "The process was like nothing I had seen in the United States," he recalled. When a machine was finished being assembled, a worker unbuttoned his shirt, dabbed some gel on his chest and applied the ultrasound probes on his body for a quick test. Then the same man wrapped the product up, put it in a box, affixed the shipping label, and placed it on the loading dock. "It would have taken a lot more people to get this done in Milwaukee," Welch noted.

The rest of the country was also catching on to the widening skills gap between the United States and some emerging economies. On June 24, 1980, NBC aired a prime-time documentary that captured the nation's gnawing self-doubt. Titled *If Japan Can, Why Can't We?*, the hour-long special explored the extraordinary manufacturing advances taking place abroad, and turned the mirror on a nation grappling with its diminished standing in the world. That same year, Jones and Welch acknowledged the need for urgent change, coauthoring a letter to shareholders. "U.S. business today finds itself challenged by aggressive overseas competitors," they wrote. "National productivity has been declining and, in industry after industry, product leadership is moving to other nations. Companies that refuse to renew themselves, that fail to cast off the old and embrace new technologies, could well find themselves in serious decline in the 1980s. We are determined that this shall not happen to General Electric."

It wasn't going to be easy for GE to thrive in this new age. And in some ways, the company, while iconic, was particularly vulnerable. When Welch took over, half of GE's earnings came from businesses dating back to the Edison era: motors, wiring, and appliances. Yet Welch, an extremist in all he did, drastically overcorrected. Instead of trying to fix American manufacturing, he effectively abandoned it, and would soon start shuttering factories around the country and shipping jobs overseas. "One of the narratives in the early '80s was 'How do we save American capitalism from the Japanese?'" said Louis Hyman, a professor of business history at Cornell University who has studied Welch and GE. "And the answer for Jack Welch was, 'Let's be more brutal.'"

In certain corners of academia and government, a related upheaval was under way. With the New Deal economics that defined postwar policy failing to deliver sustained gains after decades of success, a backlash was brewing. Conservative economists called for less government meddling, less regulation, free markets, fewer labor unions, and a world where big businesses were free to act in their own best interests. Some went further, arguing that corporations should focus on maximizing shareholder value, rather than concerning themselves with the public good. On Wall Street, animal spirits were stirring. Thanks to technology, money was beginning to move in strange new ways. A new economy was taking shape, and Welch, as chairman of GE, would have a strong hand in its design.

GE was hardly in trouble when Welch took over. Jones had overseen a steady rise in earnings, and the company had just reported an annual profit of nearly $1.5 billion. But GE's stock price hadn't budged in years, and that, to Welch, was a problem. In a memo to Jones outlining his approach should he be selected as CEO, Welch made explicit his contention that Wall Street should come first. "What we have to sell as an enterprise to the equity investor is consistent, above-average earnings growth through the economic cycle," he wrote. "The discipline to balance both short and long term is the absolute of such a strategy." Welch was effectively declaring that even if times were tough, he would find a way to make GE ever-more profitable. It was a bold mandate. Earnings don't go up endlessly, especially during economic downturns. Periods of expansion and contraction affect all companies, even GE. Welch, however, had a vision. He believed GE was going to be the most valuable company on earth, and he was determined to make that audacious goal a reality.

That raw ambition captivated even Reg Jones, who decided that Welch had what it took to be chairman. Yet as Welch himself would later acknowledge, Jones had no idea just how all-encompassing the transformation would be. "I'm not sure he knew how much I wanted GE to change," Welch said.

Jones would soon find out. Once Welch was chosen as the next

CEO, Jones summoned his successor to his office at GE headquarters. There, the outgoing CEO tried to bestow some final bits of wisdom upon the young man—just forty-five years old at the time—who had been tapped to take over, describing in grand terms a company that held unmatched sway over the U.S. economy.

"Jack, I give you the *Queen Mary*," Jones said. "This is designed not to sink."

Welch didn't miss a beat.

"I don't want the *Queen Mary*," he snapped back. "I plan to blow up the *Queen Mary*. I want speedboats."

"Generous Electric"

The company Welch wanted to blow up was part of the bedrock of the American economy, the culmination of nearly a century's worth of innovative engineering breakthroughs and careful financial stewardship. GE's scientists helped win the world wars, and won Nobel Prizes, too. The devices they invented and commercialized ushered in modern life as we know it, full of electrical conveniences and technological marvels. General Electric introduced the world to power plants and incandescent light bulbs, inventions as significant as the wheel and the printing press. On September 4, 1882, at 3 p.m., Thomas Edison himself flipped the switch at the first American power station, on Pearl Street in downtown Manhattan, illuminating four square blocks of the city, including the offices of J. P. Morgan and the *New York Times*. Edison went on to wire London's Holborn Viaduct with an array of 3,000 bulbs. And not long after that, GE installed a power plant in Japan. GE introduced or popularized electric meters, electric motors, the electric locomotive, and the X-ray machine. And that was just in the nineteenth century.

As the twentieth century dawned, GE brought to market the steam turbine, and then the electric fan. In 1909, it started selling toasters, establishing a foothold in the American kitchen. Around the same time it helped engineer the first voice radio broadcast, a transmission that included a verse from the Bible, a recording of the Largo from Handel's opera *Xerxes*, and a violin solo of "O Holy Night." In 1924 it introduced the diesel electric locomotive, revolutionizing rail transport. The next year, GE made the refrigerator mainstream. Some years after that, it started putting televisions in living rooms across the country, which, along with its ubiquitous radios, helped create the modern media landscape. In 1935, GE introduced the garbage disposal, and three years after that, the fluorescent light.

GE played an integral role in the American effort to win World War II, sending its executives to help the military, and making the vacuum tubes for radar systems and the engines for planes. In the years after the war, GE developed America's first jet engine. In the 1930s it created moldable plastics, and by the 1950s it was making transparent plastic. The plastics were used in almost every conceivable product, and in space. When Neil Armstrong and Buzz Aldrin landed on the moon, their boots were made of silicon rubber developed by GE, and the visors of their helmets were made with GE's Lexan plastic. GE built one of the world's first nuclear power plants in 1957, introduced the world's first lasers in 1962, and developed revolutionary new medical scanners in the 1970s.

It was an unprecedented run of corporate innovation and economic growth, and for the most part, workers shared in the bounty. GE was among the first American companies to offer its employees retirement plans, a share of profits, health insurance, and life insurance. GE created the first research and development lab, the first industrial park, and in 1913 the company built one of the first true corporate campuses, on a ninety-two-acre site outside Cleveland. In addition to a light bulb factory and a research center, there was a swimming pool, a bowling alley, a gym, tennis courts, a rifle range, and baseball and football fields. Dentists and doctors were on hand, as was a bank. In the evenings, employees stuck around to enjoy tap dancing and live music. A hundred years before Silicon Valley companies like Google and Facebook began showering their employees with perks, GE understood the value of taking excellent care of its workers.

It was a directive that came from the top. Gerard Swope, who became GE's chief executive in 1922, practiced what he proudly called "welfare capitalism," using the corporation's vast resources to take exceptional care of its employees—providing a profit-sharing plan, health benefits, higher wages, and more—all in an effort to boost morale and inspire workers. With the thievery and excess of the Gilded Age still fresh in the collective consciousness, GE was trying to distinguish itself as an upstanding corporate citizen, and in 1927, GE's chairman, Owen D. Young, used a speech at the Harvard Business School to excoriate businessmen who "devise ways and means to squeeze out of labor its last ounce of effort and last penny of compensation." Instead, Young called for CEOs to "think in terms of human beings—one group of human beings who put their capital in, and another group who put their lives and labor in a common enterprise for mutual advantage." In 1929, *Forbes* observed of GE that "few corporations are more progressive or better managed." GE was so magnanimous in these years that it earned the moniker "Generous Electric."

An annual report from 1953 described how GE worked "in the balanced best interests of all." The report trumpeted how much the company had paid in taxes, the virtues of paying its suppliers well, and how critical it was to take care of its employees. That year, GE proudly stated that it spent some 37 percent of its sales on pay and benefits for its workers, resulting in the "the biggest pay roll in the Company's history—with more people at work than ever before." Next to the statistic was an illustration of a grinning factory worker walking away from the assembly line, holding bags of money. Only after enumerating all the ways in which it was helping the government, suppliers, and employees did the company mention how much it allocated for investors. The sum: a modest 3.9 percent of sales. The message from the report was clear. GE saw itself as a part of an interconnected whole, one where employees and society didn't take a backseat to shareholders. "Maximizing employment security is a prime company goal," GE's head of employee benefits, Earl Willis, wrote in 1962. "The employee who can plan his economic future with reasonable certainty is an employer's most productive asset." What was good for the corporation was good for the country, and vice versa.

In 1960, the year Welch joined GE, the company's slogan was "Progress Is Our Most Important Product." It was a line repeated on every Sunday night installment of *General Electric Theater*, the mainstay television review hosted by Ronald Reagan, then merely an actor. In subsequent years, GE's slogan became "Accent on Value." And then in the 1970s, Jones introduced the phrase, "We Bring Good Things to Life." It wasn't just talk. Under Jones, the company invested 10 percent of its profits into research and development, spending heavily in a bid to invent more good things.

GE's postwar posture was in keeping with the times. The Gilded Age and Great Depression had revealed the highs and lows of modern capitalism. Great wealth could be created practically overnight, and many millions could benefit. But it also became clear that without sufficient regulation, executives could extract vast sums of wealth from corporations for themselves while undermining the broader economy. The sudden rise of the oil industry, the sugar trust, the financial system, and the railways spawned monopolies and robber barons, not to mention startling income inequality.

Following the stock market crash of 1929 and the ensuing Great Depression, the New Deal helped revitalize the economy with massive investments in infrastructure, creating millions of jobs. Wall Street was reined in with new regulations, and as workers benefited, inequality waned. It was a recipe for growth, and in the postwar years companies poured profits back into their workforces, ensuring a stable, skilled employee base. Labor unions offered employees a measure of job security and the assurance of steadily increasing wages. The gap in pay between a machinist and a manager was meaningful but not too extreme. Employers took care of their employees, understanding that by doing so they were taking care of the country, and ultimately, their own interests. The ethos was distilled in a 1932 treatise that essentially made these view sacrosanct in corporate America. *The Modern Corporation and Private Property*, by Adolf A. Berle Jr. and Gardiner C. Means, argued that companies were inextricably intertwined with their communities and ought to act with a sense of shared responsibility. Those views would shape what came to be known as the Golden Age of Capitalism, a period that lasted from the postwar boom to the stagflation of the 1970s, a stretch when many of the great American employers were at their best.

Alfred Sloan, who ran General Motors starting in 1923, drove a tough bargain with organized labor, but was generous with his employees overall. There was insurance of all sorts for GM workers—for sickness, injury, disability, and even life. And General Motors offered savings, investment, and retirement plans for factory workers, doing its part to lift its employees into the middle class.

Robert Wood Johnson, the chairman of Johnson & Johnson, crafted the company's "Credo" in 1943, just before taking the family firm public. Representative of the times, the Johnson & Johnson Credo is an artifact of the Golden Age, preserving in amber the distinctive priorities of one of that generation's most influential businessmen. Johnson stated that the company's "first responsibility is to our customers," a group the company would later define as "the patients, doctors and nurses, to mothers and fathers and all others who use our products and services." After that, Johnson & Johnson was responsible to its employees, and committed to provide "a sense of security in their jobs," adding that "wages must be fair and adequate, management just, hours short." The company's next responsibility was to its management, and it pledged that executives would be "persons of talent, education, experience and ability." Finally, Johnson turned to investors. "Our fourth and last responsibility is to our owners and stockholders," he wrote. "Business must make a sound profit . . . high taxes paid . . . new factories built . . . new products launched. . . . When these things have been done, the owners and the stockholders should receive a fair return." Johnson didn't want to make a killing. He wasn't fixated on the consistent earnings growth that Welch dreamed of. Rather, he understood the purpose of the corporation to be contributing to society, while also making a simple, reasonable profit.

Companies weren't just talking a good game back then. They were actually sharing their profits with their employees. From 1948 to 1979, worker pay grew in tandem with worker productivity. That is, as companies became more efficient and profitable, and the economy expanded, employees saw their compensation increase at roughly the same rate. Paying workers well, paying taxes, and investing for the future were seen not just as the right things to do, but as sound business practices. Per capita income rose, and millions of Americans joined the middle class, made down payments on homes, and acquired cars, TVs, and appliances, many of them made by General Electric. Wall Street wasn't measuring companies solely on the basis of their short-term profitability, allowing companies like GE to invest in the future and develop new products and services. An equilibrium existed between the interests of the men who ran the companies, the investment firms who owned those companies' shares, and the men and women who punched their timecards five days a week. Even in 1968, a year scarred by racial unrest and social strife following the assassination of Dr. Martin Luther King Jr., the public still had faith in business. That year, a survey found that 70 percent of Americans agreed with the statement: "business tries to strike a fair balance between profits and the interests of the public." And as late as 1981, the Business Roundtable—an influential lobbying group that GE had helped create a decade earlier—declared that companies had responsibilities that went well beyond quarterly earnings, observing that corporations' "importance to the well-being and quality of life of the average person has created perceptions and expectations that go far beyond what many considered their historic purpose, which was the creation of goods and services at a profit."

To use today's corporate parlance, it was a moment when all stakeholders could expect to benefit. The company wasn't being run just for investors, but for employees, customers, and communities, too. And it worked. The middle class grew, consumer spending ballooned, and new companies were founded, creating yet more jobs. It was a virtuous cycle that turned America into the world's greatest economic engine. Along the way, GE became a model employer, the kind of company where a scrappy kid from the Boston suburbs could make a career, and maybe even rise to the top.

"With my nose pressed up against the glass"

Welch was born in Peabody, Massachusetts, in 1935, the only son of an Irish Catholic family that lived in nearby Salem. His father was a conductor on the Boston & Maine railroad, a unionized job that demanded long hours. His mother, Grace, was a homemaker who devoted herself to Welch and tried to instill in him both a moral compass and a competitive streak. She took him to mass every day and made him an altar boy. She also taught him how to play poker, insisting he wager his own allowance to gain a visceral understanding of winning and losing. Welch was short, short-tempered, and had a stutter. By his own admission, he was an outsider looking in, growing up "with my nose pressed up against the glass." And from an early age, he harbored fundamental questions about his family's station in life. "I wonder why my mother didn't do better in school," he mused. "I wonder why she and her family didn't progress further."

Welch channeled these disadvantages into a restless, argumentative personality that would be well suited for an increasingly competitive economy. He learned how to throw his weight around and developed a reputation as an aggressive athlete. "He hated losing, even in touch football," remembered a childhood friend. "Jack wasn't blessed with a lot of grace or athletic ability. He trounced people by trying harder." An average student in high school, he nonetheless harbored a hunger for power, writing in his yearbook that his chief ambition in life was "to make a million." And the young Welch was impetuous. While caddying at the local golf course as a teenager, a player hit a ball into the water and told Welch to fetch it. Instead, Welch threw the man's clubs in the water and stormed off. His disposition never entirely improved. He seemed to believe that he'd been unfairly disadvantaged from the outset, and he barreled through life with a determination to prove the world wrong. "Between the stutter and being smaller, it all meant he had to scramble more," said Nicholas Heymann, who worked at GE early in his career and covered the company as an analyst for decades. "He had to try six times as hard."

Welch went to the University of Massachusetts at Amherst, then got his PhD in chemical engineering at the University of Illinois at Champaign, becoming the first doctoral student at the school to earn a degree in three years. Upon graduating in 1960, he took a job in a GE plastics plant in Pittsfield, Massachusetts. His starting salary was $10,500 a year.

Pittsfield was a relative backwater within the company. At the time, Dow Chemical and DuPont were the leaders in the plastics industry. GE was an also-ran. But Welch wasted no time getting noticed, albeit initially it was for his impulsiveness, not his business prowess. A year into his tenure, Welch's boss told him he was getting a $1,000 raise. When Welch learned that his colleagues also had gotten $1,000 raises, he was furious. Though he had not yet produced anything of lasting value, his sense of entitlement was already well developed. He believed he had been working harder than his peers, and therefore deserved more money. So he decided to quit.

Before Welch could leave the company, his boss's boss took him out to dinner and promised him more money. Welch craved validation, and the praise, plus an extra $2,000 got him to stay. "Someone told me they loved me," Welch later recalled. And even though he was no longer leaving the company, he remembered keeping the "pile of gifts" colleagues had given him as going-away presents. He never let the perceived slight go, using it as fuel in his quest for personal riches. "That standard raise I got over four decades ago has probably driven my behavior to an extreme," he wrote in his autobiography.

Business was a Darwinian competition to Welch, and from an early age he believed he was better than the rest. "Winning teams come from differentiation, rewarding the best and removing the weakest, always fighting to raise the bar," he said. This attitude at times led him to push GE to the limits. One day in 1963, Welch was at his office in Pittsfield, overlooking the factory on Plastics Avenue. Having risen to become a manager charged with developing a new plastic, Welch was impatient to bring a product to market, and had been driving his team to move faster, run more experiments—whatever it took. As Welch sat at his desk, an explosion rocked the factory.

Debris and broken glass littered the scene, and smoke shrouded the building. Somehow, no one was badly injured. But it soon became clear that Welch, as head of the plant and the one pushing his team so hard, bore responsibility for the disaster. Pressuring employees to innovate, Welch had them experimenting with an untested process, moving oxygen through a "highly volatile solution" in a large tank. Something caused a spark, setting off the explosion.

The next day, Welch drove a hundred miles to explain himself before GE executives in Connecticut. Lucky for him, his superiors were in a forgiving mood, and he escaped without facing any real consequences. The episode became a point of pride for Welch, a parable that, he believed, demonstrated a healthy appetite for risk, and gave him his first taste of impunity. "When people make mistakes, the last thing they need is discipline," he said. Welch had blown up a building and gotten away with it. An experience that might have humbled other aspiring leaders or derailed their careers embboldened him.

Not long after Welch blew up one factory, he convinced GE to spend $10 million building another factory, this one to produce a new plastic, called Noryl. The project was almost derailed at the last minute as Noryl proved more brittle than expected. But chemists working for Welch figured out a solution and were able to modify the formula, creating a more durable product. Noryl eventually became a $1 billion business. It was Welch's first big break, and it caught the attention of higher-ups at GE. In 1968, he was promoted to head of of the company's plastic business. He was just thirty-two at the time, and the company's youngest general manager. He delighted in gaining access to GE's inner sanctum, along with something even more precious: "my first stock options."

Over the next three years, Welch doubled sales in the plastics division, leading to a series of promotions. During these years, he notched significant and lasting victories. His group developed new and improved technologies for CT scanners, an achievement that earned GE titanic profits. Intoxicated with his initial victories, he began dreaming big. In his 1973 performance review, Welch declared that his long-range objective was to become CEO of the company. By this point, Welch had the attention of Reg Jones. While many other senior leaders believed Welch was too unpolished and unpredictable to be a contender for the top job, Jones himself insisted that Welch be included in the succession planning process. As a result, in 1977 Welch was made one of the half dozen most senior executives at GE and relocated from Massachusetts to company headquarters in Connecticut.

Welch was now in the race to succeed Jones, but he was hardly the obvious choice. Other, more conventional candidates were presumed to be front-runners. To test Welch's mettle, Jones gave him a portfolio of responsibilities that included the company's appliances business, and its nascent credit operations. It was a hodgepodge mix, but Welch quickly zeroed in on a strategy that he believed would distinguish himself from the other contenders: layoffs.

At the time, GE was planning to expand its appliances operations. Welch, however, believed that while the business would continue to grow, overseas competition would make it harder to turn a profit. Hoping to increase margins, he recommended significant cuts at Appliance Park, a sprawling complex in Louisville, Kentucky. Built in 1951, when GE was at the height of its postwar ambitions, this complex was the headquarters of the company's appliances division and spanned six hulking buildings, each bigger than an airport terminal. Appliance Park was so large it had its own zip code: 40225. The birthplace of millions of GE toasters, washing machines, and refrigerators, 23,000 people worked there before Welch came on the scene, so many cars coming and going during shift changes that the parking lot required a network of stop lights to maintain order. And while the appliance business was still making money and supporting thousands of good jobs in Louisville, it simply wasn't good enough for Welch, who resolved to reduce the head count at Appliance Park.

When the higher-ups approved his plan, Welch praised their "courage," which he said, accomplished their goal and "improved our profitability." Putting people out of work, he realized, was an easy way to save money and boost profits, at least in the short term. That wasn't how GE, not to mention the rest of American industry, had achieved greatness over the past half century. But it seemed to be working for Welch.

Layoffs spread to other divisions as Welch amassed more responsibility, and as he toured GE's facilities around the country he took the opportunity to remind the rank and file who was now in charge. In Cleveland, at the light bulb factory, he berated a manager for the relative high costs of GE's bulbs, screaming that competitors in communist Europe made similar products for half the price. In Bridgeport, Connecticut, he tore into another executive when he stepped on and off one of the company's new digital bathroom scales and it came back with different results. When he met a manager who failed to impress, he would snap, "What the fuck do I pay you for?" Beyond being an unsentimental cost cutter, someone who was willing to lay off a few hundred workers to meet a quarterly earnings target, Welch had never outgrown his adolescent temper. This, too, was a drastic change for a company like GE. Corporate America in those days tended to be stuffy and formal, but also respectful and decent. But with Welch shouting his way to ever-higher profits, it became harder for others to quibble with his managerial style.

Although Welch had determined that there was little future in appliances, he became enthralled with another business he took over in 1977: GE Credit Corp., the company's finance division which would eventually be renamed GE Capital. At the time, GE Credit was a small but growing part of the company. Having started as a way to provide consumers with modest lines of credit, the division had expanded into financing and leasing construction equipment, offering second mortgages, issuing some commercial real estate loans, and even managing private label credit cards. Welch immediately saw the potential. "Compared to the industrial operations I did know, this business seemed an easy way to make money," he explained. "You didn't have to invest heavily in R&D, build factories and bend metal." Instead, he realized that what mattered most was how clever your accountants were and how much money they had at their disposal. He began bolstering GE Credit's staff and looking for ways to grow the division, the beginning of a transformation that would remake the company, and ultimately the economy at large.

In three years, Welch distinguished himself from the other men vying for the top job. He was ruthless in his cuts, searing in his critiques of underperformers, and adamant in his conviction that finance was key to the company's future. It wasn't exactly the "GE Way," but it was a convincing enough performance for Welch to be named CEO. "Everybody was shocked when Jack got the job," said Ken Langone, a longtime GE board member and a cofounder of Home Depot. "He was exactly the antithesis of what you would expect Reg Jones would have picked."

Five weeks before Welch officially took over, Jones threw him a party at the Helmsley Palace, an upscale hotel in New York City. Among the sixty or so guests were CEOs from many of the nation's largest companies. As the night wore on, Welch had a bit too much to drink. When Jones asked him to address the crowd, Welch couldn't get through his remarks without slurring his words. Back at GE headquarters the next morning, Jones stormed into Welch's office. "I've never been so humiliated in my life," he told Welch. "You embarrassed me and the company."

Welch was shocked. He thought he had won over the crowd, and thought Jones was being prudish. "I was mad as hell at him because I thought he was being a stiff," Welch remembered. "I felt sorry for myself because maybe I hadn't made the great impression I thought I had." Welch claimed that Jones later walked back his criticism after hearing from several CEOs who had enjoyed the evening, but the damage was already done. At the very moment Welch was expected to comport himself with dignity, he had given the assembled chieftains a glimpse of his reckless, unpredictable energy.

"The most competitive enterprise on earth"

Less than a year after taking over as CEO, Welch took the lectern in the ballroom of the Pierre Hotel in New York to deliver a speech that he hoped would announce his arrival on the scene as a visionary boss who would chart a new course not just for GE, but for the economy at large. As Welch saw it, the postwar balance of power—and GE's part in it—was hopelessly outdated. The Golden Age of Capitalism was over. With stagflation weighing down the economy and overseas competition on the rise, the need for change was urgent. The collectivist spirit of the postwar years might have helped create the great American middle class, but such idealistic conceptions of business's role in society were no roadmap for success in the hypercompetitive economy of the 1980s. Welch foresaw a different future for GE, one defined not by electric light bulbs, but by quarterly earnings; one powered not by mechanical engineering, but by financial engineering.

Speaking to a room full of analysts from research firms and banks—the people who told investors whether or not to buy GE stock—Welch dispensed with the usual business of describing the company's financial results. Instead, in twenty minutes, he laid out his vision for the future. Titled "Growing Fast in a Slow-Growth Economy," the speech depicted a winner-take-all world, where companies were either dominating their industry or sliding into irrelevance. "There will be no room for the mediocre supplier of products and services," he said. Instead, Welch told the analysts he wanted GE to be number one or number two in each business it was in. If it couldn't achieve that kind of dominance in an industry, the company would have to ask itself a tough question. "If you weren't already in the business, would you enter it today?" he said. "And if the answer is no, face into that second difficult question: 'What are you going to do about it?'" There would be no more room for wishful thinking, Welch said. Instead, GE employees would have to "see things as they are" and face hard truths. Most of all, he wanted GE to become a financial powerhouse. Whereas in previous decades it had been expected that GE—given its size and diversity—would simply grow in line with the country's gross national product, Welch said he wanted GE to become "the locomotive pulling the GNP, not the caboose following it." GE was about to become "the most competitive enterprise on Earth."

Welch's speech portended great changes to GE and its hundreds of thousands of workers. The old rules, he made clear, would no longer apply. If a business didn't stamp out the competition, it was liable to be ousted from the GE family. If an employee wasn't directly contributing to the bottom line, he may well be fired. And buried in the speech was another clue to Welch's plans, a harbinger of what would become his all-consuming ambition: he wanted to make GE the most competitive enterprise around, the most valuable company in the world. It was a radical agenda for change, positioning GE not as the conventional industrial conglomerate the analysts knew, but as an opportunistic, aggressive company that looked for growth wherever it could be found.

Welch had worked on the speech for weeks, drawing inspiration from a variety of sources. Months earlier, *Fortune* magazine ran a series on what executives could learn from two nineteenth-century Prussian military generals, Carl von Clausewitz and Helmuth von Moltke. They promoted the concept of "total war," which eschewed detailed planning, and instead advocated a constantly evolving response to circumstances as they changed, which, for Welch, meant turning a profit however he could. He also drew upon the work of Peter Drucker, the seminal management professor who had consulted for, and studied, GE for decades. It was Drucker who had first asked the question "If you weren't already in the business, would you enter it today?"

Welch believed this aggressive strategy would wow Wall Street and make a winning first impression. But as he spoke, he could tell that his remarks were being lost on the audience. The analysts were expecting a conventional update on how GE's various businesses had performed over the past year, not some grand new philosophical framework. Welch faced blank stares and grew irritated by a crowd that seemed not just disengaged, but baffled by his performance. During the question-and-answer session, one analyst asked how the price of copper would impact earnings in the next year.

"What the hell difference will *that* make?" Welch shot back. "You should be asking me where I want to take the company!"

The speech was a flop. As the analysts filed out of the ballroom, one remarked: "We don't know what the hell he's talking about."

Though the analysts might not have appreciated it, Welch was tapping into profound changes in the zeitgeist. In the years before he took over as CEO, an intellectual revolution had been coursing through academic, economic, legal, and political circles. It began as a backlash to European socialism during the Cold War, as scholars including Friedrich A. Hayek, an Austrian economist, began to advance the theory that free markets alone were the best way to address society's needs. Only when businesses were allowed to compete unencumbered by regulation would the best ideas rise to the top, their thinking went. The profit motive, they believed, was the perfect sorting mechanism, capable of distinguishing the good ideas from the bad, and giving rise to the products, services, and systems that would benefit society at large. Competition was the paramount way to organize human activity, they stressed, and it was imperative that people stopped relying on the government—or worse, their employers—to ensure their well-being. Welfare, social safety nets, and excessive protections for workers would inevitably lead to mediocrity and apathy, they believed. These theories gained purchase in European intellectual circles starting in the postwar years, and they eventually came to influence an up-and-coming economist at the University of Chicago named Milton Friedman.

Friedman took Hayek's central thesis and ran with it, zeroing in on what this meant for corporations. As Friedman saw it, companies should focus exclusively on the profitable production of goods and services, disregarding all other supposed obligations. In a seminal essay published in the *New York Times* in 1970, Friedman declared that "the social responsibility of business is to increase its profits." That simple twist of logic—that companies should maximize profits before all else—became one of the most powerful ideas of the late twentieth century, providing intellectual justification for a wholesale rewriting of the social contract. Friedman disdained those who believed companies should do anything beyond making money. "What does it mean to say that 'business' has responsibilities? Only people can have responsibilities," he wrote. "Businessmen who talk this way are unwitting puppets of the intellectual forces that have been undermining the basis of a free society these past decades." It was a capitalistic *cri de coeur*, imploring executives to embrace the profit motive and governments to stay out of the way, and it would endure as the most influential piece of economic writing for generations.

The same year that Friedman published his essay in the *Times*, a corporate attorney named Lewis Powell delivered a speech to an audience of Southern businessmen that set the stage for a new era of corporate meddling in politics. Quoting Freidman, Powell told the executives that their way of life was under siege, that radicals, communist sympathizers, and enemies of free enterprise were poised to undermine the very ideals that made America the greatest country on earth. The next year, Powell turned the speech into a memo that made its way to the U.S. Chamber of Commerce, the influential lobbying group that represents the interests of corporate America. Again, Powell warned of the looming threats to American business, including the environmental movement, support for new social welfare programs, and the consumer advocate Ralph Nader. "Business and the enterprise system are in deep trouble, and the hour is late," Powell wrote. It was a rallying cry for the rich, an exhortation for those with power to preserve it at all costs. And rather than just sounding the alarm, the Powell memo proposed a plan of action. Business should rapidly seek to bolster its influence in politics, academia, the media, and the legal world. Instead of staying on the defense, big money needed to attack, preserving its interests and shaping government policy to its liking.

The business world quickly took heed. In the years that followed, money began pouring into politics at unprecedented rates. Billionaires funded new conservative think tanks that promoted free market economics, and shaped the policy landscape. In 1973, major companies including GE established the Business Roundtable, another lobbying group that would codify the Friedman doctrine as, effectively, the law of the land for big companies. Powell only grew more influential, joining the Supreme Court in 1972 and issuing several prominent decisions favorable to corporations. Washington, which for so long had served as a check on big business, was now doing its bidding.

All the while, Friedman's central premise—that companies exist solely to enrich their shareholders—continued to gain clout. In 1976, two professors expanded on the Friedman doctrine in their paper "Theory of the Firm," a groundbreaking work that radically transformed the way executives thought about their responsibilities. In it, Michael Jensen and William Meckling argued that if companies were insufficiently focused on maximizing profits, they might get distracted and devote undue attention to frivolities such as "the kind and amount of charitable contributions" and "personal relations ('friendship,' 'respect,' and so on) with employees." That is, companies should disregard their communities, and even their staff, and instead focus on the bottom line to the exclusion of all else. Jensen and Meckling also revamped the notion of whom executives were supposed to serve. According to their theory, shareholders were the "principals" and executives were the "agents." That is, the CEOs were working on behalf of the investors, and ought to maximize shareholder returns at any cost. Finally, Jensen and Meckling laid the foundation for the coming era of excessive executive compensation, positing that CEOs should be richly rewarded with stock to align their own incentives with their company's financial performance.

Less than a decade later, in another paper, Jensen and Meckling would go further, arguing that the only metric by which companies should be measured—more important than even profits—was their share price. It was a still more extreme view than the one Friedman had put forth, and an invitation for companies to do whatever was needed to prop up their stock. In the years ahead, more business school professors would refine these ideas, sharpening them into weaponized dogma that executives could wield to defend keeping the lion's share of wealth for investors and themselves, while paying workers a pittance. "They said essentially you're being a bad guy unless you seek to maximize shareholder value, you are ripping off the people who gave you that capital," said Roger Martin, the former dean of the Rotman School of Management at the University of Toronto, who knew Welch. "That moral argument really went a long way with CEOs like Welch. They were like, 'You're telling me that this is my job. This is a yardstick I should measure myself with.' It may be sad that I've got to shut down this town, shut down this factory, but it's the moral thing to do."

Friedman, too, continued his ascent. In 1976 he won the Nobel Prize in economics, bestowing enormous credibility on the doctrine of shareholder primacy. And in 1980, just as Welch took over, PBS ran a ten-part miniseries about Friedman and his theories called *Free to Choose*. The broadcast, beamed into millions of homes around the country, praised unfettered competition, sounded the alarm on excessive regulation, disparaged labor unions, and blamed the government for everything from declining educational performance to inflation.

Other checks on the unbridled power of major corporations were also losing their purchase around this time. In 1978 Robert Bork, the Yale law professor and future Supreme Court nominee, published *The Antitrust Paradox*, arguing that the most important consideration when evaluating potential mergers was whether or not a combination was likely to raise prices for consumers in the short term. It was a narrow interpretation of the potential harms that could arise from monopolistic behavior and gave little credence to the potential for more concentrated industries to raise prices over time. In theory, the changes were designed to protect everyday Americans. In practice, they set the stage for an era of unchecked consolidation, where big companies got bigger and bigger. It was just an idea at first, but before long the newly elected president—and former GE pitch man—Ronald Reagan helped make it a reality, installing an antitrust chief who loosened New Deal–era restrictions on mergers and acquisitions.

And with Reagan in power, the Powell memo began to come alive. Reagan stacked his administration with corporate sympathizers. John Shad became the first Wall Street banker to head the Securities and Exchange Commission in a half century. Donald Regan, the Merrill Lynch CEO, was made treasury secretary. John C. Whitehead, a senior executive at Goldman Sachs, was named deputy secretary of state. From a fringe idea hatched during the Cold War, the free market dogma had emerged as the dominant intellectual force shaping politics and economies in the West. The economic right was ascendant, and the era of financial deregulation had begun in earnest.

These professors and politicians, however, were merely enablers. With their papers, essays, think tanks, and changes to the law, they had conjured up a new set of rules and expectations that governed the way companies could behave. No longer would corporations need to act in the best interests of all stakeholders. Instead, focusing on profits alone was not just permitted, but encouraged. Rather than look after employees, companies would be forgiven for casting them to the curb in the name of better margins.

This was the genetic material from which Welchism would evolve. And yet by 1981, this insidious ideology had not found a suitable host in the business world, its true power still yet to be fully unleashed. Although investors were restless and the stock market was stuck in neutral, with economic growth slowing and inflation rising, no one had so far possessed the right combination of ambition, power, and charisma to take full advantage of a vulnerable workforce and impatient investors. No one had yet dared to explicitly, relentlessly put shareholders ahead of employees, communities, and the environment. No one until Welch. He would be the first CEO of a major company to truly embrace the agenda of shareholder primacy, harnessing the full force of GE to make it real and ushering in a new, cutthroat era of American capitalism. "Jack sort of invented it, this shareholder focus," said Gary Sheffer, who ran communications at GE for years. "When it came to the stock price, there was really nothing that got in the way." And whether or not Welch read Milton Friedman's original texts, there is no doubt about the source of his inspiration. In his autobiography, when he summarized his view of the role of business in society, he simply parroted Friedman. "A CEO's primary social responsibility," Welch wrote, "is to assure the financial success of the company."

TWO

Neutron Jack

The "Campaign Against Loyalty"

At a press conference announcing his appointment as CEO, Welch spoke warmly of some of the other executives who looked after GE's myriad businesses. "We all came to the party as good friends," Welch said of them. "It's my goal to create an atmosphere of sharing both the good and the bad, where they can grow and I can grow, and we continue to have a good time." To hear him tell it, GE was going to remain the same chummy, collegial workplace it had been for a century, where lifetime employment was virtually a given and colleagues put a premium on etiquette and decorum.

Once in power, Welch was blunter in his assessment of middle management. "Bureaucrats must be ridiculed and removed," he said, and he wasted no time culling the herd. Welch fired high performers he didn't like, and friends who weren't performing well. He shut down a whole department at headquarters that focused on long-term strategic planning. He pressured underlings to fire more people. When executives were replaced, their jobs were filled with cold-eyed loyalists. Staff at headquarters quickly shrank by more than half, from 2,100 people to 900. Entire departments that had long been integral to GE's methodical growth were all but shuttered. And in his haste to transform the company, Welch dispensed with niceties. His management style was heavy on yelling and short on empathy. He had a voluminous memory, a quick wit, and an indefatigable work ethic, and often berated managers who seemed to know less about their own business than he did. "Civility was no longer a corporate virtue," Bill Lane, Welch's longtime speechwriter, wrote in his memoir. "Spatters of blood began to fleck conference room walls. Horror shows in the field were reported."

Soon, pink slips were littering GE factory floors across the country. Employment at the company peaked at 411,000 in 1980, the year Welch was named CEO. By the end of 1982, the company had shed 35,000 employees, or almost 9 percent of its workforce. Welch fired machinists constructing power plants in Schenectady, New York, and workers assembling dishwashers in Louisville, Kentucky. The next year, GE offloaded another 37,000 employees. Communities that once flourished thanks to GE's operations began to wither under Welch.

It didn't take long for the new CEO's tactics to attract attention. In 1982, *60 Minutes* did a segment about a steam iron plant in Ontario, California, that GE had decided to close. Overnight, 825 people lost their jobs. Employees said they felt betrayed, and a local religious leader called the move "immoral." When the segment aired, it accused GE of "putting profits ahead of people." Months later, with a GE factory closing seemingly every week, Welch earned the nickname he would never shake, as *Newsweek* dubbed him "Neutron Jack." The buildings were still standing, but all the people were gone. The "Neutron Jack" moniker stung him, but he knew it was more or less accurate. "I hated it, and it hurt," he recalled. "But I hated bureaucracy and waste even more."

What made Welch's spasm of downsizing so confounding was

the fact that GE could have easily afforded to keep the employees in Louisville, Schenectady, and elsewhere on the payroll. GE was more profitable than all but nine other companies in the *Fortune* 500. Net income was up 7 percent the year Welch took over from Jones. The company had just reported earnings of $1.5 billion. But while Welch had inherited stewardship of "Generous Electric," the Golden Age of Capitalism was ancient history in his mind. Whereas previous GE chairmen like Swope and Young had embraced the company's responsibility to its workers, Welch came to the job with a zealot's conviction that GE simply employed too many people. As he saw it, a smaller workforce would lead to bigger profits. The linkage, to him, was "inescapable."

The idea that employees looked to GE for security and stability rankled Welch. "Like many other large companies in the United States, Europe, and Japan, GE has had an implicit psychological contract based on perceived lifetime employment," he said. "This produced a paternal, feudal, fuzzy kind of loyalty. You put in your time, worked hard, and the company took care of you for life." To Welch, that mentality was laughably naive. The competitive nature of the globalized marketplace demanded a new paradigm, one in which "no business is a safe haven for employment unless it is winning in the marketplace."

"The psychological contract has to change," he said. "My concept of loyalty is not 'giving time' to some corporate entity and, in turn, being shielded and protected from the outside world. Loyalty is an affinity among people who want to grapple with the outside world and win." Indeed, he directed his underlings in the communications department to stop using the word "loyal" in press releases and internal memos, a directive that became known as the "Campaign Against Loyalty." This was his overriding concern as he sought to transform GE's workforce—that his employees not expect too much from the company, that they always live in fear that they might lose their job, that they knew who was boss.

Before Welch came along, employees were regarded as a company's greatest asset. Without the rank and file, it was understood that there would be no business at all. But to Welch, labor was a cost, not an asset. And as a cost, it was to be minimized. In another departure from convention, Welch dispensed with the notion that mass layoffs were a measure of last resort, used only in times of existential crisis. Instead, he used them proactively. To Welch, downsizing was a means to improve profitability, a tool that could help him meet quarterly earnings targets. The damage to individual livelihoods, let alone entire communities, didn't seem to bother him.

To institutionalize the practice of constant downsizing, hoping to make it seem as natural as the rising and setting sun, Welch implemented a brutal mandate: each year, the lowest-performing 10 percent of GE's employees should be laid off. Managers were instructed to divide their workers into one of three groups: 20 percent in the top tier, 70 percent in the middle, and 10 percent at the bottom. Welch referred to these groups as the A, B, and C players. The bottom tier was to be let go. It was a heartless edict, ensuring that no matter how well GE might be doing, tens of thousands of its employees would be shown the door, year after year. Welch called it the "Vitality Curve." Employees, who weren't fooled by this aspirational euphemism, called it "stack ranking" or, more accurately "rank and yank." For a nearly a century, GE had enjoyed a reputation as the company that knew how to best treat, train, and develop its employees. Now, under Welch, it was devising equally sophisticated methods to fire them. And before long, many other companies were doing the same. "It was a Jack Welch idea and it got adopted by a lot of people," said Dennis Rocheleau, who led labor negotiations for Welch. "It created horrible decisions in some instances, but it got mimicked by everybody. Jack Welch was larger than life, and people just said, 'If he's doing it, well, let's do it.'"

Even as Welch used jargon to obfuscate GE's cutthroat labor practices, he insisted that he was, in fact, being compassionate. "Some think it's cruel or brutal to remove the bottom 10 percent of our people," Welch said. "It isn't. It's just the opposite. What I think is brutal and 'false kindness' is keeping people around who aren't going to grow and prosper. There's no cruelty like waiting and telling people late in their careers that they don't belong—just when their job options are limited and they're putting their children through college or paying off big mortgages." Better, Welch figured, to fire them when they were in the prime of life. As he saw it, losing their job was just "another transition in their life where they can make a new start— just like the transition from high school to college, or from college to the first job." It was a gift to be fired, he wanted them to believe. He was liberating them from the shackles of a dead-end job and freeing them to pursue, well, something else. The fired workers were taking one for the team, each layoff contributing that much additional capital to the greater pool of profits that would propel the company's stock price higher.

It was a classic Welchist sleight of hand. By whitewashing mass layoffs, he made relentless downsizing seem necessary, even natural. Welch absolved himself of personal responsibility, framing the destruction of livelihoods as an act of God, not a choice he made. He even went one step further, claiming that the people he fired were thankful about losing their jobs. "Jack loved the approval of Wall Street, but the Irish in him craved the approval and affection of the divested employees, as well," Lane, the speechwriter, recalled. "He wanted to believe they were *thrilled* at being divested."

The systematic culling of employees was a hallmark of Welch's entire twenty-year reign. Hundreds of thousands of people lost their jobs at GE while Welch was CEO. Yet he could only get so far with mass layoffs alone. After all, GE needed at least some people to work on the factory floor. So he found other ways to shift labor off the GE balance sheet. Chief among these strategies: outsourcing. Wherever possible, he reckoned, GE should let someone else do the work. "Don't own a cafeteria: Let a food company do it," he advised. "Don't run a print shop: Let a printing company do that." During the 1980s, Welch thinned the ranks of his company by firing food service workers, security guards, janitors, and more. "This is what outsourcing is all about," he continued, blithely concluding that the jobs simply "migrated elsewhere," as if the careers of thousands of Americans were birds seeking warmer climes.

Workers rarely fared so well at their new employers. Instead of having a job at GE, a stalwart of the Dow Jones Industrial Average and a reliably decent employer, the workers were funneled to contractors that typically offered inferior pay, fewer benefits, and little job security. "The idea of who belongs inside the firm and who belongs outside the firm was really pervasive in the '80s," said Louis Hyman, the Cornell professor. "That leads to workplaces where you have people who work side by side, but some are considered first-class citizens, and some are considered second-class citizens. It started with janitors and food service workers, but by the late '80s, it becomes all kinds of workers, and office workers especially."

When outsourcing didn't accomplish his goals, Welch turned to offshoring. He memorably said that "ideally, you'd have every plant you own on a barge to move with currencies and changes in the economy." That way, Welch imagined, GE factories could move around the world, chasing favorable exchange rates, tax breaks, incentives, and low wages in a seaborne race to the bottom. This was the Platonic ideal of a free market enterprise to Welch—stateless, beholden to no community, and able to hire labor in a completely opportunistic way. For the Golden Age CEOs who cared so much about their communities, it would have been a dystopian nightmare. To Welch, it was something to strive for. And he nearly accomplished as much, moving massive industrial operations from cities like Fort Wayne, Indiana, and Erie, Pennsylvania, to Mexico and Brazil.

Welch managed to accomplish all this despite GE's long and sometimes contentious relationship with organized labor. During the 1950s, Lemuel Boulware, GE's vice president of labor and community relations, took a hard line at the bargaining table. His "take it or leave it" approach to negotiating became known as Boulwarism, a term that persists today in union circles. During the 1970s, relations improved, and GE had not faced a nationwide strike since 1969. Welch had no interest in antagonizing labor to the point that workers would take to the picket line, and he managed to wage his sustained and sweeping campaign against loyalty without going to war with the unions, avoiding a major strike during his time as CEO. But he was no friend to organized labor. Rather than repeat the mistakes of Boulware and demand that unions accept the company's terms—or else—Welch simply moved jobs away from pro-labor areas whenever he could, thereby drastically reducing the proportion of the GE workforce that was unionized.

Once again Welch was on the vanguard. Around the country, unions were losing power. In 1981, President Reagan fired 11,359 unionized air traffic controllers for going on strike, emboldening companies to take a tougher line with organized labor. In 1985, employees at Hormel, the meat processor, began a strike that would last for a year after the company, which was profitable, slashed worker wages. Plants were closed, tensions flared, and the National Guard had to be called in to keep the peace. To Welch, it all served as validation to his gut instinct that GE, or at least its investors, would be better off when the company had fewer unionized workers. In 1988, he met with Governor Michael Dukakis at the Massachusetts State House. While there, he complained about unionized workers at a nearby factory who had rejected GE's latest national agreement. GE was disinclined to bring any more work to the state if organized labor was so pesky, Welch told Dukakis. "Why should I put work and money where there is trouble, when I can put up plants where people want them and deserve them?" he asked. Dukakis chuckled, according to Welch, and sent an emissary to try and smooth over relations between GE and its union.

Welch was making good on his words during these years, shifting work from unionized factories in America to foreign countries wherever he could. During the last years of the 1980s and the first years of the 1990s, total head count at GE remained essentially flat, but the geographical distribution of those jobs changed dramatically. As GE increased employment in other countries by 20,000, investing heavily in operations in India, in particular, the company's head count in the United States shrank by 20,000.

The relentless downsizing sapped morale inside GE. No division was secure, no job safe. Gone was "Generous Electric," replaced by an enterprise that seemed to lack institutional memory and was consumed with reducing costs and boosting revenues, no matter the fallout. As one manager told Welch in 1988: "If this is the best business in the world, why do I go home feeling so miserable?" It was a sentiment shared widely across GE's remaining workforce. At a factory in the Netherlands, an engineer confronted the boss about it. "The plant is nothing like it used to be," he told Welch. "It's nowhere near as much fun as it was ten years ago." Welch told the worker to make a list of all the things that used to be fun about the plant, and bring them back. It was a dismissive retort, and Welch had no intention of following up. Immediately after the conversation he caught a flight to Paris. After years of slashing and burning, Welch's tactics had sapped the joy out of what was once a proud company. "Loyalty here is 24-hours deep," complained one GE executive. "Welch has lost the dedication of a couple hundred thousand people." Even Welch knew workers were unhappy. As he recalled, "the buzz around the water cooler was not good."

Even more shocking than the ways he transformed the company was how he went about it. CEOs set the tone for an organization, and Welch was loud, cantankerous, and ruthless. Summoning a colleague, he would yell to his secretary to "Get that bozo on the line!" When he didn't like an underling's presentation, he would tell other senior executives to dispose of the hapless underling: "We've got to get rid of this fucking idiot." His leadership style had all the hallmarks of toxic masculinity. He belittled the weak, demanded total fealty, and was perennially dissatisfied, even as he grew enormously wealthy. Collegiality had been replaced with competitiveness. Loyalty was out. In its place was anxiety, a fearful understanding that the man in charge was unpredictable and merciless.

Welch was, in short, a bully. "You fuckin' guys don't know what the fuck you're doing!" he fumed at executives in the plastics division when they missed their numbers. It was what the *Wall Street Journal* described as Welch's "hazing-as-shouting-match approach, that requires managers to argue strenuously," even if they agreed with him. Said one manager whom Welch replaced: "You can't even say hello to Jack without it being confrontational. If you don't want to step up to

Jack toe-to-toe, belly-to-belly, and argue your point, he doesn't have any use for you." He worked incessantly and expected that everyone at the company do the same. And throughout his career, he often employed violent rhetoric when discussing layoffs. His favorite way to describe firing someone was to say that the person should be "shot." "Shoot them," he would say, when discussing an employee he didn't like. "They ought to be shot."

Welch had shaken GE to its core. In 1984, *Fortune* magazine named him the "Toughest Boss in America," and presented a scathing indictment of his conduct. "Welch conducts meetings so aggressively that people tremble," the magazine wrote. "He attacks almost physically with his intellect—criticizing, demeaning, ridiculing, humiliating." As one employee told the magazine, "Jack comes on like a herd of elephants. If you have a contradictory idea you have to be willing to take the guff to put it forward." Said another: "Working for him is like a war. A lot of people get shot up; the survivors go on to the next battle."

Like so many of the rich and powerful, Welch had thin skin, and he was devastated by the article. It was, he said, one of the worst moments of his career. But as had been the case when *Newsweek* labeled him "Neutron Jack," he couldn't really argue with the assessment. In fact, he believed he wasn't being tough enough. Because while GE had been turned upside down, Welch's tactics were delivering the goods. Profits were strong, sales were booming, and most importantly, GE stock was soaring. Welch would go on slashing jobs in a bid to boost his margins right up to the end. "Unfortunately," he said, "it's never over."

With Welch's campaign against loyalty getting results, other companies took note. Soon, thanks in part to the example set by GE, shedding employees became an acceptable—even routine—way for companies to improve their profitability. In the late 1960s, 27 percent of American workers belonged to labor unions. That figure began to steadily decline in the 1970s, and then fell precipitously in the 1980s. By the early 1990s, union membership was down to 13 percent, and would eventually dip below 10 percent. As labor unions declined, everyday Americans got an ever-smaller slice of the economic pie. Wage growth for workers stagnated. After growing between 5 and 9 percent annually from the late 1960s until 1981, blue-collar workers saw those gains erased. During Welch's twenty years as CEO, factory workers' wages never increased by more than 4 percent a year. Often the raises were just 2 percent, which at times lagged inflation. The share of aggregate income funneled to the middle class followed an almost identical trajectory over the last forty years of the twentieth century, falling from about 53 percent in the late 1960s to less than 47 percent in 2001. With GE leading the way, American corporations were racing ahead while leaving workers behind. "A lot of people initially were a little bit alarmed," said Nicholas Heymann, the analyst. "GE's actions spawned a lot more similar type of aggressive cost restructuring across industrial America in the late '80s and through the 1990s."

"The Pac-Man model"

Having made GE smaller through downsizing, Welch sought other ways to make GE bigger. If he was going to deliver the consistent earnings growth he so longed for, GE needed to expand, and fast. Figuring out ways to make an existing business sell more stuff—so-called organic growth—was well and good. But incremental moves would only take a company like GE so far. There were only so many power plants, jet engines, and appliances that could be sold each year. Instead, he realized that in order to get GE to grow as quickly as he hoped, he would need to rely on *inorganic* growth—that is, he would have to buy other companies. "The model Jack had was really the Pac-Man model," said Beth Comstock, a longtime GE marketing executive. "Just eat up companies. Acquire growth, acquire growth, acquire growth."

During his first years as CEO, Welch had made a few acquisitions he believed could increase sales or smooth out GE's sometimes unpredictable earnings. It was growth for growth's sake, with little regard to whether the companies GE was adding to its roster were good cultural fits. He had also sold several businesses, looking to shed employees and jettison insufficiently profitable operations. But five years into the job, he had yet to make a truly transformative deal, the kind of move that would help him create the most valuable company on earth. That changed one evening in Manhattan, when he stopped by the palatial apartment of Felix Rohatyn, an esteemed investment banker, for a drink. There, Welch mingled with the tuxedoed chairman of RCA, another American conglomerate that, in 1985, was still at the peak of its powers. At the time, RCA owned the NBC television network, a large consumer electronics business, an aerospace business, a satellite operation, semiconductor manufacturing, and much more. But it was NBC that Welch wanted most, and in a matter of weeks he had negotiated to acquire RCA for $6.3 billion, making it, back then, the largest nonoil deal in history.

The takeover was made possible with an assist from the Reagan administration. For more than half a century, GE had been expressly prohibited from owning RCA. The stipulation was a vestige of antitrust enforcement from the 1930s, when the two companies were viewed as direct competitors and GE had fallen afoul of regulators in another matter. But in 1985, with free market dogma and the spirit of deregulation sweeping the government, Republicans were looking to relax laws that constrained big business. Months before GE would make an offer for RCA, the Reagan administration conveniently threw out the consent decree that had kept the two companies apart for so long. With that technicality out of the way, the deal was easily done.

With the acquisition of RCA, GE revenues soared from $28 billion annually to more than $40 billion a year. Welch said that with RCA in the fold, GE would be "one dynamite company." But almost immediately, Welch started selling RCA off, piece by piece. He sold RCA Records to Bertelsmann, a German media group. He sold the company's satellite operations to a private equity firm. And he gave away a research center in Princeton, New Jersey, to earn a tax break. In a matter of months, through layoffs and divestitures, he had reduced RCA's head count from nearly 88,000 people to less than 36,000.

Parts of the company that Welch didn't sell came under intense pressure, too. With the addition of RCA, GE's consumer electronics business was now bigger, and theoretically stronger. But it faced growing competition from Japanese and Korean manufacturers, who were turning out superior products for a fraction of the cost. To give GE a chance to regain its competitive footing, Welch and his management team convinced workers to accept concessions—pay cuts that might help the division turn a profit. Welch said he would give the consumer electronics group a few years to prove it that it could "earn its way." His patience quickly wore thin, however, and he soon agreed to swap the consumer electronics business for the medical devices unit of Thomson, a French company. It was an impulsive deal, and he would brag of how quickly he decided it was the right move. "We didn't need to go back to headquarters for a strategic analysis and a bunch of reports," he said. "Conceptually, it took us about 30 minutes to decide that the deal made sense and then a meeting of maybe two hours with the Thomson people to work out the basic terms. We signed a letter of intent in five days."

Welch portrayed the deal as a masterstroke, believing he had traded a doomed business for one with a bright future. Soon, though, it became clear that he would have done well to look more closely. The medical systems business he had acquired was weaker than GE initially understood. Orders quickly dried up. Profits evaporated. The organization, it turned out, was nearly bankrupt. By the perverse logic of Wall Street, however, that didn't much matter. What mattered, and what Welch had achieved with the RCA deal, was making GE bigger. GE's television set business was now one of the largest in the world, fulfilling the mandate Welch laid out at the Pierre Hotel in 1981, that every group should be number one or number two in its category.

The acquisition of RCA also meant that GE had control of NBC, one of the three main American broadcast networks. Suddenly, Welch was a media mogul. He reveled in GE's ownership of NBC and delighted in schmoozing with celebrities. The fact that he cut checks for the likes of David Letterman and Tom Brokaw bolstered his already formidable self-regard. Inside the company, it was widely believed he put up the money for NBC to win the rights to broadcast the Olympic Games mostly so he could have a grand forum for entertaining clients and friends.

Yet some aspects of the media business perplexed Welch. The notion that, as one of the three major broadcast networks, NBC had some grander responsibility to the public was anathema to him. He was intent on cutting costs at NBC News, just as he did everywhere else, and scoffed at the notion that NBC was a "public trust" that should be exempt from the same profit targets that other GE divisions were held to. Instead, Welch wanted to create a new revenue stream by licensing out the NBC brand to independent producers and other TV stations, and believed the network could save money by firing much of the top on-air talent.

Just how powerful NBC could be was not lost on him though, and at times Welch tried to meddle with coverage. When the stock market crashed on Black Monday, October 19, 1987, Tom Brokaw issued an ominous report on the *NBC Nightly News*, warning of further economic carnage to come. Welch thought Brokaw was being too negative and called Lawrence Grossman, the head of the news division, to complain. "You're killing all the stocks!" he burst out.

"This is not an appropriate discussion to be having," Grossman replied.

More than a decade later, on election night in 2000, Welch reportedly planted himself in the NBC newsroom, hovered near the Decision Desk, and pressured network executives to call the election for George W. Bush. Around midnight he barked, "Okay, how much do I have to pay you assholes to call this thing for Bush!"

Control of NBC also allowed him to make one of the most fateful decisions of his career. In 1993, as he reshuffled on-air talent and producers at NBC, he tapped Roger Ailes to run CNBC, the business news channel. A conservative operative, Ailes was an unconventional choice to run a station devoted to Wall Street. He had worked as an adviser to President George H. W. Bush, and when GE hired him he was the executive producer of Rush Limbaugh's television show. Once in the GE fold, however, Ailes found ways to inject his breed of divisive political entertainment into NBC. First, he created a short-lived network called America's Talking, an early attempt to create a full-time political news channel. In 1996, Ailes was ousted following a Human Resources investigation into his inappropriate behavior. Welch nevertheless remained a friend to Ailes and agreed to loosen the terms of his noncompete agreement, thus allowing him to turn around, take a job with Rupert Murdoch, and launch Fox News.

Welch's next big acquisition took GE even further from its industrial roots. In 1986, hoping to hasten the company's transition away from manufacturing and into media and finance, he bought the investment bank Kidder Peabody. This time, there was no pretense of strengthening GE's engineering know-how. Nor did Welch want Kidder because it had a sterling reputation or deep ties with American consumers. Instead, he believed the bank would give GE a bigger role in the booming business of leveraged buyouts. Buyouts, in which private equity firms take companies off the public markets, often extracting exorbitant fees along the way, were the hottest thing on Wall Street at the time. And GE Capital was already involved in the buyout business, putting up loans for some of the biggest deals of the day. But Welch wanted more. "We thought Kidder would give us first crack at more deals and access to new distribution without paying these big fees to another of Wall Street's brokerage houses," he wrote. The acquisition of Kidder was a key element of Welch's plan to push GE deeper into finance, where, he believed, you could conjure profits from thin air—without the burden of messy factories, or unionized workers.

It seemed like easy money to Welch. But the Kidder deal was doomed from the start. Just eight months after it closed, Kidder became ground zero for the biggest scandal in finance. One of its star traders, Marty Siegel, confessed to illegally providing confidential information to Ivan Boesky, one of the shrewdest investors of his day. Siegel, already the firm's highest-paid employee, had collected briefcases full of cash from Boesky in exchange for his tips, ensnaring GE in one of the biggest insider trading schemes in history. After Siegel pleaded guilty to two felony charges and agreed to cooperate with the U.S. attorney's investigation, which was being led by a young Rudy

Giuliani, armed federal agents raided Kidder's offices and made more arrests. Welch's latest deal, and his first major foray into financialization, was already a fiasco.

Hoping to bring some order to the chaos, Welch appointed a GE board member who had previously run a tool company, but had no experience in finance, to look after Kidder Peabody. The steady hand of a loyal industrialist didn't help matters much. The next year, the stock market crashed, and Kidder's business fell apart. Losses at the firm hit $72 million in 1987, prompting GE to fire 1,000 people, or 20 percent of the investment bank's staff. In the end, while Siegel ultimately went to jail, one of Welch's deputies negotiated a deal with Giuliani that let GE off unscathed. The company paid a meager fine, agreed to cease certain types of trading, and instituted more stringent controls and procedures.

Welch took no responsibility for the malfeasance at Kidder. The criminality, he pointed out, happened before GE bought the company. Welch believed the head of Kidder, Ralph DeNunzio, was of sound moral compass and "had nothing to do with the scandal." And while the deal was Welch's idea—one he pushed through the board despite the protestations of several directors—the moment trouble surfaced, he tried to wash his hands of the whole affair. The Siegel debacle was "a kick in the teeth for those guys," Welch said, suggesting that Kidder, somehow, was not part of GE. He had only been CEO for a few years, and already his grand sense of impunity was on vivid display.

Years later, Kidder gave Welch another nasty surprise: the firm had been ginning up phantom profits through a scheme that involved trading bonds. When it was discovered, GE was hit with a $210 million charge, and $1.2 billion was wiped off the balance sheet. The shocking surprise sent GE's stock down, leading to a rare miss of the quarterly earnings forecast, and offering a preview of how deeply the financial arm could rattle the entire company. It was not the trickery that bothered Welch most, however. That he could tolerate. What really bothered him was the fact that shareholders were surprised. "Having this reprehensible scheme . . . break our more-than-decade-long string of 'no surprises' has all of us damn mad," he said.

Despite the headaches, Welch's plan was working. The additions of RCA and Kidder Peabody had diversified GE away from its traditional manufacturing businesses, making it less dependent on cyclical waves of capital spending and less reliant on its traditional customers. Even more important, the deals had shown him that there was easy money to be made in TV advertising and banking. The profit margins from Kidder and NBC were seductive, and there were no factories to maintain, no unionized workers to appease. Welch had zeroed in on a fundamental truth about the modern economy that other CEOs only dimly understood at the time: the real money was going to be made not in the factories of the American heartland, but in the office towers of Wall Street and Madison Avenue. As GE deepened its push into finance, investors began to grasp what he was up to, and the stock began ticking up. By 1987, shares in the company had risen a full 250 percent from the time Welch took over.

The deals for RCA and Kidder were pivotal in another way, too. They proved to Welch that growth could come from buying, rather than building. He could acquire his way to the top, rather than innovate his way there. Overnight, GE had become one of the biggest dealmakers in the country, acquiring major companies and chopping them up for parts. It was getting harder to see GE as one interconnected whole. Instead, the company became something of an asset manager, overseeing a range of disparate businesses that had increasingly little to do with one another.

In the years that followed, Welch would buy anything that seemed like it might turn a quick profit. "We screwed up," said Rocheleau, the longtime GE executive who worked with Welch on labor relations. "We bought businesses where we didn't succeed, and bombed in a few areas. But Welch had a vision. He was saying, 'Hey where are the markets moving? Where are we going to make higher margins?'" The constant acquisitions came at the expense of research and development, organic growth, and in-house innovation, as Welch himself acknowledged. "We are not interested in incubating new businesses," he said. Indeed, during his long tenure, the closest thing to a breakout new product that GE recorded was the debut of CNBC, the all-business cable news network that turned stock watching into prime-time entertainment.

The dealmaking boom Welch unleashed reordered the economy well beyond GE. In the years before he took over, mergers and acquisitions were relatively rare. Each year, a couple thousand transactions might take place, with an aggregate value of a few tens of billions of dollars. With Welch setting the pace at GE, those numbers exploded. By the end of his tenure, the numbers of deals soared to upward of 14,000 a year, with a combined value of well over $1 trillion. Of the companies that were in the *Fortune* 500 in 1980, a full 143 of them— 28 percent—had been acquired by the end of the decade.

At the same time, corporate raiders were on the march. Men like Carl Icahn, T. Boone Pickens, and Nelson Peltz were raising money, mounting aggressive takeover campaigns against unsuspecting companies, and—once they had control—squeezing them for profits by cutting staff and slashing costs. When companies wouldn't listen to their profit-hungry investors, the raiders would mount campaigns to replace directors, installing themselves or their cronies on the board, and then forcing the company's hand. Their exploits were glamorized in films like *Wall Street*, in which Michael Douglas, playing the sneering Gordon Gekko, proclaims that "greed, for lack of a better word, is good."

Private equity was booming, too. Buyout firms were acquiring companies with borrowed money, loading them up with debt, then slashing costs and wringing out every penny they could. Kohlberg Kravis Roberts took over RJR Nabisco and Ronald Perelman went after Revlon. The barbarians were at the gate. It was a terrifying new landscape for companies, and workers, too. At any moment, an unknown firm might appear, demanding downsizing, cost cutting, and fatter profits. But GE didn't have that problem. Because while the corporate raiders and private equity titans were squeezing companies from the outside, Welch, at GE, was doing it from within. "GE is a venture capital company," said Grossman, the former president of NBC News, and dealmaking, he added, was "what makes the light shine" in Welch's eyes. "There's no commitment to people or product."

"Eating your own mother"

If Welch was going to make GE the most valuable company on earth, he knew he would have to do it with GE Capital. From the moment he first worked with the finance division in the late 1970s, he understood a simple but powerful truth: it was easier to make money by shifting around ones and zeros than by manufacturing refrigerators. "Since I had been involved in making things all my life, pounding and grinding it out to make a nickel, I couldn't believe how easy this 'appeared' to be," he recalled of his first exposure to the world of investment banking, leveraged buyouts, and loan financing. "I was sure the opportunity was enormous. All we had to do was take the business from the back of the boat to the front." In a memo to the company's chief financial officer, Welch wrote that finance, not manufacturing, represented the future of the company. "There is no place that quantum change is needed more than in Finance," he wrote. "Finance is not an institution—it has to be . . . the driving force behind making General Electric 'the most competitive enterprise on earth.'"

In 1983, Welch began aggressively expanding into the insurance business. First, he purchased American Mortgage Insurance for $90 million. The next year, he bought Employers Reinsurance Corporation for $1.1 billion. The symbolism could hardly have been more overt. At the very moment he was selling off some of GE's signature businesses—air-conditioning and small appliances—he was gobbling up companies that had nothing to do with manufacturing. Soon after those deals, he acquired Kidder Peabody. He was laying the groundwork for the most radical transformation GE would experience under his leadership: its evolution from a company that relied on its industrial prowess to one that depended on financial engineering.

During his first decade in charge, Welch grew GE Capital at a modest clip. When he took over, the unit had $11 billion in assets. A decade later, it had $70 billion in assets, and had expanded its operations from the United States to other countries as well. Kidder Peabody, problematic as it was, had given GE a foothold on Wall Street. But the real growth was yet to come. During the second half of Welch's tenure, GE Capital grew into a colossus. By the time he retired, it had a whopping $370 billion in assets and operations in nearly fifty countries.

There was no master plan. The finance division grew by chasing money wherever it could be found. Even Welch admitted as much. "We never had a great strategic vision for GE Capital," he conceded. The result was a hydra-headed monster that grew increasingly difficult to control, let alone keep tabs on. GE Capital got into Thai auto loans. It issued consumer credit cards for companies like Home Depot. It underwrote commercial property developments in Europe. It became the world's largest equipment lessor, with more than 900 airplanes, nearly 200,000 rail cars, 750,000 automobiles, more than 100,000 trucks, and eleven satellites. It handled the credit operations for companies like Kodak, fronting the bill for customers who needed a new copy machine. It gobbled up portfolios of loans, lent out fortunes to ambitious developers, and got into arcane lending markets with razor-thin margins, but enormous volume. GE even found its way into marquee real estate. In the mid-1990s the finance unit came to own a shimmering gold skyscraper on the southwest edge of Central Park and entered into an agreement to rebrand the property with Donald Trump as the Trump International Hotel & Tower.

Even as Welch reined in spending elsewhere around the company, employment grew at GE Capital. In 1977, GE Capital had fewer than 7,000 employees and earnings of some $67 million. By the time Welch retired, GE Capital was contributing $5.2 billion in earnings to the balance sheet and employed more than 89,000 people. At its peak, GE Capital accounted for more than half of GE's profits. From 1991 to 1996, GE's revenues would have grown at just 4 percent a year without the contributions of GE Capital. Thanks to the magic of finance, however, GE's revenue growth was doubled, to more than 9 percent during those years. This, in turn, stimulated GE's stock price. From 1995 to 1997, GE stock soared 123 percent, while the Standard & Poor's 500 Index rose just 63 percent. GE Capital had nearly as much prestige as Goldman Sachs, attracting top graduates from MBA programs around the country. And it paid its executives lavishly for their work. "Every planning meeting Jack ran was always the same," recalled Gary Wendt, the longtime head of GE Capital. "He'd tell everyone else to cut costs, and he'd tell me to grow the business."

But GE Capital was much more than just a profit engine for Welch. It was also a tool he used to secure low interest rates, cut GE's taxes, and smooth out its quarterly earnings. For one thing, it allowed GE to take full advantage of its sacred AAA credit rating. That pristine financial bill of health allowed GE to borrow money at a lower cost than its competitors, giving the company an edge in an industry where fractions of a percentage point can make or break an investment. And because GE Capital was intertwined with GE's old-line industrial businesses, with their reliable earnings and tangible assets, the company was able to maintain that rating without holding too much capital. The rest of the company was collateral enough.

It was the best of both worlds for a conglomerate, allowing GE Capital to be aggressive in its dealmaking and nimble in its accounting, without being encumbered by a weighty balance sheet. "GE was unique in that it had the financial services business, and the operating businesses," said Tom Rogers, a former NBC executive who worked for Welch for years and went on to be CEO of TiVo. "The flywheel effect of how those would work together was one part of the unique combination that Jack created. The financial services businesses and operating businesses worked together to create a smoother earnings approach."

More than any other factor, it was GE Capital that allowed Welch to deliver the "consistent earnings growth" that he knew, even before he was named CEO, would prove so critical to his success. Thanks to the sprawling finance division, he could produce "earnings on demand," as one analyst put it at the time. GE's manufacturing businesses—from light bulbs to airplane engines—may have been profitable, but it wasn't easy for GE to come up with top line growth in a pinch. The same wasn't true when it came to the financial assets. The global marketplace for loans is always open, and in the last days of each quarter, GE Capital would often unleash a flurry of activity, adding profits and taking restructuring charges as needed to help the parent company meet Wall Street's expectations.

As GE grew more complex, each quarter brought a new whirlwind of divestitures, acquisitions, special gains, and onetime charges that, every ninety days, miraculously produced the precise number that Wall Street analysts wanted to see. Unrelated events were timed together in a way that magically smoothed out the balance sheet. GE Capital would take a charge for closing the Montgomery Ward chain, which it owned as part of its vast real estate holdings, and in the same period report a gain thanks to the sale of its stake in PaineWebber. It even took to reporting growth in its pension fund's investment portfolio as income.

As a result, GE's quarterly profits would look like they were going up, thanks to the pension fund's investment in the stock market, and that, in turn, would push GE shares higher. And because GE was the most powerful company in the world, a rise in GE stock would send the broader markets higher still. It was an infinite loop of speculation, and it kept GE earnings growing at steady, predictable rates, avoiding any stumbles that might send its stock cratering, or exceptional quarters that would be hard to replicate a year later. "There was very little transparency," said Beth Comstock, the longtime GE marketing executive. "GE had a financial army that was able to close the quarter the way we'd said we would."

Sometimes, managing earnings meant firing workers. In 1997, GE executed a complex transaction with Lockheed Martin, the defense contractor, that earned GE a $1.54 billion profit, and tax breaks worth $600 million. It was a windfall, but GE didn't want the huge surplus to show up on its books that quarter. Because the rest of the business was performing well, adding the profits from the Lockheed deal would have caused GE earnings to spike, disrupting the otherwise consistent upward trajectory that Welch had engineered for so long. So GE found a solution. Some of its factories were underperforming, and in the last months of 1997 it devised a plan to take an enormous $2.3 billion write-off to pay for the cost of closing those plants. While the decision made GE's earnings work for the quarter, they resulted in more than 1,000 people losing their jobs. To GE, it was the cost of doing business, with a company spokesman even acknowledging the linkage in clinical terms. "Offsetting the gain has been our practice," he said.

Welch denied that GE Capital was employed as a tool to keep the company's stock price rising. "We managed businesses—not earnings," he said dismissively. But his own deputies told a different story. Many acquisitions were conceived of by executives scrambling to hit sky-high earnings targets set by Welch and other senior managers in Fairfield. "Of course we're buying earnings when we do an acquisition," GE Capital's chief financial officer said. The CFO of the entire company also acknowledged that much of its mergers and acquisitions activity was driven not by sound strategic rationale, but by the unrelenting pressure to hit ambitious financial targets. "I see nothing wrong with someone saying, 'Look, I have an earnings objective for the year, and to achieve that earnings objective maybe I need to go make an acquisition,'" he said. "That's fine if the individual can come up with a good acquisition." Even Gary Wendt, who ran GE Capital, overtly acknowledged the earnings management, but downplayed its significance. "We do a little, not a lot," he said. Whether it was a little or a lot, Welch got away with it. For most all of his tenure, accounting rules were relatively lax and neither investors nor regulators asked too many questions. "A lot of things changed shortly after Jack, from revenue recognition rules to other things," said Rogers, the former TiVo CEO, adding that it would have been hard for Welch to "to be such a predictable earnings beast if he existed in a later environment."

In addition to smoothing out earnings, the finance division helped GE lower its taxes. In 1997, GE and other companies won a change to the law that allowed them to avoid paying billions of dollars to the IRS. Known as the "active financing" exception, the new twist in the law let GE claim that money the company made from its international financing activity was actually being generated abroad. For example, if GE Capital financed the sale of a power turbine in India, it no longer had to pay U.S. taxes on the interest income, so long as it kept the profits offshore. As a result, GE could essentially avoid paying taxes on its ever-expanding lending operations around the globe, all the while amassing additional tax credits, depreciation, and write-offs that it used to offset profits it made elsewhere in the company.

Once the change was made, GE vastly increased the amount

of profits it recorded in low-tax countries such as Ireland and Singapore. Those weren't the countries where GE was doing the most business. Instead, it was where Welch had his accountants booking the profits. From 1996 through 1998, before the change fully kicked in, GE's profits and revenues in the United States were essentially aligned. About 73 percent of its sales were in the United States., and those sales accounted for about 73 percent of total profits. But after the active financing exception was enacted, those figures began to diverge. Before long, GE was reporting that while the United States was still its largest market by revenues, only a fraction of its profits came from those sales. As Welch's army of lawyers did their best to pay the Internal Revenue Service the absolute minimum necessary under the law, other companies followed GE's lead, and the share of taxes U.S. corporations paid to the U.S. government steadily fell.

Any attempts to question what was going on inside GE Capital were complicated by the fact that Welch drastically reduced the amount of information GE released about the results in the finance division, deliberately obfuscating the inner workings of the company's moneymaking engine. Under Welch, it had become a virtual certainty that GE would hit its numbers. The cash kept flowing, and no one—not the shareholders who owned GE stock nor the Wall Street professionals whose job it was to understand how GE made its money—questioned exactly how it all happened.

Investors weren't asking too many questions in part because they didn't have a chance. Quarterly earnings announcements included bare-bones figures, and Welch eschewed the practice of holding earnings calls, which were *de rigueur* for most other public companies. GE Capital was a black box—investors could see what was coming out, but had no idea what was happening inside. "We did what we were legally required to do, but we didn't break down the businesses," said Steve Kerr, a GE executive who worked closely with Welch during the 1990s. "GE Capital was contributing a huge percentage of revenues, and a lot of that growth wasn't organic. We were getting it through acquiring other companies, at one point it was five companies every two weeks. And all this was kept from public view." Welch called it "the blob"—it was an amorphous, ever-changing collection of financial assets, available to deliver whatever adjustments were most advantageous to the parent company in a moment's notice.

Though GE made detailed financial information hard to come by, Welch understood how to sell a story. Starting in the late 1980s, he began diverting some of the company's best talent to the investor relations department, which had previously been, in his words, "a career-ending job for financial types." Welch had a different idea for what this back-office function could achieve. No longer would the investor relations department simply be the link between the company and Wall Street, keeping analysts updated on the company's performance. Instead, Welch decided, the investor relations team would become "the chief marketing officer for GE stock, constantly on the road visiting investors and selling the GE story." Once again, GE was shattering norms and ushering in a new era of unbridled corporate self-promotion. Welch said it himself. His investor relations team wasn't selling products. They were selling a narrative. Emphasizing the investor relations function had an immediate effect on priorities across the company. Suddenly, Welch said, employees "got up every morning and felt they were measured by the price of GE stock."

The best way to sell the story, however, was to keep the stock price going up, and the surest way to do that, Welch learned, was to buy back stock. With buybacks, a public company spends its own money to purchase shares from other investors at a premium. In theory, the company believes its stock is undervalued, and that by reducing the number of outstanding shares, it will consolidate its ownership at an attractive price, and make those shares that remain publicly traded more valuable. But there is another benefit, too. Wall Street analysts often measure companies on the basis of earnings per share—that is, how much profit a company makes compared to how many shares are publicly traded. When a company buys back its own stock, it automatically boosts its earnings per share, often leading to a jump in the stock price. "If I can get another cent of earnings per share if I just buy back stock and make the denominator smaller, you know, hey, what's not to like?" said Roger Martin, the Rotman School dean.

Buybacks effectively let companies manipulate their own stock price, and for that reason, they had been banned for half a century. The Securities Act of 1933, passed after the stock market crash that led to the Great Depression, barred companies from intentionally meddling with their own share price. Buybacks weren't illegal, per se, but if companies did them, they could easily be exposed to charges of manipulation. Then in 1982, the Securities and Exchange Commission blessed a change to the law that gave companies the green light to start buying back their own stock. It was another gift from the Reagan administration to the business community. Rather than invest in new products and services, or their employees, companies could now use their profits to simply repurchase their own shares, driving their stock price up. It was morning in America, and a new era of stock market gamesmanship was dawning. Welch seized on this opportunity, and he would go on to announce what was at the time the largest stock buyback program in the history of American business—some $10 billion in share repurchases. It was his down payment on a strategy that would push GE shares ever higher.

Using so much capital for buybacks—rather than research and development, capital improvements, or worker wages—was alien to many business titans of the day. As Welch forged ahead with buybacks, the CEO of U.S. Steel, one of the few American companies as iconic as GE, likened the practice of buybacks to "eating your own mother." But in time, the rest of corporate America fell in line. By the late 1980s, major corporations were spending around 30 percent of their profits purchasing their own shares. That figure rose to about 50 percent in the 1990s. In theory, the money spent on buybacks and dividends is supposed to trickle down to everyday Americans in the form of richer retirement accounts, as the fund managers who hold so much GE stock dutifully increase the value of the everyman's 401(k). In practice, however, research has shown that buybacks exacerbate inequality.

As William Lazonick, the author of one influential study on buybacks, summarized: "Corporate profitability is not translating into widespread economic prosperity." When assessing where to lay the blame, Lazonick identifies buybacks and dividends as a main culprit. Looking at the S&P 500, he found that between 2003 and 2012, companies deployed a full 54 percent of their earnings—some $2.4 trillion—to buy back their own stock. Another 37 percent of earnings during that period was spent on dividends paid out to shareholders. "That left very little for investments in productive capabilities or higher incomes for employees," he wrote. And as for those 401(k)s? At the end of the day, workers don't benefit from buybacks and dividends because on balance, they own relatively little stock. So why then, were executives so enamored with buybacks and dividends? Lazonick had an simple explanation: "Stock-based instruments make up the majority of their pay," he said, "and in the short term buybacks drive up stock prices." Given these dynamics, "the very people we rely on to make investments in the productive capabilities that will increase our shared prosperity are instead devoting most of their companies' profits to uses that will increase their own prosperity."

Had so much of the wealth created by corporations not been "reverse distributed" back to investors in the form of buybacks and dividends over the past forty-five years, and had pay kept pace with productivity, the average full-time American worker would be making about $102,000 annually, roughly double what he or she is today. And yet, despite these unsavory statistics, buybacks remain popular across corporate America, and few companies have spent more money on repurchasing their own shares over the years than GE.

Many other American companies saw GE's success with financial services and got in the game as well. John Deere, Caterpillar, and Hewlett-Packard created finance divisions, and made substantial profits not by selling their products, but by lending money. Often, the strategy backfired. Westinghouse, long one of the few conglomerates that could rival GE's size and scope, doubled down on risky real estate loans while abandoning its traditional appliances business. It was GE in miniature, but it didn't work out as well. Through a series of mergers and acquisitions, the company ultimately became CBS, but not before laying waste to thousands of jobs. National Steel acquired the United Financial Corporation of California, while Armco, another steel company, got into the insurance business. Finance had won the day. The pursuit of glory on the New York Stock Exchange and NASDAQ had become the new national pastime, with CEOs, investors, and even everyday employees tracking share prices like baseball scores. At Microsoft, workers had an application preinstalled on their computers that displayed a cartoon face on their screens—when the MSFT ticker was going up, the face smiled; when it was going down, the face frowned.

As the rest of corporate America followed Welch's lead, finance became the fastest-growing part of the U.S. economy. Big banks got bigger, trading firms proliferated, and the mergers and acquisitions boom that Welch helped ignite put thousands of bankers and lawyers to work buying and selling companies. Financial services became an ever-larger portion of America's gross domestic product, rising from just under 5 percent in 1980 to nearly twice that in the years that followed. Those who chose to work on Wall Street began to enjoy disproportionate rewards. When Welch took over, financial services workers were paid about the same as what folks in other industries made. But in time, remuneration for bankers and traders would skyrocket. And with money came talent. As Wall Street became the country's new economic center of gravity, bright graduates from top universities no longer aspired to be doctors or lawyers. Instead, they wanted to join the pin-striped army and work at a company like Goldman Sachs, Lehman Brothers, Bear Stearns, or GE Capital.

Near the end of Welch's reign, *Money* magazine took stock of GE's influence on the markets. "GE is exceptionally good at managing earnings, arguably better than any other company," it wrote. "But it is hardly alone. On the contrary, managing earnings—and expectations—has become standard operating procedure in corporate America. In a world where one quarter's results can make or break a stock, GE's methods have become the model that business follows." *Fortune* put Welch and Coca-Cola CEO Roberto Goizueta on the cover with the headline "Champs! When it comes to creating shareholder wealth, these guys are in a league of their own."

Goizueta, who also lavished his investors with buybacks and dividends, said his overarching goal was "to increase shareholder value over time," and he was consumed with it "from the time I get up in the morning to the time I go to bed," he said. "I even think about it when I am shaving."

The pursuit of shareholder value had become all consuming, and for Welch and his ilk, the layoffs, the ceaseless disposals and acquisitions, the fuzzy accounting—it was all the cost of playing the game. He had identified his goals—to keep earnings endlessly ticking up, and to create the most valuable company in the world—and he would do whatever it took to win. "Jack was very competitive," said Martin, the former Rotman School dean. "The game had been established, and he wanted to win. He knew the rules and he was going to modify his behavior in whatever way was necessary to succeed. Even though from a business strategy standpoint—in terms of the long-term sustainability of the company—he was doing the wrong thing, he was doing anything legal that would make the shareholders better off."

All the machinations worked. Financialization allowed GE to make more money with fewer employees, and in the waning days of 1993 Welch accomplished his long-sought goal. On the Big Board of the New York Stock Exchange, GE eclipsed Exxon to become the world's most valuable company, worth nearly $100 billion on the stock market. It was a mantle GE would retain more or less uninterrupted for the rest of Welch's tenure, and in the years that followed GE would grow to be worth even more, topping out at $600 billion. To Welch, it was his crowning accomplishment. Years later, on the eve of his retirement, reflecting on decades at the company that spanned the globe, he could think of no greater achievement. "The best thing you can say about GE during this period is just factual," he said. "That it became the most valuable company in the world."

THREE

That's Why They Got Hired

"Jobs may come and go"

GE was peerless in the postwar era—the undisputed pacesetter for the rest of the business world. But IBM came close. Nearly as old as GE and almost as influential, International Business Machines, or Big Blue, was a technology pioneer long before the advent of the computer, and became one of the country's most successful companies. For much of the twentieth century, IBM, like GE, fostered a "cradle to grave" culture, making it a company where workers were virtually guaranteed lifetime employment. At its campus an hour north of New York City, employees enjoyed generous benefits, salaries that kept pace with inflation, and even country club memberships. Thomas J. Watson, IBM's CEO in the postwar years, established three core company beliefs: customer service, excellence, and respect for the individual. It was IBM's own version of the Johnson & Johnson Credo, and Watson wrote a book on the topic, *A Business and Its*

Beliefs, in which he detailed the company's approach to employee loyalty. "The IBM policy on job security . . . has meant a great deal to our employees. From it has come our policy to build from within. We go to great lengths to develop our people, to retrain them when job requirements change and to give them another chance if we find them experiencing difficulties in the jobs they are in."

In the 1980s, as Welch unleashed his campaign against loyalty at GE, IBM was still clinging proudly to its legacy as a model employer. Layoffs were unheard of, and in 1985, IBM even retooled its own marketing efforts to differentiate itself from GE, unveiling a new ad campaign with the tagline, "Jobs may come and go. But people shouldn't." It was an explicit rebuke of Welchism, a rejoinder to CEOs who fetishized downsizing.

By the early 1990s, however, market pressures were too powerful for even IBM to resist. After Big Blue reported a sharp quarterly loss, the company was eager to kick-start its languishing stock price and went looking for a new CEO who could work the Welchian magic. At one point, the IBM board even tried to entice Welch to consider the job. He declined to entertain the offer. But the board was able to attract Lou Gerstner, a former American Express executive who for the previous few years had served as chief executive of RJR Nabisco, following its leveraged buyout by the private equity firm Kohlberg Kravis Roberts. Within months of Gerstner's arrival at IBM, the unthinkable happened; 60,000 of Big Blue's employees were let go at once. It was the largest mass layoff in history at the time, and an exclamation point on a new era of mass insecurity for American workers.

With IBM's burst of downsizing, one of the last holdouts from the Golden Age of Capitalism had finally given in. Welch's upside-down view of labor—that it was a cost, not an asset—was now fully accepted, and had become the intellectual justification for the wholesale reshaping of how corporate America treated its employees. In the 1980s alone, the top 500 companies in America reduced their head count by a combined three million people. Roughly a third of all middle management jobs were vaporized. With Welch leading the way, companies increasingly turned to mass layoffs to boost profits. "He took out more than a third of the people, and while I was there, the world began copying what GE did," said Steve Kerr, whom Welch appointed as GE's first chief people officer. "If Jack jumped off a bridge, half the *Fortune* 500 would have been jumping off bridges."

Lee Iacocca, another larger-than-life CEO who ran Chrysler during the 1980s and early 1990s, closed factories and thinned the ranks at headquarters even as he earned $20 million a year. AT&T was doing well, but decided to fire 40,000 people as it reshuffled divisions in a bid to create more shareholder value. "Some people find it hard to understand why we're taking these steps now while AT&T is still healthy and still a market leader," acknowledged the CEO, Robert Allen. And in 1994, Scott Paper, a producer of tissue and toilet paper, hired "Chainsaw" Al Dunlap, who had a reputation for slashing head count to boost profits.

The carnage at Scott was immediate. Dunlap announced plans to fire more than a third of employees, and more than three fourths of the company's executives. The research and development operation was cut by more than half as well. Scott, which was long a pillar of the Philadelphia business community, closed its headquarters there and relocated to Boca Raton, Florida, where Dunlap lived. His ruthless tactics worked at first. Dunlap told investors he was on track to save $420 million a year, causing Scott's shares to more than triple. As if by magic, he created $6.3 billion in new value by jettisoning employees. Then he sold Scott Paper to Kimberly-Clark for $9.4 billion, extracting a $100 million payday for himself. "Most CEOs are ridiculously overpaid," Dunlap said, "but I deserved the $100 million."

Dunlap wasn't done. In 1996, he took over Sunbeam Products, the small-appliances maker, and reprised the tactics that had earned him such a hefty payday at Scott Paper. He fired workers and squeezed suppliers, and as costs came down, the stock ticked up. But in 2001, the SEC charged Dunlap with accounting fraud, alleging he had "orchestrated a fraudulent scheme to create the illusion of a successful restructuring of Sunbeam and facilitate the sale of the company at an inflated price." He was fired for misleading investors, and Sunbeam was forced to file for bankruptcy.

Dunlap rivaled Welch not only in his willingness to cut staff, but also in his gleeful belligerence. "He was the most unpleasant, personally repulsive businessman I ever met in my life," recalled one colleague. "Every conversation began in a normal tone of voice and ended with the man yelling, red-faced and furious, at whoever was standing in front of him." It was a temperament reminiscent of Welch's own, and Dunlap looked up to Welch. When asked who, if anyone in the business world he actually admired, he had just two names to offer: Bill Gates, then at the peak of his monopolistic powers, and Jack Welch. "Myself, Jack Welch, people like that, don't really exist now. People want to be liked," Dunlap said in retirement. "I always said, in business, strive for respect. If you want to be liked, get a dog."

Other iconic CEOs of the 1990s also looked to Neutron Jack as a role model. Jacques Nasser, who became chief executive of Ford Motor Company in 1999, arrived on the job convinced that the company was hopelessly behind the times. He saw the profits being generated at GE and other companies that had doubled down on shareholder primacy, and he believed that Ford could replicate the formula. Nasser was an unabashed fan of Welch, citing the GE CEO as an inspiration for his own work, and even paying a visit to GE to learn from Welch himself.

Nasser did his best to mimic the strategies that had elevated GE's stock price to such great heights. He closed underperforming plants and sold off some businesses. And he used mergers and acquisitions to diversify into junkyards, repair shops, and more. Ford workers were rattled by those moves, but it was Nasser's attempt to emulate Welch's process of sorting employees into A, B, and C players that led to his downfall. When Nasser implemented stack ranking, Ford's managers wound up giving several middle-aged, white male employees poor reviews. That led to an age discrimination suit, which the company settled for $12 million without admissions of wrongdoing.

Nasser was ousted, and Bill Ford, the great-grandson of Henry Ford, was tapped to take over as chief executive. At a press conference announcing the management change, Ford explained that after two years under the influence of a man who revered Jack Welch, the company was in sorry shape. "We have relationships that are very important to us, and a lot of those are either broken or not healthy," Ford told the assembled press. Nasser had wrecked morale inside the company and alienated key constituents outside, and the company could bear it no longer. "The cacophony of noise and the overwhelming pressures from our constituents and from the media got to the point where to say we were distracted would be an understatement," Ford said. "It was reaching almost to the paralysis point for a lot of our management and a lot of our employees."

The wave of downsizing that Welch unleashed quickly began to reshape the distribution of wealth nationwide. Whereas productivity and worker pay had more or less risen and fallen in tandem over the years, that was no longer the case. Now, corporate profits began to explode and the earnings of CEOs skyrocketed, but the wealth of everyday workers barely rose at all. Even as thousands of people were suddenly unemployed, sapped of incomes and purchasing power, their former employers were being bid up on the stock market, creating billions of dollars in new value for investors. Nowhere was this dynamic more pronounced than at GE, where it seemed like the more employees Welch let go, the higher the stock price climbed.

These perverse economics were the inevitable result of the revolution that had begun decades before, when Hayek, Friedman, and the rest of the far-right, free market economists dreamed up their new version of capitalism. Welch had shown what could be done at GE, demonstrating that it was not just possible, but lucrative to run a major company by putting profits before people. And it was only the beginning. Welchism was a virus, and having been incubated inside GE, it was now spreading. CEOs at other companies understood that eliminating workers was an easy way to increase profits, and they eagerly followed Welch's example. The contagion had begun, and all of corporate America would soon be infected.

"I want a revolution"

For the better part of a century, long before Welch came on the scene, GE was the most influential company in the country when it came to organizational design and executive development. Charles Coffin, who took over GE in 1892, was known as the "father of professional management." In 1900, the *Wall Street Journal* declared, "General Electric is entitled now to take rank as one of the . . . best managed industrial companies known to investors." During the first half of the twentieth century, as the company grew in size and complexity, its executives devised sophisticated methods for organizing tens of thousands of workers, creating efficient layers of management, and identifying and promoting the most talented among them.

An influential Harvard Business School case study chronicled how GE became "a bellwether of American management practices." In the 1930s, GE was "a model of the era's highly centralized, tightly controlled corporate form," the study continued. Two decades later, as it diversified in the postwar years, "GE had delegated responsibility to hundreds of department managers, leading a trend towards greater decentralization." And in the 1960s, as the company grew but profits stalled, GE moved to "strengthen its corporate staffs and develop sophisticated strategic planning systems." At each juncture, other companies looked to GE for guidance, mimicking its human resources strategy and organizational charts. Over and over, "GE found itself at the leading edge of management practice," the study concluded.

GE invested heavily in the management training programs needed to support an ever more complex organization. In 1956 alone, the company spent about $40 million a year, or nearly 10 percent of its pretax earnings, on management education. As *Management Today*, a journal for org-chart aficionados, proclaimed, "No single company has made such a singular contribution to the arts and wiles, the viewpoints and the techniques, of large-scale corporate management as GE." GE was the corporation other CEOs looked to for guidance on how they ought to run their own companies, and the place where headhunters went to find talent. "When a company needs a loan, it goes to a bank," *Fortune* once wrote. "When a company needs a CEO, it goes to General Electric, which mints business leaders the way West Point mints generals."

GE even had its own elite training ground for up-and-coming stars, a retreat where white collar gladiators could hone their skills. Known as Crotonville, the campus was spread across fifty-two acres in the bucolic town of Croton-on-Hudson, just north of New York City and not far from West Point. Built by GE in the 1950s, it was an in-house business school where company executives could get a bit of continuing education and marinate in the corporate culture. At first, Crotonville was where middle managers learned to run their businesses using GE's novel organizational methods. In the 1970s, they were taught how to manage inflation and come to grips with globalization. The facility was the first of its kind, and it would inspire other companies, including IBM, Hitachi, and Boeing to create similar centers. But by the time Welch took over, Crotonville had lost its luster inside GE. It wasn't regarded as a selective club where the best managers refined their skills. Instead, it was viewed as an unchallenging in-house junket, a pit stop on the way to retirement.

Welch wanted to change that. Instead of a dowdy corporate training center, Welch wanted to make Crotonville more like a private club, a place where the company's best wanted to see and be seen. "I wanted the good ones coming up, not the tired ones looking for a last reward," he said. In January of 1981, after Welch had been named CEO but before he had taken over from Jones, he cornered GE's head of compensation and development at a company meeting in Belleair, Florida. "I want a revolution," Welch said. "And I want it to start in Crotonville." On Welch's orders, the company spent $75 million to retrofit the campus, adding posh accommodations, a state-of-the-art gym, and a high-tech conference center. Among the additions Welch insisted on: a helipad, which would allow him to avoid the drive from GE headquarters an hour away. Town officials initially refused to allow him to install it, as it violated local ordinances. But Welch gave them an ultimatum: let him have the helipad, or he would move the Crotonville facility, known as the Management Development Institute, elsewhere. The town gave in, and Welch commuted by helicopter.

These investments, at a time when he was laying off tens of thousands of workers each year, drew the ire of GE's rank and file. Welch didn't care. If he was going to run the world's best company, he wanted the cream of his managerial crop to have the best amenities. "The spending and the cutting were consistent with where we needed to go," he said. "I wanted to change the rules of engagement, asking for more—from fewer."

The refurbished Crotonville was known as "Jack's Cathedral," and its centerpiece was a 110-seat amphitheater where executives hashed out management techniques and argued about strategy. Welch dubbed it "The Pit," named after the hardscrabble playground in North Salem where he had learned, as an undersized boy, to tangle with neighborhood kids older and bigger than he. At times, executives faced the withering interrogation of Welch himself, who would swoop in every few weeks and deliver a masterclass.

Even when the boss wasn't there, Crotonville was a place where the rough edges of business were constantly on display. Locker room humor was pervasive. Bad performances in the Pit were met with a hail of crumpled-up paper balls. Food fights in the cafeteria were not uncommon. Rival cliques tossed firecrackers at each other. One evening in 1985, an observer wandered by a classroom on the campus and saw ten recent college grads, newly hired into the GE managerial ranks, crowded around a table. An argument was raging as the group debated two statements written on a flip chart at the front of the room:

Jack Welch is the greatest CEO GE has ever had.
Jack Welch is an asshole.

Another night, not long after that, an executive assembled his colleagues in the Pit, dimmed the lights, and screened a lesbian porn film, driving the class's only two women out of the room. When Welch was told of such antics, "he laughed and purred." It was just the kind of testosterone-fueled camaraderie he was looking for. He wasn't polite, and he didn't expect his minions to be, either. This was capitalist boot camp, meant to weed out those who lacked sufficient grit for the unsavory tasks at hand. "Crotonville had to become deliberately evangelical, its every graduate a missionary capable of spreading the word," wrote Noel Tichy, a University of Michigan business school professor who ran the program for Welch, and Stratford Sherman, a *Fortune* reporter, in their 1993 book, *Control Your Destiny or Someone Else Will*. Yet in the end, what was being taught was not sound business practices designed to deliver long-term value. Instead, it was a crash course in bare-knuckled cost cutting and profit maximization—Welchism 101—and the curriculum informed a generation of CEOs that was about to reshape the economy.

"No bozos"

GE's distinguished managerial pedigree and its training facility at Crotonville, colloquially known as GE University, gave Welch enormous credibility. GE executives were considered the gold standard in corporate America; executives who worked with Welch were believed to be as dependable as the company's products. And when other companies could, they poached Welch's deputies. During his twenty years as CEO, Welch personally groomed an army of protégés who internalized his tactics and took them to dozens of companies around the country.

They ran industrial and medical companies like 3M, Amgen, Arctic Cat, Boeing, Chrysler, Fiat, Goodyear, Great Lakes Chemical, Honeywell, Medtronic, McDonnell Douglas, Owens Corning, Polaris, Rubbermaid, SPX, and Stanley. They led media and technology companies like Discovery Communications, Intuit, Nielsen, Nortel, Symantec, and TiVo. They ran financial firms including Ceridian, Conseco, and Equifax. And they took over retailers such as Albertsons and Home Depot. For a time in the early 2000s, five of the top thirty companies in the Dow Jones Industrial Average were run by men who had worked for Welch. "GE was the place everyone went to recruit," said Bill George, the former CEO of Medtronic. "GE became the source, and they spread GE thinking across American industry."

Tom Neff, chairman of the executive search firm Spencer Stuart, said that thanks to the results Welch delivered, GE was a "hunting ground" that was viewed as "the preferred academy company for other businesses." There was also the fact that in the short term, hiring a GE executive was good for a company's share price. Time and again, when a public company announced that it was making an executive from GE its new CEO, the stock jumped. When Allied-Signal announced that one of Welch's closest lieutenants was taking over, its stock shot up 13 percent. When another Welch acolyte took over Goodyear, the tire company's share price jumped 12 percent on the news. When a Welch loyalist was announced as the next CEO of 3M, the company's market capitalization increased by some $4.5 billion. "That's why they got hired," said William Conaty, GE's longtime head of Human Resources. "Because they had the playbook. They had the GE toolkit. And boards back then thought that was the answer."

Larry Bossidy was practically inseparable from Welch during the Neutron Jack years. Both shared a disdain for inefficiency and a lust for profitability. But after a decade in Welch's shadow, Bossidy wanted to run his own company, and in 1991 he accepted the job as chief executive of AlliedSignal, a diversified manufacturing and chemicals conglomerate that had fallen on hard times.

AlliedSignal was in the doldrums after years of poor management and mediocre sales. Bossidy quickly began reshaping the company in Welch's image. He slashed capital spending, cut 6,200 jobs, and got tough with suppliers, winnowing their ranks and demanding better prices. Bossidy also brought Welch's brusque management style to a company that already was suffering from low morale, dismissing those he believed to be poor performers with retorts such as: "This organization needs no bozos."

Once, a foreman confronted Bossidy about his enormous pay package, yelling at the boss, "Do you deserve your pay?"

"Yes!" Bossidy shouted back. "Do you deserve yours?"

Bossidy left no doubt about who his role model was. His letters to shareholders were near-facsimiles of Welch's annual missives for GE. And when challenged about his sharp-elbowed management style, he invoked his mentor. "For years, being totally direct wasn't regarded as a plus," he said. "Then under Jack Welch, it came into vogue."

At times, Bossidy took steps that ran counter to the Welch playbook. He slashed the AlliedSignal dividend by nearly half, preserving cash and plowing it back into the company. Rather than spread AlliedSignal too thin by expanding into new business lines, he doubled down on the company's core markets. And instead of going after major deals that would radically reshape the company, Bossidy for the most part looked for smaller deals that filled holes in AlliedSignal's portfolio and were easy to integrate. Then in 1999, AlliedSignal paid $14 billion for Honeywell. The combined company took on the better-known Honeywell name and emerged as a formidable diversified industrial conglomerate. It was nowhere near the size of GE, but Bossidy had created a thriving company, with strong operations in many of GE's core business lines. AlliedSignal's business had turned around, and Bossidy's success there was seen as proof positive that Welch's disciples were the best of the best.

Welch was preparing to retire when Honeywell and AlliedSignal merged. GE was the most valuable company in the world, and he could have gone out on top. But the allure of one last megadeal captivated him. Sizing up the company Bossidy had assembled, Welch was not satisfied to admire his old friend's handiwork from afar. Instead, he wanted it for himself, and GE launched an ill-fated effort to take over Honeywell. The deal would have bolstered GE's market share in critical areas and given it new exposure to profitable industrial lines. U.S. antitrust regulators signaled their approval for the combination. By this time they were under the spell of the free market gospel, and were disinclined to challenge acquisitions that would increase concentration, so long as they didn't immediately raise prices for everyday consumers. Regulators in Europe, however, had a more nuanced view of the problems with excessive market concentration and effectively blocked the acquisition. After a year of torturous negotiations, GE walked away, foiling Welch's attempt to pull off one last coup.

Inside Honeywell, GE's efforts to take over the company were an enormous distraction. Morale slipped, sales suffered, and the stock price dipped as an air of uncertainty loomed. When the deal finally was called off, Bossidy had little patience for a deliberate turnaround strategy that might take years to accomplish. Determined to revive the stock price of the company he assembled, Bossidy went full Neutron Jack, earning his own nickname: Larry "the Knife." In the first year after the deal was scuttled, he cut 15,800 jobs, or 13 percent of the Honeywell workforce, and shut down fifty-one factories. "His strategy is to cut, cut, cut," said an analyst at the time. "And he's very good at that."

Other Welch protégés were plunged into tumult from the start. John Trani, who had risen to be head of GE medical systems, left in 1997 to become CEO of Stanley Works, the New Britain, Connecticut, based tool company. He had no experience in tools, but Stanley's board of directors believed in the Welch pixie dust and gave Trani the run of the place, along with an enormous pay package.

Stanley was founded in 1843 by Frederick T. Stanley, with a mission to create a company with "unsurpassed customer service, product innovation and integrity." The company became a New England industrial powerhouse, working its way into the *Fortune* 500. Trani exhibited little regard for that history. He started out with a bang, slashing costs, moving work to cheaper locales, and streamlining middle management. Thousands of workers in Connecticut making $14 an hour were replaced with workers in China making 30 cents an hour. He had machinery from the headquarters in New Britain disassembled, sent across the world, and reassembled for his cheaper labor force. "There are so many costs to be squeezed out of this company that it will take me years," he said.

Shares in Stanley popped on the news, as investors anticipated another GE-like rocket ride. But within a year, it became clear that the turnaround would take longer than anticipated, and Stanley stock sank once again. In response, Trani kept cutting, a few hundred jobs here, a few hundred jobs there, sending as much work as he could overseas. Eventually, Trani, like Bossidy, earned his own version of the "Neutron Jack" moniker. He was known as "The Cutter." Soon, the employees were seething mad, revenues had flatlined, and the stock was in freefall.

Taking a cue from Welch, who held GE's annual meetings in remote locales far from headquarters to discourage attendance by employees and other potential agitators, Trani did the same. In 1999, Stanley's shareholder meeting took place not in Connecticut, where the company was based, but in Columbus, Ohio. Undaunted, dozens of Stanley employees got on a bus and made the twelve-hour drive to protest Trani's management, the ceaseless cuts, the offshoring, the outsourcing. A retired employee told the CEO that the city that gave rise to Stanley was withering under his leadership. "New Britain built itself around Stanley Works, now I see it just falling apart," he said. "You're killing the city, as well as the Stanley name." Another employee lamented the fact that employees were suffering because the stock was down, and the company had invested all the funds in the 401(k) plan in company stock. "We're losing our jobs," he said. "We're losing our stock. Our 401(k)'s down the toilet." Another worker stood up and demanded of Trani: "Where is your American pride?"

Trani hit back, just like Bossidy had, just like Welch did all the time. "I look at it every day in the mirror," he replied. "I'm proud to be an American. We just have a different view of the world."

In fact, Trani was on the verge of plotting an act of economic treason. In 2001, he learned from a *Businessweek* article that certain corporations, including Ingersoll Rand and Cooper Industries, were moving their headquarters to Bermuda in a bid to reduce their tax bill. He instructed his chief financial officer to investigate the matter, and plans quickly took shape for Stanley to follow suit. The move, which would have saved Stanley from paying the U.S. government about $30 million a year in taxes, needed two thirds of investors to approve it, and was put to a shareholder vote. The big institutional shareholders appeared ready to support the move. But getting final approval for the proposal would require the votes of the shares held by the company's 401(k) plan. Employees, burned by Trani at this point, had no incentive to support a move that would further distance Stanley from its Connecticut roots, and were initially told that not voting their shares would count as a vote against the plan. Then at the last minute, Stanley changed the rules, and decided to count any unaccounted-for shares from the 401(k) plan as votes for the move. The proposal passed, and Stanley was on its way to Bermuda.

As news of Stanley's misleading communications with its employees spread, Connecticut attorney general Richard Blumenthal brought a case against the company. The penalties were potentially severe. Executives involved in the plan could have been barred from serving on public company boards. Worse, lawmakers in Washington, still reeling from 9/11, had declared Trani's tax evasion efforts unpatriotic. "During this time of war, they have chosen profit over patriotism and turned their back on the United States of America," said Congressman Richard Neal, Democrat of Massachusetts. "Here's a company pulling up stakes when the cleanup at Ground Zero is barely done," said Senator Chuck Grassley, Republican of Iowa. Trani and his allies backed down, and the move was abandoned. The next year, Trani retired early and abruptly, leaving without having named a successor.

"Wall Street gave him too much credit too soon, just because he came from GE," one analyst said at the time. It turned out that having worked under Welch did not automatically qualify someone to run a corporation. Five years after Trani left, Stanley was still suffering from his mismanagement. In 2008, just before Christmas, the company said it would slash another 2,000 jobs. By this point, workers were inured to the cuts. "It's no shock," said one machinist, who was working the evening shift when a reporter called her with the news. "Now, it's just routine, just something that happens almost every year."

It wasn't only the American heartland that suffered under the leadership of former GE executives. Welchism was going international, too. In 1998, Paolo Fresco, a native-born Italian who was one of Welch's top deputies, left GE to become chairman of Fiat SpA, the

Italian industrial conglomerate. Fresco had been close with Welch for a decade, helping him strike deals like the trade of GE's consumer electronics business for Thomson's medical imaging business, and the takeover of Tungsram, a Hungarian light bulb maker. Neither of those deals was much of a success, but they gave Fresco the confidence that he could pull off big moves.

From the outset, Fresco was clear about his mission at Fiat. He wanted to import Welchism to Italy, a country where many of the features of America's Golden Age of capitalism—lifetime employment, generous benefits, reasonable hours—still prevailed. That would mean shaking up labor relations, striking deals, and pushing into new industries, including finance. "The company that doesn't change doesn't survive," he said, channeling Welch's Darwinian view of industry. Fresco even enticed Welch to join the Fiat board, the only time Welch took such a role at another company while he was CEO of GE. "He's the best chief executive in the United States," said Fresco. "It's nice to have him around."

Among the first items on Fresco's agenda was a dealmaking spree. He spent $350 million for a tool company from Michigan, and $4.3 billion for a heavy equipment maker from Wisconsin. He tried to buy Volvo for $15 billion, but was rebuffed. And he pressed to expand the company's financial operations, while at the same time trimming staff where he could. It was all part of what he saw as his sole mandate: "I want to maximize shareholder value," he said.

But what worked at GE was less effective at Fiat. The downsizing triggered angry protests in Italy, which in turn led to strikes. With morale shaken, operations faltered and Fiat began losing market share. The stock, after jumping upon Fresco's arrival, began to slide. Fresco's answer to the crisis was further cuts, and in 2002 he proposed slashing another $1 billion in costs from the auto operation and laying off another 6,500 factory workers. That didn't work, either. By 2003, Fiat shares had fallen 65 percent, and Fresco agreed to step down earlier than planned.

Bossidy, Trani, and Fresco gave the world a preview of what Welchism looked like beyond GE. The CEOs had internalized

Welch's tactics and were determined to use them quickly and aggressively to boost the share prices of their companies. But whatever gains they achieved proved fleeting. As Welch's acolytes tried to use his playbook at other companies, they found that repeating their boss's success was harder than anticipated. And this was just the beginning. Only years later, when Welch retired, did the floodgates fully open, unleashing dozens more of his disciples across the corporate world.

Welch did have his virtues. He had boundless energy and inspired others to work ceaselessly. He demanded excellence, and often got it. Underlings were fearful that Welch himself would know more about their business than they did, which drove them to master their facts and do their homework. He reduced bureaucracy, often resulting in job losses, but also boosting efficiency and speeding up decision-making. He was brutally honest. He had a knack for strategy and a keen sense of emerging trends. And although many of his disciples emulated the worst of what he had to offer, a choice few were able to take the best of Welch and use it for the common good.

Stanley Gault grew sales and created a collaborative, innovative culture at Goodyear. Dave Cote, a senior GE executive who was among the final half dozen candidates to succeed Welch, went on to have a strong run at Honeywell after Bossidy left. Over more than a decade, Cote emerged as a durable leader who oversaw sustained growth in his company's core business, without resorting to massive layoffs or financial engineering. Honeywell stock soared during his tenure, making him one of the few Welch protégés to deliver sustained growth for investors. Another Welch disciple, Omar Ishrak, left GE after feeling like he didn't have the support to innovate and develop new products, according to Bill George, who recruited Ishrak to Medtronic, the medical device maker. Ishrak thrived there, and wound up becoming CEO of Medtronic, growing the company's market share and introducing breakthrough new offerings.

And at Polaris, a Minnesota-based maker of snowmobiles and all-terrain vehicles, Tom Tiller, who worked with Welch for fifteen years, accomplished an increasingly rare feat: growing an American company while keeping most of its manufacturing in the United States. By maintaining its factories in the upper Midwest and resisting the temptation to build vehicles with cheaper labor overseas, Tiller managed to nearly double Polaris's sales through organic growth—not acquisitions—while hiring aggressively and maintaining his workers' loyalty. Welchism wasn't going to work at Polaris, and Tiller knew it. "I'm not a communist," Tiller said. "But there's a much more competitive model, and I think Polaris exemplifies it. The maniacal focus on cost cutting really hollows out a lot of the business. We were going to do what was right for the long term. That's what America needs."

From his time at GE, Tiller knew how corrosive it could be when the CEO had a contentious dynamic with factory workers. "Jack didn't have a love affair with the individual employee at the hourly level," he said. "It was always a bit of an adversarial relationship." At Polaris, Tiller resolved to cultivate a close bond with his factory workers from the outset. "We had a fundamentally different outlook at Polaris," he said. "People were highly productive, not because they thought we were going to close a plant or move it to Mexico, but because they respected the management." For Tiller, that also meant paying his employees decent wages, while keeping his own compensation in check. "I made more money than the guy that was turning the screws, but we were all on the same elevator," Tiller said.

Over a decade, Tiller managed to nearly double sales at Polaris. Shareholders, too, were rewarded for Tiller's prudent stewardship. The stock went up steadily, posting annual returns that averaged 15 percent while the market was up just 2 percent on average during that time, a practically Welchian feat. However, Tiller did it not with downsizing, dealmaking, and financialization, but with a deliberate strategy that involved putting workers first. "The people that tried to photocopy GE, to take the Welch playbook and go hire a bunch of people from GE and take the new company and make it into a copy of GE, almost always failed," he said. "If I tried to use the same strategy at Polaris, I would have screwed up a great company."

"If it's not Boeing, I'm not going"

Besides GE itself, there is one other company that has felt most directly the effects of Welchism: Boeing. Founded by William Boeing in 1916, the company built bombers for World War II, helped put men on the moon, and brought commercial passenger jets to the mass market with planes like the 707, the 737, and the 747. For most of the twentieth century, Boeing was a company run by and for engineers. Employees—from rocket scientist PhDs to machinists on the factory floor—enjoyed strong contracts with union protections, good benefits, and a sense of purpose. Quality and safety were paramount in decision-making processes, and costs were practically an afterthought. Many talked about the company as if it was a family, and plenty of men and women spent their entire careers there. It was common for several generations of the same family to be employed by Boeing, with fathers and sons sometimes working side by side. Pilots loved Boeing planes and often refused to fly other models, saying, "If it's not Boeing, I'm not going." The same spirit prevailed at the highest levels of the company. Executives came up through the engineering ranks and didn't pay much heed to Wall Street—Boeing leadership was more focused on making good airplanes than on generating returns for investors.

Boeing hit its stride in the last decades of the twentieth century. Air travel was booming, new markets were opening up, and Boeing was the dominant force in the industry. Its only meaningful competitors were Airbus, which was created by European governments with the express intent of establishing a continental counterpart to Boeing, and McDonnell Douglas, a fading domestic rival. And while Airbus was growing stronger, Boeing still had well over 60 percent of the market for large commercial airplanes in 1997. Yet Wall Street was restless. Having witnessed what Welch did at GE, investors were demanding bigger profits from all the companies in their portfolio. So Boeing decided to acquire McDonnell Douglas for $13.3 billion. On the face of it, the deal made sense. Boeing would consolidate the market for commercial passenger jets, and acquire McDonnell

Douglas's military business. It was a victory lap of sorts for Boeing, allowing it to swallow up its last meaningful domestic rival. But the deal would transform Boeing in ways that the company could not have foreseen.

At the time, McDonnell Douglas was run by Harry Stonecipher, a former GE executive who studied at Welch's knee. Stonecipher joined GE the same year that Welch did, and made a name for himself in the company's aircraft engines division. He was cut from the same cloth as Welch—eager to extract profits, quick to slash costs, and unsentimental with his employees. Stonecipher left GE in 1987 to become president of Sundstrand, a maker of airplane and industrial parts, and in 1994 he took over McDonnell Douglas. As chief executive, Stonecipher slashed expenses and drove up the stock price. One of the few investments he made was buying a French-style country château on 286 acres outside St. Louis, which he turned into his own version of Crotonville.

The strategy produced short-term earnings gains, but within a few years the company was faltering again. Its main factory in Long Beach, California, badly needed repairs. Its airplanes were often riddled with flaws. Engineers were hired en masse when the company needed to meet a deadline, then fired when the company needed to hit its profit targets. When Boeing made its takeover approach, the McDonnell Douglas board didn't hesitate to strike a deal.

As part of the union of the two companies, Stonecipher became Boeing's president and chief operating officer. And because Boeing paid for the deal entirely with its own stock, he was also able to convert his sizable position in McDonnell Douglas into Boeing shares, instantly making him one of the combined company's single largest shareholders. He emerged with more than twice as much stock as Boeing's own chief executive, Phil Condit, and before long it became clear that Stonecipher had assumed an inordinate amount of influence inside Boeing. Though he wasn't CEO, he seemed to be running the place. Observers groused that Condit had been captured and was being held hostage in his own office. "There was a little surprise that a guy running a failing company ended up with so much power," a

Boeing executive said at the time. Disgruntled employees joked that "McDonnell Douglas bought Boeing with Boeing's money."

Once Stonecipher was installed at Boeing, changes came swiftly. First the company took a tougher line with the unions that for so long had been the bedrock of Boeing's familial culture. In 1998, a year after it spent lavishly to acquire McDonnell Douglas, Boeing said it would slash some 53,000 jobs and embrace outsourcing. Then came dystopian changes in messaging. Under Stonecipher, Boeing began talking about "A passion for affordability," code for a new emphasis on profitability and cost cutting, and not the most reassuring message in an industry where safety, not stinginess, was paramount. Then Stonecipher waged his own version of Welch's campaign against loyalty. He told employees to "quit behaving like a family and become more like a team. If you don't perform, you don't stay on the team." Indeed, he went so far as to ban the word "family." It was a direct echo of his mentor, and it sapped morale among the close-knit Boeing ranks. Stonecipher was belligerent with Boeing's engineers, calling them arrogant, and he ousted the company's head of commercial airplanes. When they pushed back, he channeled Welch's brutal honesty. "I don't give 'em hell," he said. "I just tell the truth and they think it's hell."

A year after the deal, Boeing signaled to Wall Street that it was in step with the times, launching a massive buyback program that boosted the company's stock price still higher, even as it jettisoned thousands of employees with deep institutional knowledge. In 2000, having had enough, Boeing engineers went on strike. They weren't just asking for more money. They wanted to recapture some of their autonomy, which they felt had given way to a culture that was suddenly obsessed with pinching pennies. The strike lasted for forty days, but when the engineers returned, things had only gotten worse. Managers and engineers were now distrustful of each other, relations had frayed, and in the months that followed, many longtime employees quit.

Then in 2001, Boeing made a decision that stunned corporate America. After nearly a century based in the Seattle area, the company decided to move its headquarters out of town, far from its main factories. The goal, the company said, was to create "a new, leaner corporate center focused on shareholder value." The inspiration for the move was none other than GE, which had its headquarters in Fairfield, far from its historic manufacturing centers in Schenectady, Cincinnati, and Erie. To make the announcement, Condit and Stonecipher took off on a jet from Seattle without telling the public where they were going. Only when they were in the air did they make the big reveal: Boeing was headed to Chicago.

The company had no major offices or factories in the Windy City. Indeed, its nearest commercial jet factory would now be some 1,700 miles away from the CEO. So what motivated Boeing to relocate to Chicago? Tax breaks. Boeing had played cities against each other, convincing local politicians to try and outdo one another with subsidies that might lure the company to town. The executives had also harbored an irrational belief that if managers were further away from the rank and file, they would somehow make better decisions. "When the headquarters is located in proximity to a principal business—as ours was in Seattle—the corporate center is inevitably drawn into day-to-day business operations," Condit said, as if that were a bad thing.

As Stan Sorscher, a former Boeing engineer and union leader, watched it all unfold, he lamented that the company's "safety culture" was replaced with "a culture of financial bullshit, a culture of groupthink." Longtime Boeing employees could see clearly what was happening. "What you had at the McDonnell Douglas Company is a group of corporate ninjas," said Kyle Smith, a second-generation Boeing employee who worked on the factory floor and in management. "They had continually downsized, sold off assets, made huge amounts of money for themselves and for some of their stockholders, but they decimated the company. But they'd done it profitably. So Wall Street loved them."

Even at the time, luminaries in the business world foresaw what was to come. "If in fact there's a reverse takeover, with the McDonnell ethos permeating Boeing, then Boeing is doomed to mediocrity," the business scholar Jim Collins said in 2000. "There's one thing that made Boeing really great all the way along. They always understood that they were an engineering-driven company, not a financially driven company. If they're no longer honoring that as their central mission, then over time they'll just become another company."

Condit was forced to resign in 2003, taking the fall after another Boeing executive who had come over from McDonnell Douglas was caught in a government procurement scandal. With Condit out, Stonecipher was tapped as CEO, and a boss who had learned from Welch himself was now in charge of Boeing. Firmly in power, Stonecipher began to double down on the Welch playbook. Costs were reined in. Shareholders came first. The buyback program kept going up, reaching some $10 billion per year, which was far more than the company spent on research and development. And Stonecipher was proud of it all. "When people say I changed the culture of Boeing, that was the intent, so it's run like a business rather than a great engineering firm," he said in 2004. "It is a great engineering firm, but people invest in a company because they want to make money."

Although the stock price was ticking up, Boeing was reeling inside. In the wake of the scandal that ousted Condit, Boeing performed an ethics review at the request of the Air Force. It found that employees "almost universally" longed for the days before the McDonnell Douglas merger. "In those days," the report said, quoting a worker, " 'people were treated as people, not numbers.' "

"Manager of the Century"

With GE the most valuable company in the world, with his ideas gaining purchase across corporate America, and with his own fame and fortune peaking, Welch was riding high as the twentieth century came to a close. He was a bona fide celebrity, having parlayed his success as CEO into a spot in the day's cultural pantheon. Here he was playing golf with President Clinton on Martha's Vineyard. There he was kidding around with Jay Leno on *The Tonight Show.* Donald Trump, flirting with a presidential run in 1999, told Wolf Blitzer on CNN that he would consider picking Welch as his running mate, calling him "probably the greatest corporate leader in history of a major company. He's a great man, a great guy."

Volumes of Welch quotes were published. Books glorifying his exploits became hits. *Control Your Destiny or Someone Else Will* and *The New GE: How Jack Welch Revived an American Institution* became bestsellers. His portrait graced the covers of magazines including *Newsweek, Fortune, Forbes, Businessweek,* and *Success.* During his final years at GE, some 8,000 English language articles appeared annually about Welch, most all of them fawning in tone.

Welch became fodder for business school curricula. Harvard Business School, the country's most influential training ground for future corporate leaders, practically deified Welch, its professors churning out more than a dozen case studies that lionized his exploits. A pair of academics reviewed the literature on him and concluded "that publications about him not only fulfill the same functions that legends or hagiographies have fulfilled in former centuries, but they are also similar in structure." Headlines like "How to Win" weren't uncommon. *The Economist,* normally reserved in its assessment of individual executives, called Welch "the most successful manager of the past quarter-century," and the "Princess Diana of the business press." *Businessweek* declared him the "gold standard against which other CEOs are measured." Not to be outdone, *Fortune* gave Welch the ultimate capitalist honorific: "Manager of the Century."

And Welch himself was one of the biggest winners of all. He lived in a 10,733-square-foot home on a compound in Connecticut, complete with chauffeur's quarters, squash courts, and landscaped grounds, overlooking Long Island Sound. Reg Jones's colonial brick home this was not. Welch flew in private planes, ran up tabs at the best hotels, and held GE's annual meeting at Southeastern cities that were close to the Augusta National Golf Club in Georgia. That way, the board—which mostly consisted of older white men—could play a few rounds at the home of the Masters when the meeting was done.

Like most of the rest of the country, the GE board was under Welch's spell. At one annual meeting, a minister addressed the GE directors with an impassioned plea to shower Welch with riches, warning them that if they did not, they were going to lose him to another company." The GE board didn't disappoint. By 1995, Welch had amassed more than 2.75 million shares of GE stock, worth roughly $142 million. In 1996 alone, the value of his shares increased by $83 million, making his total holdings worth some $316 million. But that was only a prelude.

In the final five years of his reign, the GE board gave him a fortune once unimaginable to a boy who had grown up in Salem's Irish Ghetto. Though he had not founded GE, he was rewarded as if he had, becoming one of the richest people on earth. In 2000, his last full year on the job, Welch's compensation package was worth $122.5 million. A career of stock-based compensation had paid off. In the end, Welch possessed a staggering 21 million shares in GE, which, at their peak, were worth roughly $1 billion. In 2001, *Forbes* ranked him 376 on its list of the 400 richest Americans. All this was before his lavish exit package, details of which would emerge only after he retired. "Jack was the rock star CEO of my era," said Lynn Forester de Rothschild, one of the rare female media moguls of the 1980s. "We all thought Jack was doing everything right, and that success was defined by meeting quarterly earnings to the penny."

Not everyone was so enamored. The stark contrast between Welch's millions and the victims of his campaign against loyalty was not lost on GE's workers. "I loved GE," said a longtime Schenectady employee. "It put a roof on all of our houses." But in the end, the loyal worker saw through the charade. "Then you look at the stock dividends and bonuses the big shots are getting, and they turned around and tell us how they had to lay off people," he continued. "They're getting these huge packages, and meanwhile we're getting laid off and losing our benefits."

And it wasn't only employees who were souring on the company. GE's reputation as a good corporate citizen suffered under Welch, too. During his two decades as CEO, Welch presided over a parade of incendiary scandals. Inside GE, the pressure to perform was relentless, and executives did anything necessary to hit their numbers.

GE brass were caught defrauding the government, fixing the price of certain products, and embezzling foreign aid that was intended for Israel. Welch personally oversaw a decades-long effort to evade responsibility for pollution in the Hudson River, where GE had dumped toxic chemicals called PCBs. But Welch was never held to account for his company's transgressions. Instead, he mastered the art of taking credit for his organization's successes while avoiding responsibility for its failures. And all the while, GE stock continued to rise along with the broader markets.

Unbridled capitalism, powered by Reaganomics, appeared to have delivered just what Friedman and his followers had promised, unleashing a roaring bull market for the better part of twenty years. The Dow Jones Industrial Average rocketed from under 1,000 to over 11,000 during Welch's tenure, making it hard for other CEOs to dispute the notion that maximizing shareholder value worked. And in 1997, the business world codified the Welchian worldview as gospel. That year, the Business Roundtable, the influential group of CEOs that GE had helped establish two decades earlier, redefined its mission statement. Gone was the nuanced view it previously held that corporations should balance the needs of workers and communities with those of investors. In its place was the assertion that profit maximization was the purpose of business. "The paramount duty of management and of boards of directors is to the corporation's stockholders," the BRT pronounced, pledging allegiance to the Friedman doctrine. "The interests of other stakeholders are relevant as a derivative of the duty to stockholders."

Nor was it just conservative economists and pro-business Republicans who embraced the free market ideology. The Democratic Party was on board, too, eager to support the Welch agenda so long as it kept the markets going up. During President Clinton's two terms, he pursued economic policies favored by corporations—championing free trade, doing little to support labor unions, and allowing the federal minimum wage to remain at poverty levels. When Milton Friedman died in 2006, Larry Summers, treasury secretary for Clinton and a senior adviser to President Obama, conceded that shareholder primacy was now dogma among not just Republicans, but Democrats, too. "Any honest Democrat will admit that we are now all Fried-manites," Summers said.

What was hard to see, amid the endless profits on Wall Street and the jubilant coverage of Welch, was the costs of his revolution. With downsizing, dealmaking, and financialization and with a rule-skirting, regulation-defying attitude that placed the interests of GE shareholders above all other concerns, Welch had redefined what it meant to be a great American corporation. Following GE's lead, more big companies turned to outsourcing and offshoring, taking steps to replace their highly paid employees with contractors or cheaper labor from overseas. These changes had a profound effect on the national psyche. Shortly after Welch took over, a large survey of Americans employed by major corporations revealed that just 14 percent were anxious about being laid off. But as American workers were asked the same question over the years, their anxiety levels steadily rose, and by 1995, even as the economy was humming, approximately half of Americans were concerned about losing their jobs, and with good reason. During the 1990s, America lost some 848,000 manufacturing jobs. The campaign against loyalty, which had begun at GE, had gone nationwide.

Blue collar workers suffered the most. As Welch retired, the gap between productivity and pay—that all-important metric for mea-suring just how the riches of our land are distributed—had become a chasm. By the turn of the millennium, American corporations were profitable as never before, with Silicon Valley at the precipice of a new, decades-long boom. Yet pay for the average American worker showed virtually no increase at all. At the same moment those at the lower end of the economic spectrum continued to struggle, senior management never had it better. Welch was one of the leaders of what amounted to a remuneration revolution that has steadily taken wealth out of the hands of workers and placed it in the pockets of managers. In 1965 CEOs were paid about 20 times as much as an av-erage employee at their company. That ratio began to balloon around the time Welch took over GE. CEOs started getting paid 50 times as much, then 100 times as much, then 200 times as much as their average employees.

Some contrarians sounded the alarm even as the party was in full swing. With the dot-com bubble inflating, Alan Greenspan, then the chairman of the Federal Reserve, famously warned of "irrational exuberance." William Bennett, who served in the administrations of Presidents Reagan and George H. W. Bush, raised the prospect that Welch's tactics, left unchecked, could ultimately do profound damage to the fabric of the country. "What I'm concerned about is the idolatry of the market," Bennett said in 1998. "Unbridled capitalism," he said, was "a problem for human beings. It's a problem for the realm of values and human relationships because it distorts things."

And Felix Rohatyn, the investment banker who had orchestrated the RCA deal for Welch, saw through the charade even before that. "We have just seen the end of the greatest decade of speculation and financial irresponsibility since the 1920s," he said in 1991. "Financial deregulation, easy credit and regulatory neglect combined with the degradation of our value system to create a religion of money and of power. The achievement of infinite wealth and fame became the ultimate standard, to be achieved at any price. The junk-bond peddlers and the raiders, the speculators and the savings-and-loan hustlers with their legions of consultants, their lobbyists and their friendly politicians, turned this country into a vast casino. Crimes were committed, crimes against the entire nation. These crimes will cost hundreds of billions of dollars. They have also undermined confidence in a system that was built up over generations. The nation will need a lengthy recovery from this madness."

Even the SEC, at last, was looking critically at the kind of earnings management that had made GE's share price growth possible for so long. In 1998, the chairman of the SEC, Arthur Levitt, cautioned that companies were treating quarterly earnings as "a numbers game." Levitt called out corporations that were chasing quarterly profits and warned that tougher enforcement was needed. "Increasingly, I have become concerned that the motivation to meet Wall Street earnings expectations may be overriding common sense business practices," he said. "Too many corporate managers, auditors, and analysts are participants in a game of nods and winks. In the zeal to satisfy consensus earnings estimates and project a smooth earnings path, wishful thinking may be winning the day over faithful representation. As a result, I fear that we are witnessing an erosion in the quality of earnings, and therefore, the quality of financial reporting. Managing may be giving way to manipulation. Integrity may be losing out to illusion."

It was a remarkable speech. The head of the SEC, the man charged with making sure corporations played by the rules, was effectively saying that the markets were rigged. "Abuses such as earnings management occur when people exploit this pliancy," Levitt continued. "Trickery is employed to obscure actual financial volatility. This, in turn, masks the true consequences of management's decisions. These practices aren't limited to smaller companies struggling to gain investor interest. It's also happening in companies whose products we know and admire." GE wasn't named explicitly, but there was little question which company Levitt had in mind.

The cautionary voices were in the minority, however, and Welch went out on top. His last day on the job September 7, 2001. GE was still among the most valuable companies in the world, and his legacy as "Manager of the Century" seemed secure.

A month after he stepped down as CEO, Welch addressed hundreds of GE's senior leaders at his final management meeting. Standing at a lectern before a blood-red curtain, he unleashed one last diatribe, a parting salvo to a company that he had enraptured and terrorized for two decades. The speech was a highlight reel of his dystopian management principles. He excoriated excessively complex organizations, issuing one last repudiation of the company he had inherited from Reg Jones. "Hate bureaucracy," he said. "Hate it every day. And don't be afraid to use the word 'hate.' Laugh at bureaucrats and get rid of layers." This set up one final effort to justify his track record of downsizing. Hoping to frame the human carnage as a moral imperative, he cast mass layoffs in religious terms. Noting that it was a leadership failure to lose a top performer, he also said "it's also a sin to keep the bottom 10 percent." And in his final address to the company where he had spent his entire career, Welch encouraged employees to mercilessly judge each other, seeking out the weak amongst their own ranks. If any GE employee identified a colleague whom they believed didn't have the right values for the company, Welch employed his favorite metaphor: "shoot them."

The room was silent, with GE loyalists hanging on his every word. He warned the crowd that such laggards were still in their midst and called for a campaign to root out the last of them. "We haven't found every one of them, but we're out with a microscope, trying to find them," he said. "And you be on the lookout every single day, every single day. Because you're going to search and get them out of here. Never, never stop looking for them." Hoping to incentivize such ruthlessness, he dangled the promises of riches, offering "big raises, lots of options." And he closed by declaring that his handpicked successor, Jeff Immelt, was, without question, the right man to take over the job. "I'm 1,000 percent certain you have the best leader in world business to lead you for the next 20 years," he said. The room erupted in applause as he finished, and he strode out of the ballroom a hero.

FOUR

The GE Glow

"The perfect selection"

During Welch's final years as CEO, the question of who would succeed him loomed over GE, and the business community at large.
Whoever was tapped as the next leader of GE would gain instant
credibility, clout that rivaled a head of state, and a compensation
package worth many millions. Yet it was also a fraught job. There had
never been such large shoes to fill, and the next CEO would immediately be under enormous scrutiny. In the end, the race came down
to three men: Bob Nardelli, Jim McNerney, and Jeff Immelt. Having
risen through the ranks of a company thoroughly transformed by
Welch, all three had the same drive that animated their boss. And
with Welch's retirement on the horizon, they were all gunning for the
top job.

Compact, pugnacious, and driven, Bob Nardelli was known as
"Little Jack." He joined GE in 1982 and worked his way up to head

GE's transportation division, which made locomotives. In the early 1990s, Nardelli took a hard line with suppliers. They would have to accept a 6 percent reduction in the prices GE would pay and a 12 percent reduction the year after that. Suppliers who didn't grant Nardelli those concessions lost GE's business. Nardelli was equally tough with his employees, unleashing a wave of layoffs across the transportation business when it became clear it would be cheaper for GE to outsource certain components than to make them in house.

In his quest to run his division as lean as possible, Nardelli banned overtime. That saved money in the short term, but made it impossible for GE workers to meet deadlines. Locomotives weren't getting delivered, and disgruntled customers threatened to take their business elsewhere. Undeterred, Nardelli doubled down on outsourcing. That strategy was bad for GE employees, but it was effective in the short term. By shifting labor off GE's payroll and relying on suppliers for a larger share of the work, Nardelli doubled annual sales in the division.

By 1995, Nardelli had been identified as a candidate to succeed Welch, and was named head of GE's power turbines business, based in Schenectady. Soon after he arrived in the city, the spiritual home of GE that had been gutted by Welch's downsizing, Nardelli met with workers and issued a series of ultimatums. Productivity for the turbines business would have to make a quantum leap in a matter of months. If the business was to have "any credibility at all with corporate," he said, "we must meet or exceed" profit goals for the next year. "Nothing else really will matter," he said, if the "numbers are not delivered. We will again be 'broad paint-brushed' as a bunch of dummies." To accomplish this rapid turnaround, Nardelli said he planned to slash costs, including through layoffs, further eroding GE's presence in Schenectady. And there would be no room for errors. "Engineering must be faster, more efficient, more productive, and get it right the first time," he said.

By the numbers, the effort was a success. When Nardelli took over, the unit was earning less than $1 billion in profits on roughly $6.4 billion in sales. By the time Welch was ready to retire, Nardelli had coaxed a $1.7 billion profit out of sales of $9.7 billion. That represented a doubling of profits and a nearly 50 percent jump in revenue. The deceptive economics of downsizing were on display once more, as Nardelli accomplished so much of his success through further job cuts, padding GE's bottom line while inflicting more damage on Schenectady's beleaguered economy.

The next of the three top contenders, Jim McNerney, arrived at GE with an Ivy League education—Yale, then an MBA from Harvard—and was gunning for the top job from an early age. His father had been president of a major insurance company, Blue Cross/Blue Shield, and McNerney regularly put feelers out with other companies and recruiters during his time at GE, looking for his big break. In the mid-1990s, McNerney was running GE's lighting business, based in Cincinnati. Thanks to misguided acquisitions and persistently high costs in the United States, the division constantly struggled to turn a profit. But McNerney found other ways to ingratiate himself with Welch.

In the mid-1990s, McNerney became one of the most zealous champions of Six Sigma, a new quality improvement methodology that Welch was pushing on the company. Inspired by the Japanese notion of kaizen, or continuous improvement, Six Sigma used a complex system of feedback and buzzwords to try and root out any lingering vestiges of inefficiency. Whether it actually helped or just created a lot of paperwork was a subject of fierce debate. But during Welch's heyday, championing Six Sigma was a must for executives hoping to stay in the boss's good graces, and McNerney embraced the cause with gusto. "It's our new global language," he said. "We're talking about the same things in India that we're talking about in Hungary that we're talking about in the United States that we're talking about in Brazil. We're using the same terminology."

Whether it was Six Sigma, favorable market conditions, or McNerney's own campaign of layoffs and outsourcing, whatever he did worked during his years overseeing the lighting business, and he was subsequently given control of GE's aircraft engines division. GE was one of the biggest producers of jet engines, and a major part of

McNerney's job involved managing relations with the unit's two most important customers, Airbus, and especially Boeing.

Not long before he took over the division, GE and Boeing had concocted a plan to sell customized versions of the 737 to corporations and billionaires. GE would supply the engines and Boeing would build the planes. It was an idea Welch himself devised with Boeing's chief executive at the time, Phil Condit, on the back of a cocktail napkin. Learjets and Gulfstreams were evidently not enough, Welch reckoned. If a company was going to buy a plane, it should buy a whole damn jumbo jet. It would be called the Boeing Business Jet, and the planes would cost $35 million each. GE estimated it would outfit 100 of the planes with engines within ten years, reaping billions in profits. GE would even take the first order, so Welch could travel in style. But while McNerney was able to grow the broader market for engines, he couldn't realize Welch's lofty ambitions for the Boeing Business Jet. After four years, just eleven planes had been sold. Nevertheless, McNerney oversaw a period of expansion in the aircraft engines business, and was solidly in contention for the top job as Welch's retirement neared.

The third and final true contender to become the next CEO was Jeff Immelt. At 6 foot 4 inches, Immelt towered above Welch. His father had worked at GE in the aviation business, and after graduating from Dartmouth, Immelt went to work for Procter & Gamble, where he shared a cubicle with Steve Ballmer, the future CEO of Microsoft. After getting an MBA from Harvard Business School, Immelt joined GE. Early in his career there, Immelt distinguished himself by deftly managing a major refrigerator recall for Welch. After that, he was promoted repeatedly, making his way up through plastics, the same proving ground where Welch made a name for himself. He was appointed head of the Americas for the plastics division in 1994, but struggled to hit the ambitious earnings targets that Welch had demanded. This was in part because the breakneck growth the division was forecasting was based on fabricated numbers.

For years, the plastics division had been misreporting inventory figures in a coordinated effort to inflate the unit's profits. Under pressure from Welch, accountants at the plants in the plastics division would essentially do business in reverse. Once they knew how much profit senior management was expecting, they would figure out the amount of sales they would need to report, adjusting inventory along the way to make it all balance out. Once again, GE employees felt that the only way to achieve the enormous increases in sales and profits that Welch expected was to bend the rules.

Immelt could have told Welch the truth—that previous management had been dishonest and the business wasn't as strong as it appeared. But Immelt was discouraged from doing so. Inside GE, executives adhered to a code of omertà, resolving not to betray one another by telling the truth. And besides, Welch was hardly a sympathetic boss. If Immelt came to him with excuses, Welch would have just replaced him with someone who would do whatever it took to hit the numbers.

It didn't take long for Immelt to embrace the dark arts of creative accounting under Welch. GE's plastic plants in Asia didn't make their own basic materials, instead receiving them from the company's facilities in the U.S. and Europe. But according to GE's accounting methods, these transfers of goods from one GE plastics unit to another were reported as sales, even though no new money was being generated. Immelt found a way to use this to his advantage. When his numbers for the quarter weren't quite adding up, he would call on the head of the Asia-Pacific region for a favor: Would it be possible for him to place a few more internal orders? Doing so would allow Immelt to meet his numbers for the quarter and keep the bosses happy. Immelt claims he didn't remember the episode that way, and broadly defended his tenure during this time. "One of the things that I felt like has been wrong about the way the company has been covered is this notion that people could just invent numbers," he said. "You had a dozen checks and balances in the system that would keep you from doing that."

As his final test, Immelt was put in charge of GE's medical division. During his three years there, he increased sales from $4.2 billion to $6 billion. To engineer that rapid growth, he used another old trick from the Welch playbook: acquisitions. He bought market share, acquiring three major companies for $1.3 billion, thereby turning his unit into what would have been a formidable company on its own. In addition to mastering the arts of financialization, he clearly had a way with dealmaking, too.

There were a few dark-horse candidates in the race to succeed Welch, including Dave Calhoun, a rising star with the same pluck that had distinguished Welch in his early years, and Larry Johnston, who was running the ailing appliances business. But in the end, it came down to Nardelli, McNerney, and Immelt. "All three exceeded every expectation we set for them," Welch said. "Their performance was off the charts." Ultimately, he settled on Immelt, boasting that "I thought he was the perfect selection."

Privately, however, Welch saw some weaknesses in Immelt. At a party at Crotonville the week before Immelt took over, Welch pulled aside Ken Langone, the GE director, and gave him a word of warning. "Ken, I want you to remember one thing," Welch said. "Jeff has a habit of overpaying for deals. Make sure you guys really study the deals he makes and the value you're getting for the price you pay."

"Very bright people"

As the race narrowed down to Nardelli, McNerney, and Immelt, other top GE executives went looking for new jobs. In April 2001, Larry Johnston, one of the long-shot candidates to succeed Welch, left GE to run Albertsons, the grocery chain. Johnston had been running GE's appliance business and knew nothing about groceries. But to the Albertsons board, the allure was irresistible. Recruiters cautioned against the decision, warning that someone who knew the industry might be better suited for the job. The board wouldn't hear it. Having considered 100 candidates, they concluded that the man who had learned from Welch was the best fit. "GE has very bright people," said an Albertsons board member, "and our business isn't that difficult. We're not building the space shuttle."

At first, it looked like a sage move. The day Johnston was announced as CEO, Albertsons stock jumped 7.5 percent. The new CEO, predictably, started divesting unprofitable stores and cutting costs. In a bid to reduce energy usage, he went so far as to turn off 25 to 50 percent of the lights in stores, a decision that only made grocery aisles seem dark and dingy. When he couldn't revive the company's core business, Johnston bought other chains, spending billions to acquire more stores, only to starve them of resources, too. And when that didn't work, he closed 165 stores and fired thousands of workers around the country. It was all part of a misguided quest for dominance in an industry where market share is highly diffuse. "We got out of markets where we weren't No. 1 or No. 2, or where we didn't have a clear path to get there," Johnston said, explaining the dizzying series of acquisitions and closings. "That perspective came in very handy when I was at GE."

As the walls closed on Johnston, he brought in a motivational speaker he had used at GE in an attempt to rally the troops. But a pep talk wouldn't stanch the bleeding. Johnston's self-inflicted wounds had doomed Albertsons, and he finally sold the company to a group led by the private equity firm Cerberus. For his troubles, Johnston was rewarded with a $105 million golden parachute.

Other Welch acolytes were struggling, too. John Blystone, a top GE executive who left to run SPX, an industrial company, resigned in scandal after he sold shares for a $25 million profit shortly before the company reported poor quarterly results. Though Blystone was not charged with insider trading, investors sued the company, alleging that the board had adjusted bonus plans to deliver unjust rewards to executives and independent directors. Soon after that, Blystone agreed to step down.

Steve Bennett, who worked at GE for twenty-three years, went on to be chief executive of two technology firms, Intuit and Symantec. At both companies, the strategies Bennett learned from Welch failed him. He abruptly stepped down from Intuit after a database problem with the company's flagship product, TurboTax, prevented thousands of people from paying their taxes on time, saying he was going to "take some time off and explore the next challenge in my life." Then a few years later, he was fired by Symantec after failing to turn the company around.

Kevin Sharer, another Welch protégé, ran the biotech firm Amgen for more than a decade. He grew revenues through a relentless series of acquisitions, but the stock price never budged. Along the way, he made $100 million or so.

And Gary Wendt, the longtime head of GE Capital, who was responsible for much of Welch's success, eventually took the top job at Conseco, a deeply indebted insurance company based in Indiana. His signing bonus was $45 million in cash. Wendt tried to right the ship at Conseco, which had made a series of ill-advised acquisitions. Instead, Conseco continued its reckless lending practices, and after twenty-eight months on the job, Wendt stepped down as the company filed for bankruptcy protection. He collected $53 million on his way out the door.

"A lot of GE leaders were thought to be business geniuses," said Bill George, the former CEO of Medtronic and a board member at Goldman Sachs. "But they were just cost cutters. And you can't cost-cut your way to prosperity."

Nonetheless, the pattern seemed to repeat itself endlessly. A GE executive was named CEO of another company. News of the appointment would send the stock of that company soaring. The men were lavished with riches when they took their new jobs, signing multimillion-dollar contracts that ensured them a gilded retirement, no matter how well they performed. A period of downsizing usually ensued, and profits often ticked up for a few quarters, or even a few years. But inevitably, Welchism exacted its price. There was little focus on long-term strategy, and a slavish devotion to meeting quarterly results. "They wouldn't know strategy if it hit them in the head," said Roger Martin, the former Rotman School dean. "All they know how to do is take what they've got and refine it, make it operationally more effective." Before long morale cratered, the business wobbled, and the stock price sank. It happened at Home Depot, Albertsons, and so many more companies. Boards believed hiring a CEO from

GE would solve their problems, but were almost always disappointed. "I watched it up close and personal," Martin said. "I watched it at Motorola. I watched it at Nortel. You see it at Home Depot, one after another. They did not have the strategy discipline. They had an operational discipline, which was basically, 'I need to squeeze it to make more money.'"

Just a few years after Welch retired, the *Wall Street Journal* took inventory of his protégés and their performance. Only two CEOs— Jim McNerney at 3M and Tom Tiller at Polaris—had managed to boost their company's stock prices. The rest had run their companies into the ground, driving down share prices by 25 percent at Albertsons, 45 percent at Great Lakes Chemicals, and 48 percent at Intuit. Welch had only just retired, and it was already becoming clear that most of the men trying to follow in his footsteps were ill-equipped to succeed. "Boards get overenthusiastic about the GE glow," said James Schrager, a professor of entrepreneurship at the University of Chicago Graduate School of Business. "They forget that there's a big divide between selling light bulbs and appliances to stores and running the stores that sell them to consumers."

"Prove Jack wrong"

After informing Immelt he had gotten the job, Welch hopped on a private jet and flew to Albany to break the news to Nardelli in person. They met in a lounge just off the runway, and Welch let Nardelli down while the plane's engines were still warm. When Nardelli learned that he had lost out to Immelt, he was livid. As Welch recounted in his autobiography, Nardelli demanded to know what else he could have done and why Welch had passed him over. He also began plotting his next move.

That Nardelli would leave GE was a given. Welch had made it clear that the two finalists who didn't make the cut would be expected to move on, to avoid any infighting after the transition. It was a measure of Welch's dictatorial style that he was unable to fathom his three protégés working together after he was gone. Nardelli wasted no time. Less than two weeks after Immelt had been selected to succeed Welch, Home Depot announced that Nardelli would be its next CEO.

Although Nardelli had no experience in the retail industry, Home Depot and GE had several close ties. The home repair megastores stocked GE appliances and light bulbs, GE Capital managed Home Depot's credit card program, and Langone, the Home Depot co-founder, sat on the GE board. Yet in important ways, Home Depot was a very different company from GE. Over the years, Home Depot had thrived on a decentralized management culture. There were regional differences, practices varied from store to store, and employees enjoyed a familial workplace that fostered a sense of camaraderie. Though it could look a bit chaotic to the executives back at headquarters, the lack of standardization served an essential purpose for Home Depot: it kept customers happy.

Sales and profits were soaring at Home Depot when Nardelli took over in 2000. The country was in the midst of a housing boom, and his job was to keep the momentum going. But the company's sometimes anarchic culture was anathema to Nardelli, steeped as he was in GE's command and control structure. He brought in additional muscle from GE to instill some discipline, and he waged his own campaign against loyalty, thinning the ranks of longtime, salaried workers and replacing them with less-knowledgeable, part-time employees. He centralized decision-making, cut costs, and gutted middle management. He demanded that shelves be stocked after closing time, making employees work longer shifts. Hoping to improve efficiency, he reduced the amount of inventory Home Depot held. Before long, customers were frustrated that items were out of stock and employees were embarrassed that their company wasn't coming through.

Nardelli also transformed what had been a convivial culture into a Darwinian one. Inventory management tools were in, while a homespun approach to customer service was out. And when Nardelli tried to strongarm suppliers into giving him better deals, as he had done successfully at GE, it backfired. Some key suppliers didn't cave, and their products were removed from Home Depot shelves. "I don't know what the hell happened to Bob," Langone said. "When all the low-hanging fruit got picked, his personality changed. Bob had a maniacal attachment to results, to numbers. And Home Depot was more than numbers. Home Depot was people."

The upheavals ate away at Home Depot. As some stores closed and employees were shuffled from one zip code to the next, long-standing relationships were frayed, and sales staff found themselves working for new managers. Morale plummeted, and only got worse when the rank and file learned the details of Nardelli's compensation. Langone and the rest of the Home Depot board had granted him a pay package that would have made Welch himself blush. He would earn a monster sum—as much as $38.1 million a year, guaranteed. The gargantuan pay on its own angered the rank and file. But shortly after Nardelli became CEO, pictures emerged of his lavish mansion with its twelve-car garage, and quickly went viral among the company's associates. Suddenly, the emperor had no clothes. Here they were on hourly wages, some of them barely able to support a family, while Nardelli was living like a king.

To close observers of the corporate world, it appeared that Nardelli was out to show Welch that he made a mistake by choosing Immelt. As one analyst said at the time, "Bob wanted to prove Jack wrong." It seemed that Little Jack was determined to show up his old boss. "One of Bob's problems, as I look back, was that he never got over the fact that he didn't get the GE job," said Langone.

Nardelli also had his grievances with Immelt, who had shown him up by winning the top job, and once Welch was out of the picture, the alliance between GE and Home Depot quickly deteriorated. Nardelli decided that Home Depot would stop carrying GE light bulbs. He also decided that GE Capital, which had managed Home Depot's white label credit card for years, would be replaced with a different provider. The moves seemed designed to needle Immelt, and they worked. Not long after, Immelt asked Langone to step down from the GE board. It was untenable to have the Home Depot cofounder there when Nardelli had grown openly antagonistic to his former employer. Making matters worse, Langone was ensnared in scandal after he approved a $187 million pay package for Dick Grasso, the former chair of the New York Stock Exchange, triggering lawsuits from then New York attorney general Eliot Spitzer. Though Spitzer charged both Grasso and Langone with wrongdoing, a court threw out the cases and neither were convicted.

Within a few years, frustrated shoppers were taking their business to Lowe's, Home Depot's main rival. The shifting sentiment allowed Lowe's to emerge as a viable national competitor, and Wall Street knew it. During Nardelli's tenure, Home Depot stock dropped 8 percent, while Lowe's stock soared 180 percent. Not even creative financial maneuvers could help. Home Depot was accused of overcharging vendors for damaged goods during Nardelli's tenure, and near the end of his reign Home Depot admitted that it had been routinely backdating stock options in an attempt to make executives' compensation packages more valuable.

After five years of mismanagement, tensions erupted at Home Depot's shareholder meeting in 2006. Nardelli turned what was usually an all-day affair into a twenty-minute face-off with his own investors. At his direction, the board didn't show up. Instead of engaging with shareholders, he made perfunctory remarks, speaking in a monotone. Following that, he cut off an investor presentation and refused to answer questions. The meeting was a disaster, and soon after, Nardelli and the board agreed he would leave the company. But not without a golden parachute. Though Home Depot investors had lost money during his tenure, Nardelli was rewarded with a $210 million exit package.

According to Jensen and Meckling, CEOs were supposed to be agents, working on behalf of stock owners to maximize shareholder value. But decades of gargantuan paydays and minimal accountability had perverted incentives in the C-suite. As Nardelli was demonstrating at Home Depot, and as Trani had done at Stanley, CEOs who studied under Welch seemed to be positively dismissive of their own investors, and primarily interested in their own fortunes.

After being pushed out of Home Depot, Nardelli was tapped to run Chrysler in 2007. The fading American automaker had been acquired by Cerberus, a notoriously predatory private equity firm. Nardelli wasn't selected on his merits alone. Nepotism had something to do with it, too. Several Cerberus executives had worked with him at GE, and while Nardelli didn't have any experience in the auto industry, just as he hadn't had any experience in retail, he was given the run of the place nonetheless and immediately put his Welchian tactics to work once again.

Out of step with the times and laden with legacy costs, Chrysler was in rough shape when Nardelli arrived. Automakers turned to Washington for help when the financial crisis hit, but as part of the initial negotiations, the Treasury Department wanted Chrysler to accept limits on executive compensation. That is, the government wanted to make sure that if it bailed out Chrysler, the executives at Cerberus wouldn't simply pay themselves a fortune and walk away. Cerberus refused, and instead tapped the private markets for what turned out to be far more expensive debt. High interest payments from those loans only hastened the inevitable, and Chrysler went bankrupt after all. Desperate not to let the auto industry collapse, Washington ultimately gave Chrysler a $4 billion loan—this despite the fact that Cerberus was flush with cash but refused to make any of it available to Chrysler. And still, Nardelli and Cerberus sold the one profitable part of Chrysler—its financial services business—as a way to pay down the debt that Cerberus had assumed to fund its ill-fated takeover in the first place. All the while, Chrysler sales were tanking—down 30 percent in Nardelli's first year, and another 45 percent the next.

As one of his final acts on the job, Nardelli defended himself and his company before the Senate, which was scrutinizing the bailout. "Bankruptcy is not something I expected to be an expert in," Nardelli said. Nor, it turns out, was he particularly good at it. Less than two years after taking the job, with Chrysler in tatters, he resigned. With his performance at Chrysler and Wendt's at Conseco, a pair of Welch's top deputies had managed to preside over two of the ten largest bankruptcies in American business history.

McNerney, the other loser of the race to succeed Welch, enjoyed the appearance of more success after he left GE. He, too, was gone within ten days of Immelt having gotten the job, hired in late 2000 as

CEO of 3M, the Minnesota-based multinational conglomerate that makes chemicals, Scotch tape, Post-it Notes, and more. McNerney was the first outsider to ever run 3M, and investors were expecting nothing less than a windfall with a GE man in charge. In the days after the announcement, 3M's stock price soared 20 percent. "The mere mention of his name made everyone richer," *Businessweek* wrote.

Having settled into his new role, McNerney pulled his own Neutron Jack move, announcing the elimination of 5,000 jobs. Before long, that figure grew to 8,000, then 11,000. From there, he continued to bring the Welch playbook to 3M. He implemented Six Sigma and tried to formalize what was at times a freewheeling, creative culture. McNerney said he wasn't trying to stifle innovation. "The DNA of this company supports idea generation," he said. "I don't want to kill that, I want to support that. I just want to make the assessment of our ideas to be more rigorous."

The new rigor extended well beyond the assessment of new products. McNerney implemented a performance review system designed to identify and remove employees who were underperforming, his own version of rank and yank. And he went on a cost-cutting binge, slashing budgets across the company. Initially, the strategies seemed to work. Profits were up, and the stock responded accordingly. To outsiders it appeared that McNerney had reinvigorated 3M. Inside the company, however, McNerney's changes were sapping spirits. 3M scientists developed new products by trying things, and sometimes failing. Trial and error was how they discovered what worked and what didn't. But with the arrival of Six Sigma, mistakes were no longer tolerated, let alone celebrated as opportunities to learn and grow. Workers who didn't follow the new regime were removed. And soon, there was open dissent among the ranks. "This was like a big family. The CEOs were from Minnesota, and we felt we had a job forever," said one long-timer. "People felt they were going to be taken care of—as long as they did their job and came to work every day and performed—that they would never have to worry about losing their job." Before long, those who knew the company best had a sense of foreboding. "There is a change in culture, and it is cause for concern," Art Fry, who invented the Post-it Note, said at the time.

After three years of upheavals, a group of former 3M employees hit back. In a landmark age discrimination suit, older workers who had been pushed out during McNerney's tenure alleged that they were systematically given lower rankings in the company's new performance review system, were disproportionately demoted, and that cumulatively this had serious negative effects on their pay, promotions, and exit packages. The suit also contended that Six Sigma was a vehicle for discrimination, as older employees were routinely passed over for younger ones when it came time to select people for the program's intensive training. 3M settled for a pittance, just $12 million, without admission of wrongdoing.

McNerney didn't remain CEO much longer. Having led 3M for just four years—a run when the stock price had risen but during which many said 3M lost its way—McNerney was hired away for an even bigger job. The man who once ran GE's aircraft engines business and counted Boeing as his most important client was headed to Seattle to run Boeing itself.

With McNerney gone, 3M reverted to its old, eccentric ways. Innovation was once again more important than financial planning. Engineers were encouraged to tinker with new products, not budgets. And 3M management said the quiet part out loud: financial engineering is ultimately a losing strategy. "Invention is by its very nature a disorderly process," said the new CEO, George Buckley. "You can't put a Six Sigma process into that area and say, well, I'm getting behind on invention, so I'm going to schedule myself for three good ideas on Wednesday and two on Friday. That's not how creativity works."

"We had no idea"

None of Welch's acolytes had a more difficult challenge than Jeff Immelt, who took over GE at the worst possible time. Immelt's second full day on the job was September 11, 2001. The terrorist attacks that day paralyzed the U.S. economy, and GE was as exposed as any company in the nation. In Welch's quest to make GE the most valuable company on earth, he had expanded into almost every conceivable industry. That meant that when things were going well for the economy overall, GE was likely to benefit. It also meant that when a black swan event like 9/11 occurred, GE was more vulnerable than most, something Immelt suddenly realized. "My second day as chairman, a plane I lease, flying with engines I built, crashed into a building that I insure, and it was covered with a network I own," Immelt said. The fallout went even further. Stock markets plunged, dragging down shares of GE, as well as the value of other assets held by GE Capital.

In the weeks following the attacks, analysts and investors began taking a closer look at GE, and they didn't like what they saw. GE Capital was bigger, more complex, and riskier than they had appreciated. The industrial businesses, from airplane engines to power turbines, looked badly exposed. When the stock markets finally opened after being closed for a week, GE's largest investor sold off half its position.

Immelt called the investor to ask for mercy. "Hey, give us a break here," he said. "This is a tough day."

The investor had no sympathy, instead making a startling revelation to Immelt. "Look," the investor said, "we had no idea that GE was so big in the insurance business."

The fact that GE's own investors didn't know how the company made its money was no accident. Welch had deliberately made it hard for them to understand GE's unnaturally smooth quarterly results, limiting the information the company disclosed. The consistent earnings growth Welch engineered had put them in a trance. But in the wake of the attacks, investors were snapping out of it, and Immelt, too, was coming to a stark realization about what kind of shape GE was really in. Two decades of underinvesting in capital improvements and R&D had left GE with a lack of innovative new products as the new millennium dawned. At a company where costs had been relentlessly cut for twenty years, there was little fat left to trim. The swelling finance operation had introduced substantial new risks to the company's balance sheet, and bamboozled Wall Street into believing GE was a company that could deliver ever-increasing profits. "It's hard to capture for you GE of 2001," Immelt said. "You'd had *Fortune* magazine's 'Manager of the Century,' a stock that was trading at

60 times earnings, and a complicated company, let's be clear. I mean, we did everything from dog insurance to TV shows."

The company had greater reach than ever before and had all the outward trappings of success, including its enormous market capitalization. But what Wall Street analysts really cared about was GE's ability to consistently meet or beat their expectations, something that was accomplished largely through the creative accounting at GE Capital.

It couldn't last forever, and breaking the run of infinite expansion and endless earnings growth was going to be hard. But in the aftermath of 9/11, Immelt had a chance. With the markets rattled and investors reassessing their portfolios, he had a unique opportunity to reset GE. He could have reined in GE Capital, offloading some of its riskier financial bets, and reinvesting in manufacturing. He could have taken a onetime charge and acknowledged that GE Capital had serious flaws that needed to be fixed. If GE had a rough quarter after 9/11, no one would have been surprised. The stock would have likely fallen, and analysts might have fretted. But after the initial hardship, GE may well have been in better shape, less dependent on the magic of GE Capital and more transparent with its investors.

Immelt didn't appear to have that kind of resolve. The allure of another blowout earnings report, especially in the wake of the terrorist attacks, was too powerful to resist. He didn't want to be the one to break GE's sensational run of quarterly earnings, especially not in his first days on the job. So rather than do the tough but necessary work of resetting expectations and repositioning the company, Immelt turned to GE Capital for profits in a pinch and beat earnings once more. While almost every other company had a rough quarter immediately after the terrorist attacks, GE was a rare exception. "Despite a global recession and the September 11 terrorist attacks, we delivered double-digit earnings growth," Immelt said, announcing a $14 billion quarterly profit. "This is a tribute to our great global team and the strength of the GE business model."

Not everyone was convinced. Bill Gross, one of Wall Street's savviest investors, a billionaire known as "the bond king," was about to turn on Immelt. Gross, the cofounder of Pacific Investment Management Company, or Pimco, a major institutional investor, was known for his discursive memos and prescient timing. Six months into Immelt's tenure, in early 2002, he posted a bombshell on his company's website. Pimco had just sold off $1 billion of GE bonds because, he believed, GE's "honesty remains in doubt." Gross was smarting over some of GE's recent financial decisions, which had hurt investors like himself. But he also leveled a more fundamental critique that clearly impugned Welch's credibility as well. "GE has been shrouded in mystery for a number of years," Gross said on CNBC. "Institutional investors have wondered why a company can continue to produce 15 percent earnings growth year after year, quarter after quarter."

He didn't stop there. GE's success, Gross argued, was due not so much to the underlying strength of its industrial businesses, but GE Capital's wheeling and dealing in the short-term paper business, as well as its ceaseless acquisitions using the company's own stock. GE, he said, "grows earnings not so much by the brilliance of management or the diversity of their operations, as Welch and Immelt claim, but through the acquisition of companies—more than 100 companies in each of the last five years—using high-powered, high-multiple GE stock or cheap near-Treasury-Bill-yielding commercial paper." And Gross identified a crucial vulnerability at the heart of GE Capital, one of the country's biggest lenders. Its debt amounted to a whopping $127 billion, but the company only had credit lines totaling $31 billion.

Gross had said the quiet part out loud. In the event of a crisis, GE would be dangerously exposed. The strategy Welch had used for so long, to such great effect, which Immelt adopted as his own, was faltering. "So much was depending on Welch himself individually," said Tom Tiller, the longtime GE executive who turned around Polaris. "I think that if Jesus Christ himself would have gone in after him, he would have had a tough time."

"I had the world by the ass"

While Nardelli was toiling away at Home Depot, McNerney was trying to reinvent 3M, and Immelt was wrestling with GE, Welch was living it up. As he began retirement, it would not be enough for him to disappear to Florida and golf away his days. Instead, he was gearing up for a second act, preparing to cement his legacy as Manager of the Century. In his first weeks away from GE, Welch prepared for his book tour. His autobiography, *Jack: Straight from the Gut*, went on sale on September 11, 2001. That morning, Welch was at Rockefeller Center to promote the book on the *Today* show, which aired on NBC, a network GE owned. For nine minutes, Welch and Matt Lauer engaged in light banter about Welch's run as CEO. Lauer asked him about the "Neutron Jack" label but was mostly deferential to his former boss. Welch was his usual self, charming and cantankerous at the same time.

An hour later, Lauer and his cohost, Katie Couric, cut away from their regularly scheduled programming to bring viewers live shots of black smoke pouring from the World Trade Center. That was the end of the *Straight from the Gut* publicity tour. For the rest of that morning, the most prominent mention of Welch's name on NBC came when *New York Times* columnist Thomas Friedman remarked that Osama bin Laden was "a bizarre combination of Charles Manson and Jack Welch."

"I'm not sure Jack Welch would really appreciate that," offered Couric, in the anchor's chair. Friedman clarified, saying he intended Welch "no insult," but was rather trying to suggest that bin Laden had "the organizational skills of a corporate *Fortune* 500 manager."

While the attacks rattled the global economy, they hardly fazed Welch. After all, GE was no longer his problem. His book, for which he received a $7 million advance, went on to be a bestseller. He was incomprehensibly wealthy and about to meet the woman of his dreams.

Before he retired, *Harvard Business Review* had asked him for an interview. The magazine—a must read for corporate leaders around the country—wanted to put Welch on the cover and reflect on his legacy. Initially he balked, preferring to control his own narrative with the release of his book. But when he learned that *HBR* allowed interview subjects to read articles before they went to press, and even make changes, he agreed. In October, with Ground Zero still smoldering, the editor of *HBR*, Suzy Wetlaufer, came down from Boston to interview Welch in his New York office. Wetlaufer had cut her teeth as a local reporter, and published a novel, *Judgment Call*, which told the story of an attractive, sassy female reporter who becomes romantically involved with one of her sources, a cocaine dealer from Miami. Now, as Wetlaufer walked into Welch's office, she came face-to-face with the biggest corporate kingpin of them all. Though Welch was still married to his wife of thirteen years, Jane Beasley, he was immediately smitten with Wetlaufer. Within weeks, despite their twenty-two-year age difference and Welch's marriage, they were romantically involved. All the while, Wetlaufer continued working on her Welch cover story, even getting a photographer to take a picture of them together that would run with her editor's letter in that issue.

As the copy was going to press, however, Wetlaufer got a call from Jane, who had found out about the affair. Wasn't Wetlaufer compromising her journalistic integrity by writing a puff piece about a man she now was sleeping with? The call rattled Wetlaufer, who then informed her superior at *HBR* about the situation and suggested the magazine spike the story. When Wetlaufer's *HBR* colleagues found out, they staged a mutiny, declaring they had lost confidence in their editor. "For some of the true business journalists on the staff, it was like I had linked up with the enemy," Wetlaufer said. "We were supposed to be reporting on these people, and 'What, you're like running off with one of them?'" Wetlaufer agreed to take a leave of absence and ultimately left *HBR*. A new team of reporters was assigned to redo the Welch profile, which was published as "Jack on Jack."

Jane filed for divorce. She and Welch had had a prenuptial agreement, but it had expired, and Welch had offered her a settlement of $35,000 a month, plus a onetime payment of $10 million. Beasley, however, had grown accustomed to a gilded lifestyle that even those generous sums would not cover. So she pressed for more, enumerating the perks she enjoyed as Welch's wife in a court filing, which included new details about his retirement contract with GE.

Though Welch had stopped working for GE in September of 2001, GE never really stopped working for him. Before he stepped down, the Manager of the Century secured a retirement package unlike any other in the history of corporate America. Even after he left the company, Welch would be entitled to live off the largesse of its shareholders until his dying day. The legalese that codified this arrangement appeared innocuous enough. In 1996, as the board restructured Welch's contract, it slipped in language stipulating that Welch would receive, "for the remainder of his life, continued access to company facilities and services comparable to those provided to him prior to his retirement." It was a throwaway line, and it went unnoticed for years. But when Beasley brought it to light, it was suddenly clear that, in practice, it meant that GE shareholders were footing the bill for Welch's extravagant retirement.

In exchange for agreeing to consult for the company for thirty days a year, Welch would receive a daily rate equal to his salary when he was CEO, an annual retainer, and innumerable perks. Among these were Welch's apartment at the Trump International Hotel & Tower, with its sweeping views of Central Park, as well as the considerable expenses associated with such a regal home, including fresh flowers, housekeepers, and laundry services. All told, that alone represented $80,000 a month in value. When the Welches were on the go, GE also covered the tab. In Manhattan, there were box seats at the Metropolitan Opera at Lincoln Center and courtside seats to see the Knicks at Madison Square Garden. GE paid for nearly a dozen country club memberships, helicopter and limousine services, and rental cars. It provided Welch with computers, fax machines, car phones, cell phones, satellite communications, appliances, and even light bulbs. It paid for landscape designers, architects, and security guards. It picked up the tab at Michelin starred restaurants like Jean-Georges in Manhattan, and when the Welches traveled by air, GE made available the company's Boeing Business Jet—the 737 that Welch himself had dreamed up. In the filing, Beasley estimated the cost of the 737 alone to be $3.5 million a year.

The details set off an uproar when they became public. Even Welch's longtime allies felt the retirement package went too far. "I think it was wrong for the board to have given those kind of perks," said Walter Wriston, the onetime CEO of Citicorp and a former GE director who had personally approved many of Welch's gargantuan packages. "He had a pension of $7 million to $8 million a year. Why do you then need an apartment, a maid?" Wriston continued. "And the use for free of the corporate jet for life seems to me to be excessive." Welch feigned contrition. He penned an op-ed for the *Wall Street Journal* explaining the arrangement, and he agreed to reimburse the company for many of the expenses. Yet in the end, as always, Welch was unrepentant. "The contract was not only open, but also economically sound for GE and its shareowners," he said. In other words, he seemed to be saying: *I was worth it.*

As with most everything Welch did, his retirement package set a precedent. Within months, other companies gave their chiefs similar deals. Less than a year later, Larry Bossidy got an almost identical agreement written into his contract at Honeywell, entitling him to "company facilities and services comparable to those provided prior to his retirement," for the rest of his life.

After Welch and Beasley divorced, with Beasley pocketing $183 million, Welch and Wetlaufer married. Between the exit package scandal, the affair, the abrupt turn in the fortunes of GE after 9/11, Welch was brought back down to earth in the months after he retired. The New York *Daily News* put Welch on the cover with a banner headline: "GREED!" *Money* magazine said he was among those "responsible for the market's nosedive." The man who had been anointed Manager of the Century just months before suddenly had a target on his back.

Yet this is a land of second and third acts, at least for those who can afford them. The nineteenth-century robber barons tried to atone for their monopolistic business practices with philanthropy, endowing foundations and universities with so many billions that, decades on, the names Rockefeller, Carnegie, and Mellon are associated more with charities than they are with monopolies. Some of Welch's peers were similarly dexterous. Michael Milken, the junk bond king of the 1980s, was convicted of racketeering and fraud, sentenced to ten years in prison, and barred from the securities industry. After his sentence was reduced for cooperating with prosecutors, he reinvented himself as a philanthropist and would-be public intellectual, footing the bill for a major economic and policy conference where he entertained celebrities including Tom Brady and former president George W. Bush, repairing his reputation one photo op at a time. Donald Trump was a well-known fraud by the early 2000s. Bankruptcies trailed him, most major banks wouldn't do business with him, and his buffoonery was the stuff of lore. That didn't stop NBC—under Immelt's control at the time—from greenlighting *The Apprentice*, giving Trump a new lease on fame, as well as a new fortune.

So it was for Welch. His first year of retirement was bumpy, and the cracks in GE's foundation may have started to show. But he remained the swaggering, unapologetic, uber boss who had ruled GE with an iron fist, and he wasn't about to let some pesky, moralizing headlines get him down. Not long after leaving GE, he confided in magazine editor Tina Brown, telling her how much he loved living at the top of the Trump International, the gold-hued monolith that GE Capital and Trump developed in the mid-1990s. As he looked out the window at night and saw the sparkling lights of Manhattan encircling Central Park, he told Brown, "I felt I had the world by the ass."

FIVE

Rotten Apples

"Terrible excesses"

Under pressure to produce endless growth, GE began bending the rules. Creative accounting became the norm, and the company's sprawling finance operations were sufficiently vast and complex to blind regulators to the misdeeds, at least for a time. And GE wasn't alone. In the last years of the twentieth century and the first years of the twenty-first, a slew of major corporations were engaged in similarly dubious practices.

At Waste Management, the garbage collection company, founder Dean Buntrock led a years-long effort to deceive regulators and shareholders. From 1992 to 1997, executives would predetermine earning targets—numbers they felt would be sure to impress Wall Street analysts and keep the stock moving higher—then falsify company records however needed to hit the mark. With Waste Management stock hitting new highs quarter after quarter, the executives were lavished with options and saw their personal net worth skyrocket. When a new CEO took over in 1997 and ordered a review of the accounting practices, the fraud was revealed, and the company restated the previous five years' earnings by $1.7 billion, the largest such correction ever at the time. The stock plunged, and it cost the company $3.5 billion in pretax charges and earnings restatements. The SEC indicted Buntrock and his associates, describing the scheme as "one of the most egregious accounting frauds we have seen" and alleging the Waste Management executives "cooked the books, enriched themselves, preserved their jobs and duped unsuspecting shareholders." Though Buntrock and his accomplices had been caught red-handed, they never admitted wrongdoing and never went to jail, settling the case and getting Waste Management to pay for most of the nearly $31 million in fines.

Then Enron collapsed. Before its implosion in 2001, the Texas energy company was considered one of the best-managed firms in the nation. Enron threw off money, making its founder, Kenneth Lay, and its chief executive, Jeffrey Skilling, fabulously wealthy and revered in the business community. And by the early 2000s, much of Enron's success was coming from a secretive commodities trading program. The company was racking up enormous losses and resorting to duping investors and regulators with fraudulent accounting in a bid to cover up the debacle. Eventually, Enron went bankrupt. Lay and Skilling were arrested and convicted. And Arthur Andersen, Enron's accounting firm, was forced out of business.

The next year, Tyco International, an industrial conglomerate, collapsed. Dennis Kozlowski, Tyco's CEO, had been feted as a corporate superhero and named one of the "Top 25 Managers of the Year" by *Businessweek*. Just a few months later, Kozlowski was facing ruin. He had turned Tyco into a $114 billion company using the Welch playbook—relentless dealmaking and ceaseless cost cutting. Kozlowski even cited Welch as his inspiration, saying he aspired to be a "combination of what Jack Welch put together at GE and Warren Buffett's very practical ideas on how you go about creating return for shareholders." With one deal after another—some 900 in all—

Kozlowski created a sprawling company that made everything from home security systems to submarine parts. Tyco also used the same kind of earnings management that had become commonplace at GE Capital, and often went further. And in the midst of that breakneck growth, Kozlowski turned to crime. As the CEO of a major American corporation, he was already in line to receive many tens of millions of dollars. That was a given, but it wasn't enough. Kozlowski began stealing from the company, and ultimately fleeced the corporate coffers of some $150 million. He was found out, convicted, and sentenced to prison. In the wake of his arrest, investors realized that Tyco was not worth more than the sum of its parts, that in fact, the company was a collection of disparate businesses that didn't belong together at all. With new management in place and Kozlowski behind bars, Tyco was sold off in pieces.

Also in 2002, WorldCom, a major long distance telephone company, collapsed amid an accounting scandal. The company's founder, Bernard Ebbers, had been systematically inflating earnings in order to prop up WorldCom's stock price. Over the years, he had orchestrated a scheme to report $3.8 billion in fraudulent earnings and overstated the company's assets by more than $11 billion. Falsifying earnings and lying about the value of assets was outright criminality, and Ebbers was sent to prison. Thanks to the example set by Welch, the pressure to drive share prices ever higher was all consuming, and many CEOs would do anything to get ahead.

The ignominies kept coming in the years that followed. Freddie Mac, the government-backed lender, was caught misstating earnings by $5 billion from 2000 to 2002. Once again, the fraud had been perpetrated by executives who were intent on creating the impression of endless growth, inflating the stock price, and reaping the rewards for themselves. (Freddie Mac and the executives settled without admitting or denying guilt.)

And in 2005, New York attorney general Eliot Spitzer brought charges against Maurice "Hank" Greenberg, the CEO of AIG, one of the world's largest insurance companies. AIG had gone to great lengths to mislead the public about the size of its reserves and the overall health of the company. It was forced to restate four years of financial results, leading to a multibillion-dollar loss for shareholders. AIG paid more than $1.6 billion to settle, without admitting guilt. Greenberg settled too, but ultimately admitted to his role in the fraud and paid a $9 million fine.

With so much of corporate America ensnared in scandal, GE itself was no longer immune from scrutiny. The SEC began looking into GE's accounting in an effort to determine whether it was hiding profits—or losses—through accounting chicanery, an investigation that took years to complete. By the end of 2002, Congress passed the Sarbanes-Oxley Act, a sweeping law that cracked down on corporate fraud and demanded a new level of transparency and accountability from companies and executives. "Before Enron, neither analysts nor investors ever asked us how GE Capital worked," Immelt said. But with CEOs around the country under the microscope, Immelt, too, found himself facing intense new scrutiny from investors and regulators alike.

After decades when it seemed like big business could do no wrong, the relentless trickery had tarnished corporate America's sterling reputation. Some of the country's most illustrious companies were found to be deeply corrupt. The lust for short-term profits often led executives to bend the rules, and sometimes break the law. And while Welch, newly retired, didn't seem to appreciate his own role in creating a culture where such malfeasance was commonplace, it was clear even to him that something had gone awry. "It seemed to the public as if all of business was filled with bad people—a whole orchard of rotten apples," he said. "The long running boom economy brought out terrible excesses, and dishonest acts were perpetuated by handfuls of people."

"The employees will still be cowering"

By the early 2000s, even Boeing, which for so long had been one of the paragons of American industrialism, was mired in scandal. In

2004, the company's chief financial officer was imprisoned for trying to bribe a Pentagon official. The next year, Harry Stonecipher, who took over Boeing after a stint at McDonnell Douglas, was forced to resign after having an affair with a subordinate. Although Stonecipher had been CEO for only a few years, he had inexorably altered Boeing in that time. A proud engineering culture had been replaced with one focused on the bottom line. The strong bonds that tied workers to the company had frayed. Now, as the Boeing board looked for a new CEO, they turned to one of the men who almost won the race to succeed Welch: Jim McNerney.

While McNerney's tenure at 3M had been controversial inside the company, it had delivered results for shareholders. And though the former light bulb executive wasn't an engineer himself, he had ended his time at GE running the aircraft engines business, an experience that gave him strong relationships at the highest levels of Boeing and a working knowledge of the aviation market. Running a company that designed and built airplanes, however, was a quite different task. At its best, the Boeing engineering culture thrived on radical transparency, a willingness to call out mistakes and a freedom to spend time—and money—to get things right. It was the kind of laborious, innovative work for which McNerney had exhibited little patience at 3M, where he was accused of stifling innovation by imposing Six Sigma and cutting costs. And soon after taking over Boeing in 2005, he began making similar moves.

From his time with Welch, McNerney understood how compensation could be used to transform a culture. And in an effort to get mid-level Boeing employees to prioritize the reduction of costs, he made a subtle but powerful change to the company's pay plan. Under the new system, managers' compensation would be tied not just to the company's stock price, but to the financial performance of their own business groups. While that made intuitive sense—rewarding strong performance at the team level—it had a perverse effect: managers suddenly had a personal incentive to cut costs however they could. They were thinking not just about making a great product that would help the company, let alone a safe airplane, but about how they could pinch pennies along the way. The new compensation scheme initially had the intended effect. Costs came down. Efficiency improved. Yet in time, incentivizing Boeing employees to fret about costs would have disastrous consequences.

McNerney made other moves to throttle Boeing's familial culture, too. He slashed wages and did away with the company's pension plan. He moved more jobs out of Seattle and went to war with the unions. He squeezed suppliers, pressuring them to lower their prices or lose Boeing's business. And he said that uncooperative suppliers would wind up barred from working with the company. "If a certain group is not working with us . . . they'll be on a no-fly list," he said. "They'll not be allowed to bid on new programs with Boeing."

McNerney also shared Welch's delight in making his employees tremble. During a 2014 conference call with analysts, McNerney said he didn't intend to retire immediately because "the heart will still be beating, the employees will still be cowering." One labor leader at Boeing called that remark a "new low" in relations between the company and its employees. McNerney passed it off as a bad joke, but at least one astute observer understood the origins of his contemptuous attitude. Tom Buffenbarger, a union leader, said that McNerney's remarks were a reminder that "the Jack Welch style of anti-personnel management is still alive and well at Boeing."

Not long before McNerney took over, Stonecipher had made one of his most consequential decisions as Boeing CEO, approving the creation of an entirely new jet. It had been decades since the company created a new plane from scratch, but Boeing couldn't postpone the work any longer. The international travel market was booming, airlines were flying longer routes, and Boeing wanted to deliver a midsized, fuel-efficient plane that could fly more than 7,000 miles without stopping. It was a multibillion-dollar opportunity that would be ferociously expensive, but it was essential work. Without major new investments, the company would fall behind the times and fade into irrelevance. Stonecipher had tried to resist taking on such an enormous project. He wanted Boeing to keep plowing its profits into buybacks and dividends. If the company did proceed, he argued, it should do so with an eye toward minimizing expenses. His opposition delayed the project for a couple years, but he ultimately approved the development of what would become the 787 Dreamliner.

The 787 program was in its infancy when McNerney arrived, but the new boss saw an opportunity to make his mark. It would be Boeing's first brand-new jet in decades, and the new CEO thought he could do things differently. With previous Boeing planes, around 35 percent of parts were outsourced to contractors, while Boeing fabricated most components itself. McNerney flipped that ratio. Now, some 70 percent of Dreamliner parts would be outsourced. The goal, naturally, was to cut costs. McNerney believed he could drive a hard bargain with suppliers, boosting Boeing's profitability. He also thought outsourcing would speed development of the new plane, with projections estimating that the Dreamliner's development could be completed in just four to six years, for as little as $6 billion to $10 billion if everything went right. Both predictions turned out to be wildly optimistic. Development of the new plane would take nine years and cost more than $32 billion.

Outsourcing also gave Boeing substantially less control over the quality and timing of components, and ultimately of the Dreamliner itself. Rather than taking full ownership of the new plane's design and engineering, Boeing let its subcontractors do much of that critical work. The 787's fuselage would be made from carbon fiber instead of aluminum alloy, a change intended to reduce the weight of the plane and improve its durability. But using carbon fiber for fuselage was an unproven new technology, adding a new level of complication to the program. The result was a cascading series of delays and glitches. Things got so bad with one supplier which was supposed to build the rear fuselage that Boeing purchased the factory in question for $1 billion. And in his most extreme attempt to keep costs down, McNerney went so far as to construct an entirely new Boeing factory in South Carolina, the state with the lowest union representation in the nation.

Orders started pouring in once Boeing formally unveiled the

plane in 2004. At $200 million apiece, the Dreamliner promised to be a success. But the decision to hire cheap labor quickly created more problems for Boeing. In a bid to prevent a possible unionization drive, managers in South Carolina were told not to hire workers with a history of participating in organized labor. Boeing got what it paid for. There was no historic aviation manufacturing base in South Carolina, so few of the workers at the new factory were familiar with the intricacies of building planes, and errors quickly piled up. Shoddy workmanship resulted in sharp metal shavings being left dangerously close to wires in the cockpit. Random objects—tools, strings of lights, and even ladders—were left inside the bowels of finished planes. One plane was flooded when it was almost finished, and another plane's engine caught fire on the assembly line. There were so many problems with the Dreamliners from Charleston that Qatar Airways, a major Boeing customer, stopped accepting planes from the factory. Even the workers making the mistakes knew something was deeply amiss. Whistleblower complaints emerged, the Federal Aviation Administration launched investigations that led to Boeing paying $6.6 million in fines, and morale slumped. Many employees harbored serious concerns about the safety of the Dreamliners coming out of South Carolina. "I've told my wife that I never plan to fly on it," said Joseph Clayton, a technician at the factory. "It's just a safety issue."

The Dreamliner finally debuted in late 2011, years late and significantly over budget. Then, just over a year after it entered service, the entire fleet was grounded because the plane's batteries were catching fire. The grounding was costly and embarrassing and a harbinger of much more serious problems to come. Yet before the Dreamliner could even take flight, Boeing faced another critical decision.

"Winning"

While former GE executives were wrecking American companies in virtually every sector of the economy, Welch was freed from managerial responsibilities, newly in love, and shockingly rich. With Suzy at his side, he became a multimedia juggernaut. Together the couple struck a deal to write a new book, *Winning*, which fused business war stories with self-help bromides. A few years later, they put out a companion volume entitled *Winning: The Answers: Confronting 74 of the Toughest Questions in Business Today.* And in 2015 the Welches published their last book, *The Real-Life MBA: Your No-BS Guide to Winning the Game, Building a Team, and Growing Your Career.* They began writing a weekly column—first for *Businessweek*, and then for Reuters and *Fortune*—each week's installation offering a lesson on competition, grit, and determination.

They worked the speaking circuit, commanding six-figure fees for hour-long appearances. But Welch wouldn't give speeches; that required too much work. Rather, he would charge an event $150,000 to have an approved moderator conduct a Q&A with him. Here was Welch at the Shale Gas Insight conference in Philadelphia. There he was at the Boston University MBA Symposium. Next it was off to Ecuador for the Business Decision Makers Program. Event organizers would upsell attendees, with $800 tickets buying access to a cocktail reception with Welch. He became a regular commentator on CNBC and other networks, opining on the business news of the day. He would gab for hours with Charlie Rose, join panel discussions on talk shows, and sit for interviews with anyone who came calling. "No question Jack Welch, the retired CEO of GE, is one of the most successful corporate executives in the history of American business," Dan Rather purred when he featured Welch and Wetlaufer on *60 Minutes* in 2005. "And he is obsessed with winning, which happens to be the title of his new book."

Donning a sweater instead of a suit and tie, Welch launched a multipronged effort to soften his rough edges. He and Suzy recorded an audiobook with Dan Goleman, the author of *Emotional Intelligence*. Goleman's work focused on the role of empathy, mindfulness, and compassion, hardly characteristics that defined Welch's time as CEO, and the resulting audiobook portrayed Welch as a corner office guru, deftly navigating the business world with wisdom and grace. "No one knows leadership like Jack Welch," the promotional material for the audiobook read. "Key elements of emotional intelligence, from self-awareness to the ability to instill core values in a team, are part of that success."

In reality, Welch had hardly toned down his rhetoric. Everywhere he went, he continued to preach the gospel of shareholder primacy, suggesting that companies put investors first and remain unsentimental in the face of layoffs. "You know exactly who the turkeys are, and they're right amongst you," Welch said at the MIT Sloan School of Management. "Baseball teams do it every day. It's the way it is. Why should business not have cuts?" During a panel discussion with Nobel Prize–winning economist Joseph Stiglitz, Welch made the risible assertion that no successful industry had ever flourished with a highly unionized workforce, disregarding the glory days of the American auto and steel industries, to name but two examples.

Warren Bennis, founding chairman of the Leadership Institute at the University of Southern California and a friend of Welch's, said that when Welch married Suzy, he "reinvented himself." "Without her ignition, I don't think he would be as productive," Bennis said. "They're co-leaders. She's part of the energy behind that brand. Their relationship is a key to who he's become." And the press lapped it up. In 2005, *Newsweek*—the publication that coined "Neutron Jack"—splashed Welch on the cover with the headline, "How to Win." *Success* magazine put him on the cover with the banner, "What It Takes to Be a Great Leader."

While success in one domain does not guarantee success in another, that never stopped men like Welch from trying. If he could run GE, what was to stop him from lending his managerial expertise to other ventures in need of reform? Brimming with confidence, Welch in 2003 became chairman of the NYC Leadership Academy, an organization created to coach New York City public school teachers and train new principals. The academy had been dreamed up by Joel Klein, the technocratic schools chancellor under Mayor Michael Bloomberg, and was meant to bring the competitive spirit of corporate America to the world of primary education. At its unveiling, Welch tried to instill fear into the aspiring principals with the same tough-nosed tactics he used at GE. "We used to say in the corporation, 'Any one of you jerk managers who's got a dull crowd hanging around with you don't deserve your job,'" Welch said. "Well, we'll say that to principals. We'll challenge principals in the same way."

Soon after the program began, Welch brought the principals to Crotonville for a weekend retreat. At one point, he was promoting the notion that teachers' compensation should be tied to their students' test scores. It was the kind of accountability he'd expected as CEO, and he couldn't imagine why it wouldn't work in a classroom. But the concept was anathema to the educators, who knew firsthand that children learn in different ways, and not all of them test well. "Children are not products," said one aspiring principal during an exchange with Welch at Crotonville.

"Oh yes they are!" Welch shot back, silencing her.

Despite his efforts to bring Welchism to New York City public schools, the program did little to change the fate of the country's largest school system, which remained segregated, underfunded, and unable to deliver consistent educational outcomes to children throughout the city, irrespective of their family's net worth. The Leadership Academy was unceremoniously shuttered in 2017, and the city's educational leaders took the opportunity to remark upon the program's misguided approach. "It takes specific things to run GE, but it's a different thing than running a school," the deputy chancellor of schools said at its closing.

Welch had believed that he could help fix the New York City public schools not because he was an expert in public education. He thought he could do it because he had been a successful CEO. He suffered from the delusion that his money was representative of some greater intelligence, as if his ability to wring profits from a hyperfinancialized multinational corporation bestowed him with the gifts of an educational reformer. It's a delusion common to the wealthy, and Welch has hardly been the only one to turn his attention to repairing our public schools. The Bill and Melinda Gates Foundation, flush with a $50 billion endowment made possible by Microsoft's early monopolizing, tried to use technology to overhaul curriculums in Washington State. Amazon founder Jeff Bezos has launched the Bezos Academy, a preschool designed to cultivate entrepreneurial thinking. Facebook founder Mark Zuckerberg donated $100 million to revamp the Newark public school system, an effort later deemed unsuccessful. And Adam Neumann, the WeWork cofounder, started a high-priced school for his children and their friends and let his wife design the curriculum. These expensive efforts were largely unsuccessful, making clear that improving how children learn and teachers teach takes more than money.

Although Welch's attempt to reform the New York City public schools turned out to be beyond his grasp, he was not done with his forays into education. Welch soon became convinced he could teach future business leaders, too. At a party in 2009, he met Michael Clifford, a businessman who, after a career in broadcasting and stints working with popular evangelical Christians including Pat Robertson and Jerry Falwell, grew convinced there was a fortune to be made in online education. Clifford began buying accredited schools that were struggling financially, rebranding them, and charging high fees for degrees earned via the web. At times, he tried to recruit homeless people to sign up, because they would be eligible for federal student loans which could have helped the bottom line. Clifford understood the power of Welch's brand and saw an opportunity, and soon after they met, Clifford pitched Welch on the idea of creating an online MBA.

Welch was initially skeptical. But after Clifford made $50 million through another online education venture, Welch—encouraged by Suzy—wanted in. "Suzy was the ball bearing that made it happen," Clifford said. It would be a for-profit Crotonville, and a chance to spread Welchism further still. Before long, the men launched the Jack Welch Management Institute, an online MBA program that featured occasional instruction from Welch himself, and from some of his trusted acolytes, including Jim McNerney.

To promote the MBA, Welch went on *The Apprentice* with Donald Trump, awarding one lucky contestant a scholarship to the institute. The morning after their co-branded episode aired, Welch and Trump appeared together on the *Today* show, standing in the plaza at Rockefeller Center and making small talk with Matt Lauer, Al Roker, and Ann Curry. The men were an odd couple, Trump towering above Welch, both of them hungry for attention.

"Donald has been extremely helpful," Welch said.

"There's nobody better than Jack," said Trump.

Today, the Jack Welch Management Institute lives on, with students still paying $50,000 a year to receive an online degree with his name on it. It is but one reminder of Welch's enduring influence in the global marketplace of bad ideas. His books are still in print. And from San Diego, to Sydney, to Kansas City, to Prague, groups of aspiring executives get together to discuss Welch's legacy and study his books. In Dhahran, Saudi Arabia, one such group was organized by Muath Bin Hussain, who got a degree from the Jack Welch Management Institute and went on to work for Saudi Aramco, the state oil producer that in recent years assumed the mantle of the most valuable company on earth. "I love Jack Welch and I consider him as my mentor," Bin Hussain said. "I am spreading what I have learned at his institute to our clients."

Just as Welch had transformed GE from a sleepy industrial giant into a turbocharged diversified conglomerate, he transformed himself. He wasn't just a retired CEO. He was a self-help guru, a policy expert, and an entrepreneur. There was no unifying agenda to his post-GE work. He did not champion a worthy cause or devote himself to helping those in need. He did not give away great sums of his fortune or reflect deeply on how his time leading a titan of American industry had shaped the country's fate. As had been the case when he was CEO, Welch was not concerned with the common good. Instead, his main interest was self-promotion. He found ways to defend his legacy, promote the myth that CEOs could do anything, and evangelize for his fellow bosses however he could. As Jimmy Lee, the vice chairman of JPMorgan and close friend of Welch's said: "His agenda is being Jack."

"You could feel his presence"

When Immelt decided to double down on Welchism in the wake of 9/11, it was, on one hand, a perfectly logical decision. Immelt didn't want to be the one to break GE's long string of remarkable quarterly returns, and thanks to the magic of GE Capital he was able to sustain the success, even with the economy in shambles. But by forgoing the opportunity to reset the company, Immelt ultimately was setting himself up for failure, effectively promising Wall Street that earnings would continue to rise indefinitely, just as they had under Welch. Pulling that off would prove to be impossible, especially with regulators scrutinizing GE and analysts wary of the company following the critique by Bill Gross, the outspoken bond investor. But Immelt was going to try, and to do so, he would lean on Welch's favored tactics of downsizing, dealmaking, and financialization in the years ahead.

In 2003 alone, ignoring Gross's critique that GE's growth was fueled by unending dealmaking, Immelt spent roughly $30 billion on acquisitions. GE bought the film and TV unit of the French media conglomerate Vivendi, a Finnish medical device company, and a British life sciences company. Those deals followed the $5.4 billion acquisition of a commercial lending business in the Netherlands. GE was buying up everything from medical technology to media assets in an unending quest to grow the bottom line at the expense of all else. The years that followed included more profligate spending, as Immelt signed off on deals for data management companies, environmental software makers, and more.

The acquisitions rarely paid off. In the aftermath of 9/11, GE bet big on security technology firms, buying two explosive detection companies for $1 billion. The businesses never grew much, however, and in 2009, Immelt offloaded majority interests in the firms for a significant loss. Those were rounding errors at a company the size of GE, but they were emblematic of Immelt's seemingly poor acquisition skills. He was often too early or too late to an emerging trend, frequently paid too much, and seemed incapable of changing his mind once he was set on a target. Welch's warning to Langone on the eve of his retirement—that Immelt was an irresponsible dealmaker—appeared to be spot on.

As Immelt diversified into any number of new industries, he had less and less regard for several businesses that were once pillars of GE—plastics, appliances, and lighting. The plastics business was sold off to Saudi Basic Industries, a Riyadh-based chemicals company, for $11.6 billion. It was a good price, more than most analysts expected the business would fetch. Yet it also took GE further away from its industrial roots. Some years later, Immelt sold the appliances business to a Chinese company, Haier, for $5.4 billion. As part of the deal, he licensed out the GE name. The result was a feature of globalization that Welch probably never saw coming: American workers now came and went from Appliance Park in Louisville still making products affixed with the GE logo, but working for a Chinese company and earning less than they had when the factory was actually owned by GE. Eventually, GE would sell its lighting business, too—again licensing the GE name—completing the nearly wholesale dismantling of the conglomerate that Welch had made the most valuable company on earth.

All the while, GE Capital just kept growing. Immelt continued to acquire niche financial businesses, paying $4 billion for a real estate finance operation, Security Capital Group, in December 2001. GE acquired commercial loan portfolios from Boeing, and car loans from South Korea. It gobbled up more private label credit cards and invested in banks from Turkey to New Zealand. And in 2004, GE Capital waded into riskier territory, acquiring Western Asset Mortgage Capital, or WMC, a subprime mortgage lender, for $500 million. At the time, subprime mortgages were on the rise as American homeowners with questionable credit loaded up on low-interest debt. There were obvious and glaring risks to the business, but the profits were there, and no one understood just how disastrous the loans might be. At the time of the deal for WMC, GE's entry into the industry, far from raising questions, seemed like a seal of approval, conferring on subprime mortgages some mainstream credibility.

Meanwhile, the global economy appeared to be on the mend.

After the shock of 9/11, the capital markets regained their strength. And with the boom times back, GE Capital borrowed extensively and produced enormous profits. GE Capital had topped out at $425 billion in assets under Welch. Within five years of Immelt taking over, it had grown to more than $550 billion in assets, and it would grow larger still. GE Capital wasn't just bigger, it was an increasingly important part of the overall mix at GE, too. Financial services had never contributed more than 41 percent of GE's profits under Welch. Under Immelt, that figure soared to nearly 60 percent. And of course, Immelt continued to use GE Capital to bolster GE's earnings. Quarter after quarter, the finance arm came up with unusual—and sometimes improper—ways to make the numbers work just well enough for the company to deliver another quarter of stellar earnings.

As innovative as GE was when it came to creative accounting, there were growing signs that the company had lost its edge when it came to industrial innovation. Welch, with his relentless trimming of costs and his obsession with reporting favorable results to Wall Street, had sapped the company's entrepreneurial spirit. And however much Immelt might have wanted this to change, it was too late.

Aaron Dignan, a consultant who helps companies navigate organization challenges and difficult transformations, worked with GE for years under Immelt, trying to get the company to think big. Dignan found that GE executives were myopically focused on their own business lines, doing whatever was needed to meet their numbers quarter after quarter, and thinking little about the company's overall strategy. When Dignan tried to talk about innovation, GE executives talked about their order backlog. When he asked the business leaders of different units what the purpose of the company was, he said, their answer was always about delivering for shareholders. "When you tried to get anything done, you would feel the imprint of Welch," he said. "The impact that man left was profoundly deep."

For years, Dignan burrowed into GE, encouraging Immelt to pursue 3D printing, self-driving cars, anything that might give the company relevance in the years ahead. Dignan kept telling Immelt and the board what any student of business understands: there would be up-front costs, but that if the investments paid off, the rewards could be enormous. "This is going to hurt before it gets better," he would tell them. "We actually have to dismantle the garden from the roots up and rebuild a business for the twenty-first century. And then it can be a $1 trillion company. But you're not going to get your quarterly returns for the next five years. Do you want to do that?" The alternative, he explained, was a slow march to irrelevancy. "The answer was always like, 'No. We want our dividend,'" Dignan said.

Eric Ries, a consultant and author of *The Lean Startup*, was also brought in to work with Immelt and his team. Ries, an expert in entrepreneurial culture, was there to try to jump-start innovation inside the company. That meant trying new things, being willing to fail, and possibly investing in technologies that might not immediately pay off. Inside GE, however, Ries found a deep-seated aversion to risk taking. At every turn, people were afraid to go out on a limb, worried they might fail, and most of all, paranoid that whatever they tried would prove insufficiently profitable. Long after Welch had retired, his ghost still haunted the halls of GE. "He had the same status inside of GE almost like Thomas Edison," Ries said. "Nobody spoke his name directly, but you could feel his presence. His ideals were lurking around every corner."

The closest GE came to innovation under Immelt was a marketing campaign known as "Ecomagination." The effort was little more than greenwashing. While GE had a nascent wind energy business and tried to improve efficiency in some of its products, it kept churning out turbines, locomotives, and jet engines that ran on fossil fuel and continued fighting efforts to clean up the Hudson River, which GE had polluted with PCBs for decades. "I wasn't an environmentalist, per se," Immelt said. "I like looking at a pristine beach as much as the next guy, but I wasn't coming at this from a tree-hugging perspective." Rather, Immelt, always the salesman, understood that the market for green products was poised to take off. "Ecomagination fooled many when the real strategy was quarterly earnings and gas turbines," said Paul Polman, the former chief executive of Unilever.

Even Tina Fey saw through the charade. As Immelt launched

Ecomagination, *30 Rock*, Fey's sendup of NBC and GE, skewered the effort, with Jack Donaghy—the CEO character played by Alec Baldwin and inspired by Welch—promoting his own environmental push. The slogan: "Saving the earth while maintaining profitability! The free market will solve global warming—if that even exists!"

SIX

Bad Trades

"I almost fell out of my seat"

GE helped popularize some of the most influential products of the modern age, innovations that changed untold numbers of lives: the light bulb, the refrigerator, the television, the jet engine. And there is one more item that belongs on this list: the subprime mortgage.

In the early 2000s, with a housing boom in full swing and interest rates low, banks and other lenders were handing out so many mortgages to borrowers with bad credit that a whole new enterprise was created: the subprime mortgage industry. It was an unlimited gusher of free money for anyone who believed they could flip a house while the market was still rising. Lenders knew that many of these borrowers would have a hard time making good on their payments. That reality was embedded in the very name of these dubious loans: the borrowers were "subprime." As in, less than optimal. As in, they had bad credit. But despite the risks, lenders issued millions of subprime mortgages in the years after 9/11, knowingly offering big loans with adjustable interest rates to virtually anyone who wanted one, almost regardless of income or occupation. Then creative financiers took things even further. Wall Street firms packaged these questionable loans into mortgage-backed securities, sold them to investors, and created a whole universe of dubious financial products. Without anyone quite realizing it, more and more of the global financial system was dependent on overstretched American homeowners' ability to meet their monthly mortgage payments.

Under Welch, GE Capital had expanded into trading, private equity, and high-interest credit cards. But it had never gone so far as to market mortgages to homeowners who had little chance of making their payments. Yet in 2004, with GE chasing profits wherever they could be found, Immelt agreed to acquire Western Asset Mortgage Capital, a major subprime player, for $500 million.

The deal had all the hallmarks of Immelt's rashness. It was executed quickly, the price was high, and due diligence was minimal. Had GE looked closely, it might have realized that WMC was hiring unqualified shoe salesmen and porn stars as sales reps, then rewarding them with huge bonuses for signing up new borrowers. It might have discovered that the company was riddled with fraud, as salespeople forged documents to get unqualified borrowers approved for jumbo loans. It might have found out that WMC employees were falsifying documents in order to bundle those bad loans and sell them to Wall Street. It might have noticed that many of the mortgages WMC issued wound up facing foreclosure. But GE appeared none the wiser, and the subprime mortgage boom rolled on.

Under GE's ownership, WMC became one of the biggest subprime lenders in the country over the next two years, originating about $65 billion in loans to tens of thousands of unqualified homebuyers. And by 2007, all those bad bets were catching up with the economy. Borrowers were defaulting, triggering a massive subprime mortgage crisis and leaving GE—a company most people still thought of as the reliable producer of refrigerators and light bulbs—dangerously exposed. That summer, WMC reported a $1 billion loss. GE scrambled to stanch the bleeding, winding down positions, firing most of the staff, and agreeing to sell WMC for a steep discount. Two decades earlier, Welch had bought himself a headache when he acquired Kidder Peabody. The investment bank, it turned out, was a den of insider trading that ensnared GE in years of scandal. Now Immelt had bought a similar mess in WMC. "I wish we'd never gotten into the business," Immelt said.

It was too late. The contagion in the financial markets was spreading well beyond the United States, and GE Capital's strategy of chasing deals around the globe suddenly looked like folly. Lake, a Japanese company that financed consumer loans and that GE had acquired during Welch's last years, was also in trouble, and reported a $1.2 billion loss before GE sold it. Immelt's history of questionable dealmaking was finally having an acutely negative impact, and GE Capital, for so long the company's secret weapon, was suddenly its chief liability. But Immelt himself still appeared to be blind to this fact.

That summer, he commissioned the consulting firm McKinsey & Company to produce a study assessing GE Capital's vulnerability in the event of a sharp economic downturn. McKinsey's verdict: *Everything was fine!* The consultants believed that even if capital markets in the United States seized up, there would be enough liquidity in the global financial system to sustain GE Capital's frantic dealmaking and lending operations.

That was just what Immelt wanted to hear. If anything, Immelt figured that a broader economic downturn might give GE the opportunity to acquire distressed companies at fire-sale prices. Bankers from Goldman Sachs echoed McKinsey's assessment, assuring the CEO that GE would be able to handle whatever came its way. Heartened, Immelt continued to project optimism. Just months before the economy's darkest days he proclaimed, "Our financial businesses should do well in a year like 2008."

The next month, Immelt fielded questions from investors, and confidently assured them that—as always—the company was on track to meet or beat expectations when it reported earnings. But just three days later, the investment bank Bear Stearns collapsed, sending the first serious convulsions through the broader financial markets.

In April 2008, GE reported first quarter profits far below Wall Street's expectations. GE missed its target by $700 million—a catastrophic failure. "I was on the train, and I almost fell out of my seat," said a top analyst who covered the company. "People thought it was a misprint." GE shares fell 12 percent as investors offloaded the stock. In the aftermath, Immelt admitted that GE Capital had suffered from an "inability to do transactions in the last two weeks that normally could get done." It was a remarkable public confession that in the last days of each quarter, GE Capital had a habit of doing whatever deals were needed to meet the numbers.

For decades, GE Capital had been the magician backstage, conjuring tricks that consistently dazzled Wall Street. Investors didn't ask too many questions. The fact that it wasn't entirely clear how Welch, and then Immelt, made it all work was part of what made the act so enticing. It was easier to suspend disbelief and enjoy the show. But now the wizard had been exposed. "Investors now understand that GE uses the last couple weeks in the quarter to 'fine-tune' its financial service portfolios to ensure its earnings objectives are achieved," Heymann, the GE analyst, said at the time. "It turns out it really wasn't miracle management systems or risk-control systems or even innovative brilliance. It was the green curtain that allowed the magic to be consistently performed undetected."

By September of 2008, the world was in a full-blown financial crisis. Two of the Big Three automakers needed a bailout from Washington. Fannie Mae and Freddie Mac were put into conservatorship by the federal government. Bank of America was forced to acquire Merrill Lynch. Lehman Brothers filed for bankruptcy. The Dow Jones Industrial Average was in free fall. AIG was on the brink and had to be bailed out. As the global financial system teetered, it was getting more expensive for GE to borrow money, and the company needed all the cash it could get to handle its short-term debts—approximately $90 billion worth. More banks were failing, others looked poised to follow, and the ripple effects were putting an enormous cash crunch on GE.

Immelt was cornered by late September. A prominent analyst cut the earnings forecast for GE, causing the stock to drop 9 percent. In the bond markets, investors signaled that GE's debt—long protected by the company's pristine AAA credit rating—was flirting with junk territory. It was hard to fathom, but for a moment it seemed that GE, one of the pillars of American industry, could fail, too.

In the end, Immelt was bailed out by one of the nation's most famous investors. On the afternoon of September 30, Warren Buffett agreed to loan the company $3 billion. The cash itself was important, but the show of support from Buffett was what mattered most, giving other investors faith in GE. "I am confident that GE will continue to be successful in the years to come," Buffett said in a statement.

Days later, Immelt was in Washington asking for more help. This time, he needed the Federal Deposit Insurance Corporation to guarantee approximately $139 billion of its loans, essentially bestowing on GE the credibility of Uncle Sam himself. Just how badly GE needed the cash became clear less than two weeks later, when it reported a 22 percent drop in profits for the quarter, with GE Capital notching a stunning 38 percent drop in earnings. Without liquid capital markets, its black box financial wizardry was useless. Worse, GE looked just as vulnerable as every other company, maybe more so. Besides having industrial businesses that were shaky in a downturn, Immelt was also saddled with an unregulated bank that held a grab bag of bad loans.

GE would never fully recover. The backstop from Buffett and the FDIC stopped the bleeding, but the government designated GE a systemically important financial institution (SIFI), imposing additional regulations on the company and adding a mountain of costs. Immelt, chastened by the experience, resolved to get rid of GE Capital once and for all. It was a harrowing experience, but Immelt had been well paid for his effort. Over three years, from 2007 to 2009, he received $25 million in compensation.

"Get a gun out and shoot him"

When Welch retired, he suggested that his "success will be deter-mined by how well my successor grows" the company "in the next 20 years." By that measure, he was shaping up to be a failure. GE's market capitalization had shed hundreds of billions of dollars on Im-melt's watch, and the news kept getting worse.

In public, Welch refrained from speaking ill of his chosen suc-cessor. When asked to assess GE's performance, Welch would praise Immelt and profess faith in the company and its future. But in pri-vate, Welch was fuming. He would tell confidants that Immelt was a disaster. "He said, 'The biggest single decision I had to make as chair-man and CEO of GE was my replacement, and I blew it,'" Langone remembered. Relations between Welch and Immelt had soured in other ways, too. When Immelt had pushed Langone off the GE board, Welch—who recruited Langone and remained a close friend—took it personally.

After biting his tongue for seven years, Welch's reserve finally broke after Immelt's earnings miss at the onset of the financial crisis. The Manager of the Century's protégé was failing at the worst pos-sible moment, and Welch assailed Immelt on national television.

"Here's the screw-up," Welch said on CNBC. "You made a promise that you deliver this, and you miss three weeks later. Jeff has a cred-ibility issue. He's getting his ass kicked." When the host asked what would happen if Immelt missed an earnings forecast again, Welch employed his favorite murderous metaphor. "I'd be shocked beyond belief, and I'd get a gun out and shoot him if he doesn't make what he promised now," he said. "Just deliver the earnings. Tell them you're going to grow 12 percent and deliver 12 percent!"

The next day, Welch called Immelt in hopes of making peace. Immelt was in no mood though, and finally let his old boss have it. "Following you has been no fun," Immelt told Welch. "I've kept my mouth shut about the problems you left me. I bolstered your legacy, when I could easily have shot it full of holes. And because I've done so, you are still 'Jack Welch, CEO of the Century.' But now, when I need your help, you stab me in the back? I just don't get it."

"Look, I'm sorry," Welch said. "You fucked up, but I shouldn't have said what I said on air."

Welch tried to walk his comments back in the days that followed, but Immelt stewed about the incident long after it was over. "This essentially ended our relationship," Immelt said. "I'd finally realized that he was using his criticisms of me to promote his own brand." Welch, Immelt understood, had left him "a bag of shit." For years, Immelt had refrained from publicly criticizing the former CEO. After that episode, however, he was less cautious. The next year, he bad-mouthed Welch at a party hosted by the *Financial Times*. "Not only could anyone have run GE in the 1990s," Immelt said, "his dog could have run GE. A German shepherd could have run GE." What Immelt faced now, he told the crowd, "will be really, really, really hard."

Within months, more of Welch's sins would come back to haunt the company. Early in 2009, GE announced that it had settled sweeping accounting fraud charges with the SEC. For two years just after Immelt took over, GE had overstated profits in a bid to jack up its share price. The company had developed myriad ways to fudge the numbers, detailed in an extensive SEC complaint. For example, as GE's short-term lending business had ballooned in early 2003, the company modified its accounting practices at the last minute to avoid reporting a $200 million pretax charge. According to all generally accepted accounting standards, the move was highly improper. But the change allowed GE to once again meet its quarterly expectations.

In other instances, Immelt's accountants found ways to let GE record revenue before products were actually sold. One particularly audacious move involved the company purporting to have sold some $400 million worth of locomotives in the fourth quarter, helping the company make its numbers for the year. But rather than actually selling the trains to railroad operators, GE had entrusted them to other financial institutions for safekeeping, until the actual customers would be ready to buy them the next year. In each case, the impetus was clear.

"The motivation was to increase earnings," said David Bergers, the SEC official who led the investigation. And while the settlement was for transgressions that occurred in the years after Welch departed, the tactics appear to have been well honed. In its complaint, the SEC noted that GE met or beat analyst expectations every quarter from 1995 through 2004. The suggestion was unmistakable: at the height of Welch's powers, the same sort of tactics were being employed. As the SEC documented, this wasn't a one-off anomaly. Distorting earnings had apparently become something of an art form at GE. "GE bent the accounting rules beyond the breaking point," said Robert Khuzami, director of the SEC's Division of Enforcement.

GE agreed to settle with the government and pay $50 million—a relative pittance—to resolve the matter. The deal allowed GE to claim the wrongdoing was an honest mistake, that any impropriety was the fault of a few bad apples. It was the same excuse Welch made when his underlings were ripping off the Air Force, the same excuse other executives used when trouble occurred on their watch. But the settlement made it harder for GE to deny what so many had suspected for so long—its picture-perfect earnings were a little too perfect. The company seemed to have made a habit of fiddling with the numbers to keep Wall Street happy.

The financial crisis wasn't the fault of GE alone. Predatory lenders, greedy banks, and overleveraged homebuyers deserve most of the credit for that. Profit-hungry corporations sold naive consumers on loans they couldn't afford. Banks packaged the loans and sold them off, bundling risk and passing it to the next unsuspecting party. When the music stopped, the government bailed out the banks, but left the homeowners hanging out to dry. Everyday people reaching for the American dream through the time-honored tradition of homeownership went bankrupt, while none of the major architects of the subprime crisis went to jail. And though it wasn't Welch or Immelt who bore responsibility for the crisis, when the dominoes started to fall, GE was deeply enmeshed with a toxic financial system.

At its inception, GE Capital was designed to support the middle class, offering low-interest loans to people trying to buy their first refrigerator. It was a benign financing arm, intended not to unleash profits but to nurture a new generation of consumers. Now GE Capital seemed to be preying on the same sort of consumers it was originally designed to help. GE Capital had become the very opposite of what it was meant to be, knocking the middle class down instead of building it up.

Even beyond GE's own role in the crisis, the primal forces that led so much risk to be amassed by so few reflected the Welchian worldview. The appetite for endless growth—no matter the risk—was ripped straight from the GE playbook. The embrace of financial complexity—credit default swaps, collateralized debt obligations, and mortgage-backed securities—was an extension of the black box culture that GE Capital helped create. And investors' enduring faith that the markets could always go up—even the housing market—was nurtured over the years by Welch's quest for consistent earnings growth.

At the end of the day, the purported solutions to the crisis were Welchian. To shore up the financial system, policymakers and executives set off a wave of consolidation—Bank of America taking over Merrill Lynch, Wells Fargo taking over Wachovia—allowing big banks to get even bigger. Those who suffered the most were the ones who could least afford it—tens of millions put out of work, hundreds of millions who saw their savings decimated. And the ones responsible for provoking the crisis—the bankers, financiers, and executives who saddled homeowners with unsustainable debt, who ratcheted up interest rates, who packaged bad mortgages into products so toxic that they poisoned the entire economy—went unpunished, enjoying the impunity our criminal justice system so often affords white-collar offenders.

"The dumbest idea in the world"

In the wake of the financial crisis, the full scope of the carnage became clear. The housing market was gutted, unemployment had spiked, retirement accounts were obliterated. That such economic destruction could come about so swiftly, seemingly out of nowhere, exposed some of the fundamental injustices inherent in the modern economy. How was it that subprime mortgages and the predatory lending practices of a handful of Wall Street firms could destabilize the entire economy? How was it that so many people were living on the brink of catastrophe, liable to face foreclosure and bankruptcy at any moment due to the aggressive profiteering of greedy mortgage brokers?

In response to the crisis, a new generation of activists began railing against yawning inequality and the systems that create it. Politicians from both sides of the aisle called for more checks on big corporations. Even some CEOs conceded that it was time to pay more heed to just how exactly an economy that put profits above all else was affecting society at large. And as the true impunity of those responsible came into focus—no one who had a major hand in causing the crisis faced real consequences—that outrage spilled onto the streets.

Egged on by the anti-capitalist magazine *Adbusters*, a group of protesters descended on Zuccotti Park in lower Manhattan in September 2011, and the Occupy Wall Street movement was born. With the slogan "We are the 99 percent," one protest spawned another, and what started in New York spread to Oakland, London, and dozens of other cities around the world. People were outraged that wages were so low and employment seemed so tenuous for so many. They were furious that corporations got bailed out, and that none of the parties responsible for the financial crisis had been held accountable. They were angry that health care was so expensive and so complicated. Most of all, they were righteously indignant that bankers and traders and executives had it so good, while so many teachers, waiters, and machinists struggled to get by. What began with drum circles mushroomed into a global series of protests, many of them provoking violent police crackdowns, as crowds around the world took to the streets to protest the consequences of Welchism.

While protesters saw the Occupy Wall Street movement as a vessel for their rage, many companies saw a ripe messaging opportunity. Clearly, people were livid. And clearly, the status quo was part of the problem. So companies put their best marketers to work convincing the 99 percent that multinational corporations were, in fact, on their side. Soon, companies were sporting idealistic acronyms like merit badges, touting their CSR (corporate social responsibility) and ESG (environmental, social, and governance) bona fides. They would cut emissions, promote diversity, and clean up their supply chains. These were noble goals, to be sure, but the targets were often vague, the promises unenforceable.

Nonetheless, the conversation about what was wrong with our economy persisted, and eventually made its way into the C-suite itself. Some CEOs began tepidly acknowledging that all was not right with capitalism today, and that a few judicious reforms might be in order. Buzzwords like "conscious capitalism" and "stakeholder capitalism" were bandied about by executives hoping to distinguish themselves from the perpetrators of the heist that had shifted trillions of dollars of wealth from the working class to a small band of millionaires and billionaires. And among those appearing to reassess the promise of shareholder primacy in the wake of the financial crisis was, improbably, Welch himself.

In 2009, with the world economy still reeling and GE itself teetering on the brink, Welch was interviewed by the *Financial Times* about the future of capitalism. When asked about his long history of prioritizing investors above all else, he tried to distance himself from his singular contribution to the modern economic system. "On the face of it, shareholder value is the dumbest idea in the world," he declared, eschewing the very priorities he embodied. "Shareholder value is a result, not a strategy. . . . Your main constituencies are your employees, your customers and your products."

Coming from Welch, the assertion was laughable. He had been the first CEO to focus on shareholder value to the exclusion of all else, and he knew it. It was right there in his 1980 memo to Reg Jones as he vied for the top job. But just as he had reinvited himself in retirement, he was now rewriting his history as CEO, too.

Not long after Welch made his remark to the *FT*, he joined Larry Kudlow—the conservative business commentator—and expounded on his revelation that pleasing investors was, perhaps, not all that mattered. Kudlow, a first-rate cheerleader of free market dogma, seemed uncomfortable with Welch's questioning the status quo, and tried to steer the conversation back to safer ground. "But we've got to have profits," Kudlow said. "Profits are the mother's milk."

"Absolutely!" said Welch.

This wasn't the only way Welch was seeking to recast his legacy. He regularly took to LinkedIn, the social network for professionals, to publish essays disavowing his own managerial innovations. One of his posts was titled "'Rank-and-Yank'? That's Not How It's Done." In it, Welch described his beloved Vitality Curve as "a media-invented, politicized, sledgehammer of a pejorative that perpetuates a myth about a powerfully effective real practice called (more appropriately) differentiation." But he didn't deny doing it. As had been the case when *Newsweek* dubbed him Neutron Jack, he was complaining about the semantics, rather than the substance. In another post, "Six Deadly Sins of M&A," he offered up some commonsense chestnuts ("Don't pay too much"), while failing to acknowledge his own disastrous history of dealmaking. There was no mention of the way he took over RCA then sold it for parts, no mention of the den of thieves he had bought himself in Kidder Peabody. Welch was engaged in a grand campaign to buff out the blemishes in his career and perpetuate the myth that he was indeed the Manager of the Century.

Nothing, however, compared to his pronouncement that shareholder value was "the dumbest idea in the world." Many commentators remarked on the rich irony when Welch made his remark. But repeat a lie often enough and it becomes the truth, and with time Welch's quote has been accepted at face value, to the point that today it's common to find Welch cited as one of the leading critics of the very movement he pioneered. *Forbes* has run headlines such as "The Dumbest Idea in the World: Maximizing Shareholder Value," and Welch is sometimes given credit for "seeing the light" and becoming "one of the strongest critics of shareholder value."

"Go, go, go"

In 2011, Boeing CEO Jim McNerney received a call that shook him to
the core. On the line was Gerard Arpey, the chief executive of American Airlines, one of Boeing's best customers. For decades, American
had only bought Boeing planes. But that was about to end, Arpey told
McNerney. American was preparing to place a massive order with
Airbus for a fleet of new A320neos, the European rival to Boeing's
stalwart single-aisle 737.

McNerney was stunned, and he assembled his top brass to plot a
response. For years, Boeing had been considering designing a successor to the 737 from scratch. But the messy development and rollout
of the 787 Dreamliner had made such a project seem more daunt-
ing than ever. Now American Airlines had forced the issue. Would
Boeing take the time to design a new plane, likely losing out on the
American order? Or could it somehow extend the life of the 737 program once more? In a matter of days, Boeing had a decision: it would
redesign the 737—a plane that was first introduced in the 1960s—yet
again, a process that would be faster and much cheaper than designing a whole new plane. McNerney relayed the news to Arpey, and
promised that the new version of the 737 would be able to match
the A320neo's fuel efficiency. Arpey was persuaded, and American
decided to split the order between Boeing and Airbus.

Scrapping plans for an altogether new plane made sense in the
short term. Missing out on the American deal would have been an
embarrassment and likely would have sent Boeing's stock price down
sharply. But McNerney was effectively committing Boeing to another
several decades with the 737, setting in motion a chain of events that
would ultimately leave 346 people dead and the company on the ropes.

McNerney, who retired in 2015 after a decade in charge, didn't
stick around to witness the fallout from his decision. Boeing stock
had surged in the final years of his tenure, thanks largely to a massive buyback and dividend campaign he orchestrated. The return of
capital program boosted the company's share price and also sent the
value of McNerney's shares surging to some $250 million.

McNerney's replacement was Dennis Muilenburg, a Boeing lifer who had made his name in the company's defense business. Choosing an engineer, and someone from inside Boeing's own ranks, suggested that perhaps, after almost two decades, the GE culture was beginning to wane. But that would not be the case. Before McNerney left, he took steps to ensure that the Welch lineage would remain intact, bringing in several GE executives who had worked with Welch. Dave Calhoun, one of the dark-horse candidates in the race to succeed Welch, was added to the board. And the year after taking over, Muilenburg hired GE's head of airplane engines, Kevin McAllister, to oversee Boeing's commercial airlines business, which included the new 737 project, now known as the Max.

When the Max was introduced in 2011, it was an immediate hit. Boeing pitched the plane with the slogan, "Max Efficiency, Max Reliability," and airlines around the world placed orders for thousands of the new jets, quickly making it Boeing's best-selling plane in history. But the decision to revamp the 737 posed an immediate challenge to Boeing's engineers. In the 1960s, when the plane was first designed, jet engines were smaller, and the entire airframe was shorter. As a result, the body of the 737 sat low to the ground. But the new fuel-efficient engines needed to power the Max were much larger than their predecessors. And because there was no easy way to make the 737 sit higher off the ground, Boeing had to mount the engines further forward on the wings, so they wouldn't scrape the runway when the plane landed. This simple design change had a cascading series of consequences.

When engineers started testing a scale model of the Max in a wind tunnel, in 2012, they noticed that with the engines mounted further forward, the plane's nose tended to pitch upward in certain extreme turns. To compensate, Boeing engineers came up with a software fix known as the Maneuvering Characteristics Augmentation System, or MCAS. Now when the plane's sensors detected that the nose was pitching up, the software would automatically push the nose down. But Boeing committed a cardinal sin in the final design of MCAS: engineers made the system reliant on just one flimsy piece of metal protruding from the fuselage known as the angle of attack sensor, which measures the plane's pitch. In doing so, they gave the 737 Max a single point of failure, something that is verboten in aviation engineering, where redundancy is baked into every critical safety system.

Given that MCAS was a new feature on the Max, Boeing contemplated playing up the system and making it integral to pilots' understanding of the updated plane. At one point, engineers considered adding an MCAS alert to the primary flight display in the cockpit, which would inform pilots if the system engaged. And for a long while, a description of MCAS was included in the pilot's manual. But at Boeing's request, the FAA removed mention of MCAS from the pilot's manual, concealing the new system from pilots and its airline customers. The MCAS alert was never added to the cockpit. Another alert that could have helped pilots diagnose an MCAS malfunction was sold at extra cost. And the FAA never fully reviewed the final version of MCAS that was added to the Max.

There was a powerful motivator for this obfuscation. It was a companywide priority that the Max be as similar as possible to the previous generation of the plane, the 737NG. Part of the pitch Boeing made to airlines was that pilots who flew the NG would be able to handle the Max without extensive new training. In the event that there were substantial changes that pilots needed to know about, they would have had to go through simulator training in order to fly the Max, a time-consuming and expensive process. Boeing assured airlines that this wouldn't be the case. Instead, an hour-long iPad course would be sufficient (though the iPad course contained no mention of MCAS). The company put real money behind these promises. Boeing told Southwest Airlines that if pilots needed simulator training to fly the new plane, it would take $1 million off the price of each Max.

Inside Boeing, pressure to produce the Max quickly and cheaply was intense. The company was already playing catch-up with Airbus, and every extra month it took to bring the Max to market was another month of money lost. One engineer said that managers would tell subordinates that even a one-day delay was costing the company, reminding him that, "You don't want to be upsetting executives."

Engineers were driven hard and forced to submit technical draw-
ings twice as fast as they normally would. Budget constraints led the
Max program to hire employees away from other projects within the
company. "The timeline was extremely compressed," said one engineer, "It was go, go, go."

In documents released by Congress following an inquiry into the
company, the test pilots working on the Max were shown to have lost
faith in their colleagues, questioning the design of the plane and the
people who built it. "This airplane is designed by clowns, who are
in turn supervised by monkeys," read one message. "This is a joke,"
read another. "This airplane is ridiculous." Another wrote, "I honestly
don't trust many people at Boeing."

And on the factory floor in Renton, Washington, where hundreds of Max jets were being assembled, workers were under intense
pressure from their managers. Even as they flagged safety violations,
pleaded for more time, and requested protocols that would ensure
quality, executives demanded that they keep production up, and dis-
regarded their concerns. "Frankly right now all my internal warning
bells are going off," Ed Pierson, a senior manager in the Max factory,
wrote in an email to the head of the 737 program in June 2018. "And
for the first time in my life, I'm sorry to say that I'm hesitant about
putting my family on a Boeing airplane."

It was the same sort of pressure Welch had brought to bear inside GE's factories, but this time, lives were at stake. As late as mid-
2018, colleagues were lamenting the state of their company to one
another. "I don't know how to fix these things . . . it's systemic," one
employee emailed another about the Max. "Sometimes you have to
let big things fail so that everyone can identify a problem . . . maybe
that's what needs to happen rather than continuing to scrape by."

"Unbelievable jobs numbers"

The American economy rebounded from the financial crisis with
surprising speed. Massive bailouts from the Obama administration

saved the auto industry and the banks, and as a result, much of the rest of the economy, too. And while homeowners and workers were overlooked in the government's response, the stock market was humming again within a few years of the crisis, and even companies like GE and Boeing were prospering once more. By 2012, with President Obama running for a second term, hiring was picking up and the economy was doing well overall.

To Welch, who was at this point more than a decade into retirement, it seemed like it was going too well. He was a lifelong Republican and toed the party line on economic issues such as taxes (they should be low) and regulations (they should be minimal). He would set aside politics for the opportunity to rub elbows with the most powerful man in the world. (He and Bill Clinton were golf buddies.) And when Democrats embraced the free market agenda of low taxes and minimal regulation, as happened when Clinton championed the North American Free Trade Agreement (NAFTA), Welch was quick to lend his support. But for the most part, he was a shameless partisan.

When he came across a news report that George Stephanopoulos, then an adviser to President Clinton, was being considered for a job as a commentator on NBC, he drew a picture of a human hand with its middle finger raised on the story, then faxed it to the head of the network. "Stephanopoulos!" he snapped. "That liberal asshole!" And he had such a keen interest in seeing George W. Bush defeat Al Gore that he lorded over the NBC News Decision Desk on election night, reportedly pressuring executives to call the race for Bush, and prompting a congressional inquiry into the incident. In retirement, however, Welch veered from the merely partisan to the downright conspiratorial.

On October 5, 2012, the Bureau of Labor Statistics released the monthly jobs report numbers, a routine economic disclosure that rarely generates much interest beyond the business press. On this day, late in Obama's first term and just a month before election day, the news was good for the incumbent: the unemployment rate had dipped below 8 percent for the first time in four years. Welch couldn't believe it. "Unbelievable jobs numbers," he posted on Twitter. "These Chicago guys will do anything . . . can't debate so change numbers."

In effect, Welch was alleging that the Obama administration— the "Chicago guys"—were so desperate to win the election that they tampered with the jobs report for political gain. Welch had no basis for his accusation. It simply seemed unfathomable to him that the economy might actually be growing under a Democratic president. The irony was as rich as Welch himself. GE enjoyed its greatest run-up in value during the Clinton administration. And Welch, who had presided over a company where fiddling with the numbers was commonplace, was now accusing the Obama administration of doing the same with righteous indignity. Evidently the only way he could explain genuine success that didn't comport with his political views was to insinuate rampant corruption.

The backlash was swift. "You've lost your mind," retorted Austan Goolsbee, an economist who had served as chairman of the Council of Economic Advisers. The mainstream business press systematically dismantled Welch's claim. Venerable economists picked apart the Welch myth, correctly noting the enormity and implausibility of the conspiracy necessary to pull off a wholesale fabrication of the federal jobs report. Writers at *Fortune* magazine, where Welch was publishing his column at the time, were among those to debunk the claim.

Welch spent the next day doing damage control, appearing on CNN with Anderson Cooper and other shows to explain that, no, he didn't have any evidence, and offering up halfhearted apologies. But once Welch's lie was out there, it was impossible to contain. Right-wing pundits picked up on the conspiracy theory and amplified it. "In regards to today's jobs report, I agree with former GE CEO Jack Welch," tweeted Allen West, the Republican congressman. "Chicago style politics is at work here." Laura Ingraham, the Fox News host, called the numbers "total pro-Obama propaganda." Former House speaker Newt Gingrich said the Welch lie "rings true." Even Donald Trump, then merely a reality television star, joined the chorus of conspiracy theorists, calling Welch's bogus accusation "100 percent correct" and accusing the Obama administration of "monkeying around" with the numbers. "I don't believe the number and neither do any of the other people that have intelligence," Trump said on Fox News. "Because that number came out of nowhere." The lie went viral, with "jobs report truthers," as they became known, insisting that the Bureau of Labor Statistics figure was a fabrication designed to bolster President Obama's reelection hopes.

Welch himself seemed to realize that forging ahead with the lie was a better course than trying to walk it back. Annoyed that *Fortune*—the same publication that crowned him Manager of the Century—would turn on him, he said he would no longer write for the magazine, claiming he would get better "traction" elsewhere. He wasn't all wrong. Fabricating conspiracy theories, he realized, gave him far more influence than a column in a staid business magazine. So he doubled down on his bogus claim, asserting that he would do it all over again if he had the chance and continuing to expound on his little lie at paid talks around the country. "In order for the employment numbers to be where they were said to be, the economy would have to be operating at breakneck speed," Welch told an audience at the North Carolina CEO Forum, a week after his tweet. "Do you think the economy is operating at breakneck speed? All I'm trying to do is show this number is nonsense!"

As the lie festered, conservative media outlets tried to prop it up, with the *New York Post* publishing an article citing a "reliable source" who claimed that the Obama administration had, in fact, meddled with the numbers before the election. There was no substance to the erroneous claims. An investigation by the Census Bureau's Office of Inspector General "did not find any evidence to support allegations that supervisors in the Philadelphia Regional Office manipulated, or attempted to manipulate, the unemployment rate prior to the 2012 presidential election." But it didn't matter that Welch was wrong. In fact, the more zany stuff he tweeted, the more followers he gained. He called climate change "mass neurosis" and "the attack on capitalism that socialism couldn't bring." He suggested that Hillary Clinton was compromised as secretary of state because of the Clinton Foundation. Once again he was ahead of his time, recognizing that on Twitter, salaciousness translated to followers, and followers amounted to power.

Welch was at the vanguard of a disinformation revolution, but he was not alone. A year earlier, Trump had launched his Birther campaign, falsely alleging that Obama hadn't been born in the United States, and was thus an illegitimate president. Together, Welch and Trump had come to understand just how powerful lies could be in the age of social media. At the time, their antics were written off as buffoonery and bluster, the mad musings of washed-up tycoons. But their falsehoods found a willing audience, helping propel Trump to the Oval Office, and laying the ground-work for Pizzagate, QAnon, and the endless cascade of falsehoods that would soon come from President Trump himself.

Reflecting on the loony news cycles sparked by Birtherism and the jobs numbers conspiracy, the news anchor Chuck Todd fore-saw the insanity to come. "The idea that Donald Trump and Jack Welch—rich people with crazy conspiracies—can get traction on this," Todd said, "is a bad trend."

"The richest people made the most mistakes"

GE survived the financial crisis, but only barely. Had Buffett not come to the rescue, had Washington not backstopped its loans, GE Capital could have collapsed, taking the General Electric Company, and a significant swath of the broader economy, down with it. It was a near-death experience, brought on by an addiction to chas-ing ever higher earnings and an unwillingness to go through the painful process of withdrawal. In the aftermath of the crisis, Immelt himself conceded that the country had lost its way, becoming over-reliant on risky bets like the ones made by GE Capital. "While some of America's competitors were throttling up on manufacturing and R&D, we deemphasized technology," he told a crowd at West Point in late 2009. "Our economy tilted instead toward the quicker profits of financial services." "Rewards became perverted," he continued.

"The richest people made the most mistakes with the least account-ability."

If Immelt appreciated the irony, it didn't show. No company better embodied the country's turn away from manufacturing and toward financialization than GE. Who besides Welch and Immelt himself better exemplified the capacity to fail with impunity?

Things would only get worse. Now that GE Capital had its hands tied by regulators, there would be no last-minute magic at the end of each quarter. Some of the industrial businesses, such as wind tur-bines and health care, were growing. But that wasn't enough to offset declines in major areas like power turbines. So Immelt made what looked like a series of increasingly desperate moves in a last bid to revive GE.

He spent lavishly buying up oil and gas companies when energy prices were high, then watched as the value of those assets plummeted when energy prices came down. Then in 2015, GE paid $10.6 billion for Alstom, a French company that made power turbines. It was GE's largest ever deal, and was to be one of its worst, too. Profit margins at Alstom were thin to begin with, and antitrust regulators forced GE to sell off Alstom's most profitable business lines. What GE did get was tens of thousands of highly paid new employees, who—thanks to Eu-rope's labor laws—were virtually impossible to fire. That pricey new labor force might have been worth it had Alstom's fossil fuel turbines been in demand, but Immelt's timing proved faulty again. Just as the deal closed, renewable power became more cost competitive as the price of solar panels and wind turbines dropped, and GE was making expensive gas turbines at a moment few wanted them.

Unable to produce durable growth through the business itself, Immelt once again turned to buybacks and dividends in hopes of raising the stock price. In 2015, GE launched a $50 billion buyback program, one of the largest such commitments in history. To meet that massive new obligation, Immelt announced that the company would begin dismantling GE Capital once and for all. Piece by piece, the company started selling off its financial assets—the $7 billion sale of its vehicle management business here, the $12 billion sale of its leveraged lending business there. Proceeds would go directly to share-holders in an effort to prop up the stock. Meanwhile, the company's pension fund was withering, depriving its 600,000 former employees the payouts they had been counting on in retirement. By the end of 2016, the pension fund was facing a $31 billion shortfall.

More than a decade after Immelt took over, GE was a shell of the company Welch had made the most valuable in the world. GE Capital was being disassembled. The once profitable power business was failing. The dividend had been cut. Stalwart businesses like plastics and appliances had been sold off. And no matter what, the stock wouldn't rise.

With the news out of GE only getting worse, Nelson Peltz, one of the original corporate raiders, bought a minority stake in the stock and began agitating for change. Meanwhile, Bernie Sanders, the Vermont senator who was running for president, had Immelt in his sights as well. In an interview with the New York *Daily News*, the senator said greedy companies were "destroying the moral fabric of the country." When asked for an example, he cited GE. "General Electric was created in this country by American workers and American consumers," Sanders said. "What we have seen over the many years is shutting down of many major plants in this country. Sending jobs to low-wage countries. And General Electric, doing a very good job avoiding the taxes. In fact, in a given year, they pay nothing in taxes. That's greed. That is greed and that's selfishness. That is lack of respect for the people of this country."

Sanders kept going, leveling an indictment against Welchism itself. "If you are a corporation and the only damn thing you are concerned about is your profits—let's just give an example of a corporation that's making money in America, today, but desiring to move to China or to Mexico to make even more money—that is destroying the moral fabric of this country."

Immelt retorted with an op-ed in the *Washington Post*, arguing that GE was a force for good. "GE has been in business for 124 years, and we've never been a big hit with socialists," he said. "We create wealth and jobs, instead of just calling for them in speeches." But the spectacle of Immelt and Sanders quarreling in the media only served to further undermine the CEO's credibility.

It didn't help Immelt's case that even as GE was falling apart, he was growing enormously wealthy. He drew a titanic salary, routinely ending the year as one of the highest-paid CEOs in the country. In 2015, the year he struck the disastrous deal for Alstom, he made $33 million. And when Immelt traveled the world in GE's corporate jet, he routinely had an extra jet follow behind, just in case the one he was on broke down. When it was revealed, this "chase plane" became a metaphor for all that was wrong with GE—a company obsessed with appearances, run by a CEO who was out of touch, wasting resources on something that added no value. Immelt, said one prominent analyst, was "the imperial CEO," noting that "not even heads of state get that kind of treatment." If GE was squandering money on a second plane, he wondered, what else were they doing? "You really have to question the financial oversight and controls and internal audit," he said. "You have to question the entire organization."

By 2017, the board had had enough, and Immelt was pushed out. During his time as CEO, GE was the worst-performing stock in the Dow Jones Industrial Average. A half trillion dollars in shareholder value had been wiped out. Admittedly, Immelt was dealt a difficult hand to begin with. When he took over, GE's value was inflated by the magic of quarterly earnings miracles, while at the same time holding a host of industrial businesses that were starved for investment. Sixteen years later, many of the same problems still plagued the company. Revenues had grown as Immelt acquired new companies and diversified the overall mix of the businesses where GE operated, but he couldn't chart a new path forward. From failing to wind down GE Capital after 9/11, to betting big on oil and gas and power turbines at just the wrong moment, his tenure was marked by a succession of bad decisions. Along the way, he spent $93 billion on buybacks. The Manager of the Century's handpicked successor had turned out to be a dud.

When news of Immelt's ouster was announced, Welch released a chilly statement. "Jeff brought his best every day for 16 years," he said.

"I wish him the very best in the many good years ahead." Immelt was similarly terse in reflecting on the man who tapped him for the most coveted job in corporate America. "Jack was a very good CEO, and I appreciate everything he did for me," Immelt said at the time.

The two centimillionaires were doing everything they could to avoid blaming each other for the mess GE had become, but their mutual animosity was unmistakable. "There is very bad blood between these two former GE CEOs," said Jeffrey Sonnenfeld, dean of leadership studies at the Yale School of Management. "Welch has regrets about Immelt given choices Immelt made, and Immelt has been disappointed about some elements of the Welch legacy."

Immelt's successor was John Flannery, a GE lifer who had spent much of his career executing deals for Welch and Immelt in GE Capital. Flannery had been a core member of GE's mergers and acquisitions team, mastering the art of Welchian dealmaking, and ultimately looking after Asian markets for the company. Given Flannery's pedigree, he approached his responsibilities not with a holistic view of how he might revive a once great industrial giant, but with the grim industriousness of a bean counter. After decades spent swapping assets and fiddling with financial instruments, the only thing he could do, once he had control of GE, was treat it like a restructuring job. The focus, he said, would be on three core businesses—power, aviation, and health care. Everything else, in an echo of Welch's "fix it, close it, or sell it" mantra, would be jettisoned. He sold the transportation division, which still made locomotives; the lighting division, which represented the company's roots; and the oil and gas business, on which Immelt had spent so much to gain so little. While many investors felt these actions were long overdue, Flannery failed to restore faith in the company, and the stock kept falling.

A few months after he took over, Flannery also got a couple of nasty surprises. Though GE was supposedly out of the insurance business—something Immelt had trumpeted when he was CEO—that wasn't actually true. GE still held substantial long-term-care policies, the sort of arrangements that cover nursing homes, and was ultimately responsible for approximately $15 billion in coverage. After spending so much on buybacks, GE didn't have easy access to that kind of cash. The SEC opened an investigation into the shortfall, and GE ultimately paid a $200 million fine. The next month, the Justice Department said it was investigating WMC, the toxic subprime mortgage business GE had never managed to fully unload, leading the company to say it might put the unit into bankruptcy. Long after Welch had left the building, GE was still paying for his sins.

On June 19, 2018, with all of Welch's bad decisions catching up with the company, GE was removed from the Dow Jones Industrial Average, the bluest of blue-chip indexes and a bellwether for the American economy. Over the years many great companies joined the Dow and were subsequently dropped when their fortunes faded. Bethlehem Steel, Sears, and Kodak all enjoyed turns in the Dow. Yet for the entirety of the twentieth century, through the Great Depression, two world wars, the dot-com bubble, and other upheavals, GE remained. It was a stubborn reminder of America's proud industrial past and the great wealth that was created and shared during the Golden Age of Capitalism.

In the end, however, Welchism caught up with the company. Decades of underinvestment had left GE with no breakthrough new products. Impulsive dealmaking had saddled the company with money losing divisions. And GE Capital had long ago stopped coming to the rescue with last-minute earnings. S&P Dow Jones Indices, which owns the Dow, said that dropping GE would "make the index a better measure of the economy and the stock market." That was hard to argue with. Over the previous year, GE shares had fallen 55 percent, while the Dow itself had gained nearly 50 percent, despite GE weighing it down. The company that would replace GE was Walgreens Boots Alliance, the drugstore chain. It was a selection rich with symbolism. After all, America was no longer a country that made appliances and jet engines, so much as it was one that consumed prescription drugs and processed foods. And still, to see General Electric laid so low was a jarring reminder of the company's proud past, and its sorry state in the present. As one senior money manager succinctly put it, "GE no longer qualifies as one of the most important companies in our country."

Seventeen years after Welch retired, GE was still reckoning with

Neutron Jack's legacy. The infatuation with finance, the addiction to buybacks—it all had led to this moment, and there was only so much the new CEO could do. Even as the broader markets went on a bull run during the first years of Trump's presidency, GE stock continued to slide with Flannery in charge.

A few months after GE was removed from the Dow, Flannery was fired. As GE's board of directors contemplated who would become the company's third CEO in as many years, it seemed to finally grasp that another disciple of Welch, the man who bore singular responsibility for the company's problems, was probably not the best choice. And for the first time in its 126-year history, the GE board turned to an outsider. Larry Culp, who had run a small industrial conglomerate called Danaher and briefly served on the GE board, was named the next CEO. With his hiring, the Welch lineage finally had been broken.

SEVEN

Negative Externalities

"We're not treated as human beings"

Arthur Cecil Pigou, contemplating the trajectory of modern capitalism a century ago, foresaw what was to come. Pigou, an English economist who worked as a professor at the University of Cambridge, was concerned not just with how goods and services changed hands, but also with what effect all that economic activity had on society at large. In 1920, he published his seminal work, *The Economics of Welfare*, putting his finger on a core truth about capitalism that was as resonant then as it is today: individuals running corporations are incentivized to maximize their own self-interest, not take care of the rest of the world. *The Economics of Welfare* also expanded on the concept of "externalities" in business, a term for the side effects of commercial activity. Where previous economists had mostly considered the positive externalities of a growing economy—the cost of goods going down as supply increased, for example—Pigou turned his attention to *negative* externalities: all the harm that companies might cause in their pursuit of profits. If industrialists couldn't be trusted to look out for the common good, Pigou understood, it was only a matter of time before the consequences of their actions began to spill over into the wider world. In his book, Pigou identified a handful of obvious negative externalities that were already clear to see, among them pollution in London. (He concluded that chimney smoke was obscuring a great deal of sunlight.) And he proposed some obvious solutions, including regulation and taxation, that might create disincentives for companies to run roughshod over their communities.

Yet on his leafy Cambridge campus a hundred years ago, Pigou could not have imagined the great variety, scale, and impact of the harms that would be arising from the business world today. From runaway climate change to steep inequality, to hollowed-out communities abandoned by companies seeking cheap labor elsewhere, it can at times seem like corporations do as much harm as they do good. These are the negative externalities we now live with, and while Pigou may not have been able to articulate the specifics a century ago, he knew what was coming.

Under Welch, the negative externalities emanating from GE started piling up. No longer could GE's impact on the world be measured simply by all the good things it brought to life. Instead, it became necessary to also account for the hundreds of thousands of people GE laid off, the PCBs it dumped into the Hudson River, and the many ways it bilked the U.S. government. And today, even after Welch and most of his protégés have retired or died, Welchism's three main features—downsizing, dealmaking, and financialization—are all endemic in the modern economy, producing an endless font of negative externalities all their own.

Take downsizing. Two generations after Welch began his campaign against loyalty, CEOs have not let up their attack on workers. Hardly a week goes by without a major American employer announcing a round of layoffs as part of a new "restructuring plan" designed to "improve profitability." American Express was flush with cash in 2015, but ordered a round of layoffs in a bid to quickly boost its profit margins and stock price. It didn't work—AmEx stock slid some more and stayed down for the following two years. Sprint was minting money in 2016 but slashed thousands of call center jobs to reduce expenses, a move that simultaneously wreaked havoc on workers and led to inferior customer service. Offshoring continues, too. Carrier, the air-conditioning company, sent jobs to Mexico in 2017 even after President Trump intervened. And Nabisco, AT&T, and Brooks Brothers all shifted jobs overseas in recent years.

Executives' faith in the easy math of mass layoffs—that fewer employees will mean higher profits, that labor is a cost, not an asset—persists in spite of a growing body of research debunking that dogma. "The research evidence has not found any support for the overall idea that layoffs help firm performance," said Peter Cappelli, a professor at the University of Pennsylvania's Wharton School of Business. "There is no evidence that cutting to improve profitability helps beyond the immediate, short-term accounting bump." One study showed that when retailers cut staff, any short-term cost savings were overshadowed by long-term losses. It turns out that when stores are staffed by a skeleton crew, sales dry up quickly. And still, Cappelli writes, layoffs are common thanks to "an emphasis on minimizing payroll expenses and an emphasis on meeting short-term (often monthly) performance targets."

In recent years, companies have found still new ways to marginalize their employees that go well beyond routine downsizing. No longer is the campaign against loyalty simply about mass layoffs and stack ranking. Today, companies are engaged in a broader effort to redefine what it means to have a job at all. What began with Welch's forays into outsourcing—shifting workers off GE's payroll and on to service providers—has been taken to a new extreme, with companies now turning to contractors, freelancers, and the gig economy for as much labor as possible. For companies, the incentives are unchanged: lower labor costs mean higher profits, they insist. What is new is that a whole infrastructure has been created to support this liminal state of employment, normalizing economic insecurity. Even at some of the country's largest employers, there is a concerted effort to keep workers as close to temps as they can possibly be, with the aspiration of making people as interchangeable as the parts of a machine.

The new downsizing takes many forms, depending on the industry. The rise of the gig economy has allowed new multibillion-dollar companies to be built on the backs of a shadow workforce. There are millions of drivers for Uber and Lyft, hundreds of thousands of deliverymen for Instacart and Seamless, and many thousands more offering themselves up for part-time work on sites like TaskRabbit and Upwork. Some of these workers treat the jobs as side hustles, occasional gigs that provide a bit of pocket cash. But for many, gig work is a full-time occupation, only without the security of a steady paycheck, decent benefits, or an employer to hold accountable. The gig economy, which began as a way to connect people who needed an odd job done here and there with locals looking to make a little extra cash, has given rise to an entirely new kind of labor force. Corporations worth tens of billions of dollars, such as Uber, classify their primary workers—drivers—not as employees but as contractors, and they treat them accordingly. Gig economy companies have taken Welch's fantasy—to "have every plant you own on a barge"—to an extreme he likely would have relished. Now they can operate while having practically no employees at all.

Nor is it just gig economy employers playing havoc with the lives of their workers. At fast food restaurants, employees have their schedules jerked around by chains that are looking to minimize inefficiencies and make the most of lean workforces. Workers at Taco Bell sometimes have mere hours of free time between seven-hour shifts, leaving little time to care for their families or themselves. Companies like Starbucks have put workers on call for shifts that could be canceled at the last minute. Hourly employees have been scheduled to work the late shift, then open the same restaurant the next morning on just a few hours of sleep, a practice known as "clopening." New York municipal authorities sued Chipotle for erratically changing workers' schedules without notice, even after a law was put in place to ban the practice. Research shows that erratic schedules had deeply deleterious effects on workers and their families, extending all the way to the development and emotional health of the employees' children. All the while, many companies took to having hourly workers sign noncompete agreements, depressing wages across the industry.

In offices, too, Welchist ideals persist. The Vitality Curve is still in use at companies large and small. In the years after Welch popularized stack ranking at GE, the practice became widespread not just at companies like Ford and 3M, where it led to lawsuits, but also in the tech industry. The practice flourished at Microsoft for years under Steve Ballmer, Immelt's former cubicle-mate. Unsurprisingly, it led to mass disaffection and an erosion of cooperation, as colleagues were pitted against each other. "This caused people to resist helping one another," said one Microsoft employee. "It wasn't just that helping a colleague took time away from someone's own work. The forced curve meant that 'Helping your fellow worker become more productive can actually hurt your chances of getting a higher bonus.'" Microsoft phased out the practice after it led to broad disillusionment within the ranks, but newer companies have not learned the lessons of history. At WeWork—the shared office space company—cofounder Adam Neumann set a goal of laying off 20 percent of the company's workforce every year. "We met those expectations, and I'm not proud of it," said one member of WeWork's human resources staff.

And at Amazon—one of the world's largest corporations—worker well-being seems to be but an afterthought. Amazon manages more than a million employees across its vast fulfillment centers, fleets of delivery trucks, and office parks, eclipsed only by Walmart, which employs two million people. The e-commerce giant is among the most prolific recruiters and employers in the country. Yet even while employing such a significant swath of the populous, Amazon's overriding concern is not the resilience and economic security of the many souls that don safety vests emblazoned with its ubiquitous curved arrow logo. Instead, after many years running a loss as it built market share, the company is now focused on churning out ever-larger quarterly profits for investors.

Like Welch before him, Amazon founder Jeff Bezos seemed to arrive on the job with a zealot's conviction that workers were fun-

damentally expendable. According to an executive who helped design Amazon's warehouse systems, Bezos articulated early on that he
wanted to avoid having an entrenched, loyal workforce. If employees grew too comfortable, Bezos believed, it would be an inevitable
"march to mediocrity." Without the threat of dismissal, his employees
wouldn't work their hardest, Bezos reasoned, explaining that "our nature as humans is to expend as little energy as possible to get what we
want or need," the executive said.

To ensure that Amazon workers not become too complacent,
Bezos devised a strategy he believed would keep them on their toes:
he would make their employment status as tenuous as possible. Indeed, Amazon's human resources strategies are designed to ensure
that the vast majority of employees have only the thinnest connection
with the company, a transactional relationship that might be severed
at any moment. Whereas Welch had to rely on stack ranking to en-
force his mandate, Bezos uses technology, and has turned Amazon's
warehouses into laboratories where workers are subjected to ever
more dystopian forms of management, where people are treated like
machines, workplace injuries are common, and any vestige of senti-
mentality is snuffed out. "We're not treated as human beings, we're
not even treated as robots," said one worker. "We're treated as part of
the data stream."

That's more than just a metaphor. At Amazon, employees are increasingly managed not by other people, but by software. The financial advantages of having computers look after humans are reflected
in Amazon's profits, which continue to swell, billions upon billions
every quarter. For the workers themselves, however, having an al-
gorithm for a boss can be problematic. When an employee has an
actual question, there is sometimes no one there to answer it. Workers who just clocked fifty-five-hour weeks can suddenly be assigned
mandatory overtime, with no one to appeal to. Sometimes, the algo-
rithm accidentally fires workers, who, despite begging to remain employed with the company, are out of a job. Cameras and computers
are watching Amazon employees every minute of the day. Workers
on the warehouse floor are tracked constantly, with sensors recording

how fast they pack boxes and how long they linger, perhaps catching their breath. Time spent using the bathroom can result in lower performance reviews. Any lag in productivity is assumed to be the fault of a lazy worker. Drivers have resorted to peeing in bottles, and factory workers who walk too slowly have been disciplined. Some workers have taken to reminding management that they are not, in fact, merely part of the data stream. "It is very important that area managers understand that associates are more than just numbers," an employee wrote on the internal feedback board of Amazon's Staten Island warehouse. "We are human beings. We are not tools used to make their daily/weekly goals and rates."

Treating humans like cogs in a machine—expendable parts that can be replaced at will—has had predictable effects on Amazon's attrition. The company loses about 3 percent of its hourly workforce every week, translating into a turnover rate of some 150 percent a year. Yet that astronomically high churn is a feature, not a bug. The company seems to be designed to chew workers up and spit them out. To disincentivize workers from growing too comfortable at Amazon, Bezos eliminated mandatory raises after three years and looked for ways to push insufficiently motivated employees out the door. Amazon is so committed to the idea of a permanent temporary workforce that it offers hourly workers cash bonuses to quit. It is exactly the kind of transactional relationship Bezos wants to have with his employees, the very opposite of the social contract that bound employers and workers during the Golden Age of Capitalism. And it leaves workers adrift, impoverished, and physically broken.

Despite these inhumane labor practices, there is no sign that Amazon might run out of workers anytime soon. Given the evaporation of manufacturing jobs—and the decimation of local retail thanks to Amazon itself—the company has an easy time recruiting. In so many zip codes where factories once flourished, warehouse jobs are just about the only options for employment, and local politicians try to outdo one another with bigger tax breaks in hopes of landing the next Amazon fulfillment center.

But it is not only the Amazon workers in warehouses and on the road who suffer from Bezos's apparent campaign against loyalty. As was the case at GE, even those in management must endure a state of perpetual anxiety. While Amazon executives are well paid, generous compensation is no guarantee of lifetime employment. Like GE under Welch, Amazon employs a system of ranking its employees. And while the company has denied that it used stack ranking, the contours of the program are much the same as Welch's Vitality Curve. Amazon expects managers to rank 20 percent of their employees as "top tier," 75 percent as different gradations of "highly valued," and 5 percent as "least effective." Those ranked well are eligible for perks and promotions, while those at the bottom of the rankings are put into performance improvement programs, and often shown the door.

Bezos could even be considered the Jack Welch of his day, wielding unmatched financial, political, and cultural power. Where Welch controlled NBC, Bezos personally owns the *Washington Post* and has control of Amazon Prime's TV and film offerings. When Bezos left his longtime wife, MacKenzie Scott, for Lauren Sanchez, a helicopter pilot with supermodel looks, the tabloids ate it up. Not since Welch left Jane for Suzy had there been such a sensational CEO divorce.

Welch seemed to sense the kinship, coming to Bezos's defense after the *New York Times* published an investigation into Amazon's harsh working conditions in 2015. The *Times* story described executives under such intense pressure that they regularly cried at their desks and blue-collar workers under constant electronic surveillance. It was a damning portrait of one of the country's most powerful companies, and Bezos responded with a letter to Amazon employees defending the culture. "The people we hire here are the best of the best," Bezos wrote. "You are recruited every day by other world-class companies, and you can work anywhere you want."

Bromides from a billionaire were cold comfort to Amazon employees, but Bezos found at least one sympathetic ear. "Love Jeff Bezos' response to ridiculous NYTimes article on Amazon," Welch wrote on Twitter, throwing in a couple chest-thumping hashtags for good measure. "#leadership #winning."

"We've sort of put it all together"

Dealmaking and financialization are also now firmly established features of the modern economy. And when it comes to big corporations' insatiable appetite for mergers and acquisitions, no company better represents the frequently misguided lust for inorganic growth than AT&T.

By 2015, a wave of megadeals reshaped the media business. Comcast had taken full control of NBC Universal, buying it from GE some thirty years after Welch had acquired NBC as part of the RCA deal. Netflix was ascendant. Disney was expanding its content library and readying a streaming service. After decades when content and delivery were seen as distinctly different businesses, media companies suddenly wanted to control both at the same time. So that year, AT&T—which was still, for the most part, a phone company—acquired DirecTV, the satellite television provider, for $67 billion. Shortly after that, AT&T spent another $85 billion to buy Time Warner, a prized collection of television and movie assets that included HBO, CNN, and Warner Bros.

They looked like good deals at first, bringing a huge amount of content and distribution together under one roof. These acquisitions made AT&T a behemoth on the stock market, creating what was briefly one of the most valuable companies in the country. Then Randall Stephenson, AT&T's empire-building chief executive, went into full Neutron Jack mode. He slashed 20,000 workers a year while drawing a $30 million salary, ramped up the company's buybacks and dividends, and was rewarded with a payday approaching $100 million upon retirement in 2020.

Not long after Stephenson stepped down, the true costs of his strategy became clear. AT&T was struggling under a mountain of debt. Workers were dissatisfied, and DirecTV was losing subscribers. When a new CEO took over, another spasm of dealmaking ensued. This time, the company would be offloading the assets that it had acquired just a year before. The company agreed to sell DirecTV to private equity for a massive loss. And in 2021, AT&T agreed to combine its entertainment properties, including the recently acquired Time Warner, with Discovery Communications, which for years had been a second-tier cable provider. The man who orchestrated the deal and would oversee what would instantly become one of the biggest media companies on earth was David Zaslav, who had come up inside NBC under Welch. Billions of dollars would trade hands. Bankers and lawyers would earn tremendous fees. Zaslav was in line to earn at least $100 million; likely much more than that. And as companies are reshuffled in the years ahead, as divisions are combined and synergies are pursued, as profits are used to pay down debts, it is almost inevitable that tens of thousands of workers will lose their jobs.

The Discovery deal with AT&T was more than a power move by a Welch protégé. It represented the apotheosis of corporate America's infatuation with dealmaking. Ever since Welch acquired RCA, mergers and acquisitions have been booming. In 1985, there were just 2,300 deals in the United States, worth $300 billion. By the time Welch retired, those figures had both roughly tripled—nearly 10,000 deals in 2001, worth $1 trillion. And the numbers just kept growing. In 2019 there were more than 18,000 such deals worth nearly $2 trillion, a wholesale reordering of the economy driven by private equity firms and public companies alike.

As a consequence, today there are only about half as many public companies in the United States as there were in Welch's heyday. That is partly the result of new rules that have made it more onerous to be a public company. Young companies are also waiting longer to go public these days thanks to large pools of venture capital that make it more feasible to postpone a public listing. But the evaporation of some 4,000 public companies over the past thirty years is largely the result of the decades-long mergers boom that has made a few companies bigger, and many industries more concentrated. Whether it be cable television, cell phone service, airlines, sunglasses, supermarkets, or health insurance, consumers have fewer choices than they did a generation ago. In industry after industry, a few big companies have gobbled up market share, creating industries where dominant players compete with only a few meaningful rivals. Today, three quarters of

American industries are significantly more concentrated than they were twenty-five years ago.

The rise of market concentration across the economy has real effects on ordinary people. By some measures, corporate consolidation has depressed average American salaries by some $10,000 a year. Companies in highly concentrated industries also spend less on capital expenditures, which tend to create jobs, than they did before the deals boom—down to just 3 percent of revenues, from 9 percent a year in 1990. During this time, profit margins at the biggest companies have climbed from 7 percent to 18 percent. And overall, a more concentrated economy is less dynamic. There are fewer new businesses getting started these days than there were in the second half of the twentieth century. With fewer companies hiring, workers switch jobs less frequently. Small business makes up less and less of the country's gross domestic product. And when just a few big companies dominate an industry and face only nominal competition, prices are more likely to rise, a dynamic known as "monopoly rents." The dealmaking boom that Welch kicked off never really subsided, and we all keep paying the price.

While AT&T has thrived on the kind of torrid mergermania that fueled so much of GE's growth, other companies have managed to incorporate elements of Welch's downsizing, dealmaking, and financialization all under one corporate umbrella. Consider the case of 3G Capital, a private equity group that controls brands including Budweiser, Burger King, and Kraft Heinz. Founded by a group of Brazilian financiers, the men behind 3G Capital are the Neutron Jacks of the twenty-first century, relentlessly acquiring companies, slashing costs and head counts, and extracting profits for themselves and investors while seeming to ignore the well-being of their workforce and the need for research and development.

The leader of the group, Jorge Paulo Lemann, was a tennis star before going into business, representing Brazil in the Davis Cup and competing at Wimbledon. He was just as competitive in the office as on the court, and quickly parlayed his entry-level experience in banking into a remarkable run of acquisitions—taking over a broker dealer, a retailer, and a brewery in less than twenty years with the help of his two partners. The brewery proved the most decisive move. With it in hand, the trio went on an international shopping spree, forming Ambev, Brazil's largest beer company, in 1999. Five years later, they bought Interbrew, the Belgian brewer, and three years after that, the company bought Anheuser-Busch, maker of Budweiser and Bud Light, to create the world's largest brewer. Along the way, the Brazilians developed a reputation as savage cost cutters and merciless downsizers. Upon taking over new companies, they would routinely reduce head count by thousands. Immediately after acquiring Anheuser-Busch, the company fired 1,400 workers in St. Louis. AB InBev became notorious for unsentimentally switching suppliers to reduce costs, raising prices on consumers whenever it could, and brewing beers in whatever market was cheapest—so, for example, a "Belgian" beer might be produced in St. Louis. Then in 2016, AB InBev completed the takeover of SABMiller, further enlarging what was already the world's biggest brewer. The result was a huge company, but not a particularly nimble one. In the wake of that deal, shares of the company were depressed, AB InBev had more than $100 billion in debt, and innovation had stalled.

There is no mistaking the provenance of the 3G management techniques, and Lemann didn't try to hide it. When asked in 2014 to explain his influences, he got straight to the point: "We'd read everything about Jack Welch," Lemann said. "GE's annual reports were our Bible." There were other influences as well—Goldman Sachs ranks highly—but to the Brazilians, Welch always came first. And while there is no shortage of Welch imitators in the corporate world today, the men behind 3G Capital stand out not only for the degree to which they replicated the GE playbook, but by their willingness to say so. "We're a copycat, really," Lemann said. "That's what we are. Most of the stuff we've learned has been from Jack Welch, Jim Collins [the author of *Good to Great*], from GE, from Walmart. We've sort of put it all together."

For a time, the business press lapped it up. Lemann and the other 3G executives were celebrated in glowing profiles. Investors swooned

over the group's relentless acquisitions and shrewd financial management. And all the while, 3G found ways to give Welch's tactics new
life. Going beyond the rampant dealmaking, the Brazilians adopted
other management practices pioneered by Welch. They employed
stack ranking, replicating the 20/70/10 split that Welch dictated. "Yes,
there will be people at the bottom," said Carlos Brito, one of Lemann's
top executives. "And that's the idea; that the people at the bottom feel
bad, and they want to go to the top."

The Brazilians also put their own spin on the effort to cut costs,
embracing a system known as zero-based budgeting, or ZBB. Rather
than a traditional budget, which is based on the previous year's expenditures, zero-based budgeting requires managers to start from
scratch every year. Each expenditure must be justified, nothing is a
given. While the system is effective at lowering costs across an organization, it can also lead to unending disruption. Business units
and whole departments can be slashed overnight if, during a budget
review, they are deemed insufficiently beneficial to the bottom line.

Having conquered the beer world, Lemann and his partners set
their sights on food. They formed 3G Capital, a private equity firm,
and in 2010 they struck a deal to buy Burger King from its owners, a
consortium of private equity firms. Two months after the deal closed,
more than 400 people were laid off at Burger King's headquarters in
Miami. Those who remained led a spartan office life. Just one personal item was allowed at each desk, and employees were expected to
work Saturdays. More Welchian maneuvers followed. The company
slashed the R&D department, ramped up outsourcing, and took a
hard line with suppliers, demanding discounts of up to 20 percent.
Four years later, 3G acquired the Canadian donut chain Tim Hortons
and combined it with Burger King, forming a new company, Restaurant Brands International. Just as had been the case at Burger King,
Tim Hortons employees were jettisoned, costs were slashed, and vendors were squeezed.

In 2013, 3G made its biggest move to date, agreeing to buy Heinz,
the iconic ketchup maker. This time, Lemann and his associates were
joined by another investor: Warren Buffett. Though Buffett enjoys a

folksy reputation as an everyman with heartland values and modest tastes, he is just as shrewd as Welch was. Buffett's portfolio includes mobile home parks that charge poor tenants exorbitant interest rates and stakes in fast food companies like Coca-Cola and McDonald's that peddle unhealthy food and beverages. He also runs his companies lean, demanding the same relentless focus on profits that Welch expected at GE. In the Brazilians from 3G, Buffet saw kindred spirits, lauding their "competence and integrity." "3G is a perfect partner," he said. And Heinz, they thought, was a perfect target.

Founded in 1869, H. J. Heinz helped pioneer the processed food business in the United States, becoming a pillar of the Pittsburgh business community. In an echo of some of GE's early moves, Heinz took good care of his employees and gave them benefits that went well beyond a paycheck, becoming a model employer during the Golden Age of Capitalism. There was a library, a swimming pool, and showers for employees, and the company was a generous local philanthropist. While much of that was the stuff of history by the time 3G and Buffett came along, the company still had its headquarters, as well as significant manufacturing, in the Pittsburgh area.

3G promised to maintain a presence in the city, but little more. After the new 3G-appointed CEO gave his first speech to the company's top fifty executives, he brought them into a room and one by one told them whether they still had a job—eleven of the top twelve were sent home. Overall, more than a quarter of the employees in Pittsburgh were laid off. Real estate was consolidated, employees were crammed into shared workspaces, and working long hours, including weekends, became the norm. The penny-pinching went all the way down to the office printer. Employees were not permitted to print more than 200 pages per month. Minifridges were banned. But as 3G tried to wring costs from Heinz, it discovered that there were only so many new efficiencies it could find. Heinz was already running lean, and cutting back on printer paper was only going to take 3G so far. Lemann, however, was doing quite well. With well-timed stock sales and his ongoing ownership stakes in many of the companies he cobbled together, he was worth $26 billion in 2021, making him one of the seventy richest people in the world.

3G's companies tended to get larger not through organic growth but through acquisitions, and before long the financiers were looking for a takeover target they could merge with Heinz. In 2015 they found one, and 3G and Buffett agreed to acquire Kraft, the maker of boxed macaroni and cheese and Oscar Mayer hot dogs. The combined company, Kraft Heinz, instantly became one of the biggest food companies in the world. The familiar cost cutting commenced. This time, workers were told to make sure their printing was double-sided, and the company stopped distributing free Jell-O. Within a month of the deal closing, the workforce was slashed by 2,500, or 5 percent. Two years later, 20 percent of employees were gone. But again, a lack of new products quickly resulted in anemic sales growth.

Critics of Kraft Heinz said it was a house of cards, that unless the company found yet another acquisition, the business would go into a tailspin. Before long, the doubters were proven right. Sales were slumping. The company wasn't innovating. And in 2019, Kraft Heinz announced a $15.4 billion write-down of its iconic Kraft and Oscar Mayer brands. It was arguably an admission of mismanagement. And there were still more problems to come. Kraft Heinz was running short of cash, and said it would slash its dividend. Next, an investor sued the company, alleging that 3G executives engaged in insider trading before the avalanche of bad news. (The suit was ultimately dismissed, but fed the perception that executives were bending the rules at 3G.) Not long after that came another write-down, this time for $1.2 billion. Then in 2021, federal regulators announced a settlement with the company over what it claimed were years of financial misrepresentations. From 2015 to 2019, the SEC alleged that Kraft Heinz had been using Welch's full arsenal of shady accounting practices to smooth out its results—recognizing unearned discounts from suppliers, maintaining false and misleading supplier contracts, and inventing cost savings where there were none. The company, which agreed to pay $62 million in fines, had been deliberately reporting false earnings, then boasting about the purported gains to the analyst community, according to the SEC. The company's Brazilian chief operating officer, who had personally signed off on the schemes, agreed to pay a civil penalty of $300,000 without admitting or denying guilt.

Two decades into the twenty-first century, the signature tactics of Welchism—downsizing, dealmaking, and financialization—were still being employed at one of the biggest companies in the world.

And 3G is hardly alone. The earnings management Welch pioneered at GE Capital remains a favorite tactic with companies intent on delivering their own version of "consistent, above-average earnings growth." Under Armour, the Baltimore-based athletic apparel company, posted sales growth of 20 percent or more for a stunning twenty-six straight quarters until 2016. But the numbers were a mirage. The company had been reporting future sales early, pressuring retailers to accept orders before the products were ready, and shuffling inventory from one location to another in order to make it look like items were flying off the shelves. "It was all in the name of hitting the number, and it would happen out in the open," said one merchandising executive from the company. "They didn't think there was anything improper about it."

This was hardly the result of a few bad apples. Kevin Plank, Under Armour's founder and CEO, was aware of the moves. Ultimately, Under Armour got off with a slap on the wrist. The company settled with the SEC for $9 million without admitting or denying wrongdoing, and no executives were held accountable. Thanks in part to such weak enforcement, the practice of earnings management remains widespread today. A study by McKinsey found that 61 percent of companies that profess to have a "long-term" orientation would, faced with the prospect of a quarterly earnings miss, take measures to make the financial results better than they actually were, even if it meant breaking the law.

Amazon, 3G, AT&T, and Under Armour are hardly the exceptions. Welch's fingerprints can be found all over today's economy. At company after company, the Jack Welch way of doing business—and sometimes Welch's own tutelage—has left a trail of destruction. The negative externalities are endless, and can be seen in the companies themselves, in the employees who suffer, and in data that confirms that the riches of this land are not evenly distributed, not even remotely so.

Corporations, which once generously shared profits with their workers across the country, now funnel the lion's share of the wealth they create to institutional investors and executives. Whereas in the 1980s less than half of corporate profits were going back to investors, over the past decade, that figure has soared to 93 percent.

The wealth is being clustered geographically, too, with superstar companies concentrated in urban centers, rather than the Rust Belt cities and rural areas that had thrived during the Golden Age. Places like Erie and Schenectady—where GE once employed thousands— are languishing, while Denver and Boston boom. Coders, management consultants, and tax attorneys all do well, while workers without advanced degrees, and those toiling in e-commerce warehouses and big box stores, are worse off. That's not only because only a tiny sliver of workers receive stock as part of their compensation. It's also because wages have been falling for decades now.

Had the federal minimum wage simply kept up with inflation since 1968, it would be more than $24 an hour. Instead, the minimum wage remains just $7.25, an hourly rate that will not keep someone above the poverty line in most of America. A 2019 study found that some 44 percent of working Americans are employed in low-wage jobs that provide median annual incomes of just $18,000 a year. The poorest 50 percent of Americans essentially own nothing. These aren't teens at the ice cream shop making a little money before college. Most are in their prime working years, between the ages of twenty-five and fifty-four, and are earning an average of just $10.22 an hour. "Nearly half of all workers earn wages that are not enough, on their own, to promote economic security," the authors of the study wrote. The economic hardship facing so many Americans is having measurable impacts not just on the quality of life, but on how long people live. In the United States, life expectancy has fallen in recent years, reversing a century's worth of progress. Americans—mostly the working class—are dying earlier from suicide, drug overdoses, alcoholism, and poor health, what economists Anne Case and Angus Deaton refer to as "deaths of despair."

Meanwhile, senior management has reaped rich rewards. For about three decades after World War II, the pay ratio between CEOs and employees remained consistent. As executives made more money, so did everyday workers. Then, right around the time Welch took over GE, those trend lines began to diverge. Worker pay flatlined, and in some years even fell when adjusted for inflation. Executive compensation, on the other hand, skyrocketed. Whereas a CEO during the Golden Age of Capitalism might have made ten or fifteen times as much as an average worker at his company, today that figure stretches into the hundreds or even thousands.

The chief executive of a major American company now makes in one year what it would take a typical worker in that company 320 years to earn. The median annual pay among top CEOs is $12.7 million, and that's the middle of the pack. At the top companies, CEOs make in a year what it would take a millennium for their employees to earn, enjoying annual incomes in excess of $100 million. At Walmart, an employee earning the median salary of $19,177 in 2017 would have had to work for more than a thousand years to make the $22.2 million that Doug McMillon, the Walmart CEO, was awarded that same year. And when the cash isn't being lavished on executives, it is being sent out the door in the form of dividends and buybacks. Today, the richest 1 percent of Americans possess almost 45 percent of the country's wealth, with a median net worth well above $10 million.

At the very top, the stratification is even more pronounced. Wealth concentration among the richest Americans now exceeds even the excesses of the Gilded Age. In 1913, the top 0.00001 percent was represented by four of the wealthiest men ever to walk the planet; John D. Rockefeller, Henry Clay Frick, Andrew Carnegie, and George Fisher Baker accounted for some 0.85 percent of the total wealth in the United States. In 2020, the 0.00001 percent was represented by just three men: Jeff Bezos, Bill Gates, and Mark Zuckerberg, who together accounted for some 1.35 percent of total U.S. wealth. Three men who founded technology companies possessed as much wealth as the entire bottom half of the United States combined. The wealthiest 0.01 percent of American households, around 18,000 families, also possess proportionally more capital than they did in the Gilded Age, today owning about 10 percent of the country's wealth, compared to 2 percent in 1913. Perhaps most startling is how fast they have achieved this sudden concentration of wealth. In the late 1970s, just before Welch took over, the top 0.01 percent of families held just 2 percent of the country's wealth.

Such glaring statistics are the inevitable result of four decades of Welchism. Before Welch took over, productivity and worker pay rose in tandem; following his campaign against loyalty, they diverged, and worker pay has never recovered. Until Welch came on the scene, CEOs were well-paid managers; after his gargantuan paydays, other bosses came to expect extraordinary compensation packages, too. With workers earning less and CEOs earning so much more, income inequality began to soar. Manufacturing jobs in America peaked just as Welch took over, then began to decline as he sent work overseas. Mergers and acquisitions ballooned on his watch, concentrating power in the hands of just a few companies in sector after sector, leading to higher prices, fewer options for employees, and a less dynamic economy overall. And the amount of taxes paid by corporations has plummeted, while buybacks and dividends have exploded.

This is the world Welch bequeathed us. One where Jeff Bezos can afford to send himself to space, while hourly employees at Amazon warehouses are monitored by robots. One where a handful of private equity executives can buy up iconic American food companies and squeeze them dry. One where a media company can go $80 billion into debt buying up rivals, then lay off tens of thousands of workers in the name of profitability. Welchism has made America poorer, less equal, and more insecure. It has hollowed out factory towns while filling Wall Street's coffers. It has left corporations unaccountable for their failings, while leaving more of the population vulnerable to the whims of highly paid executives. And it has created an economy where once proud industrial companies lose their way, with sometimes fatal consequences.

Two Crashes

Early on the morning of October 29, 2018, Lion Air Flight 610 took off from Jakarta with 189 people aboard, bound for a nearby island in Indonesia. The plane was a brand-new Boeing 737 Max, one of dozens purchased by Lion Air, a low-cost Indonesian airline. Moments after takeoff, the captain and first officer began to have trouble controlling the plane. Without warning, the nose of the Max would suddenly dip. The pilots pulled back on the yoke in hopes of bringing the plane back to level and continuing their ascent. But time and again, the Max pushed its nose toward the ocean below. Thirteen minutes after takeoff, the plane plunged into the water, killing everyone aboard.

When Boeing executives learned of the crash, they wrote it off as an unfortunate accident in a country with a shoddy aviation safety record. Indonesian airlines had a reputation for poor training and dubious maintenance, and Lion Air had lost planes before. Within days, however, Boeing understood from the recovered flight recorder data that MCAS, the new system installed on the Max, had played a role in the crash. Something had caused one of the angle of attack sensors protruding from the fuselage to malfunction, the onboard computer believed the plane was pointing up at a dangerous angle, and MCAS repeatedly nudged the nose of the Max down, ultimately sending it into a nosedive. The 737 Max, Boeing's most important jet in a generation, had a terrible flaw.

Yet at the highest levels of Boeing, there was a perplexing inability to grasp the severity of the crisis the company now faced. Rather than truly wrestling with the implications of the crash and what it might portend for the company, Boeing executives essentially dismissed it as a regrettable anomaly. Executives believed that the Lion Air pilots simply couldn't handle whatever had happened in the cockpit and that faulty maintenance had left the plane vulnerable to a malfunction. Boeing insinuated as much in public statements, and, in private meetings with pilots from American Airlines, senior Boeing executives reiterated that the Max was safe. The crash, Boeing implied, was due to pilot error.

Boeing issued a reminder to pilots about how to handle a scenario like the one that unfolded on the ill-fated Lion Air flight. Yet even then, after having omitted MCAS from the pilot's manual, there was no mention of MCAS in the reminder. Boeing said it planned to update the MCAS software, a tacit admission that the plane was flawed, but that was the extent of the company's response.

Had Boeing fully appreciated what actually happened off the coast of Jakarta, it would have had a full-blown crisis on its hands. If that plane had crashed as a result of MCAS, then hundreds of other new Max jets might also be vulnerable. And if that was true, the plane would likely have to be grounded, a drastic step that would cost Boeing billions of dollars and decimate the company's share price.

Rather than investigate the crash's cause and ensure that Boeing's engineering was sound, the company's executives turned their attention back to Wall Street. Less than two months after the crash, on December 17, citing "Boeing's strong operational performance, financial health and positive future outlook," Dennis Muilenburg, the Boeing CEO, announced that the company was increasing its dividend by 20 percent and would spend $20 billion on stock buybacks. It was the apex of two decades of unwavering devotion to investors that began in 1997, when Stonecipher joined the company, and it further clarified Muilenburg's priorities. In the few years since he had taken over, Boeing had spent more than 90 percent of its operating cashflow on buybacks and dividends.

As shareholders enjoyed the early windfalls from Boeing's latest return of capital program, the Max kept flying. For months, thousands of flights took off and landed safely, and more airlines kept accepting new deliveries of Boeing's latest jet. The MCAS software update, which was expected early in 2019, was repeatedly delayed.

Then, on March 10, 2019, a 737 Max departed Addis Ababa, Ethiopia, en route to Nairobi, Kenya. The regular flight was popular with diplomats and aid workers and was known as the "U.N. Shuttle." On this day, 157 people were aboard, many of them on their way to a United Nations environmental conference. But minutes after takeoff, the plane began pushing itself down. The pilots tried to intervene, pulling back on the yoke and taking other steps to regain control of the plane. But their efforts were futile. Just as had happened less than five months earlier in Indonesia, MCAS had gone haywire. Six minutes after takeoff, the plane crashed into a remote field, killing all passengers and crew.

This time, the global aviation community took notice. Within days, regulators in almost every country had grounded the Max. The similarities between the two crashes were too glaring ignore, even if it wasn't yet clear what exactly had happened. The Max kept flying in the United States for several days more, with the FAA reluctant to ground Boeing's most important plane. Muilenburg called President Trump and assured him that the Max was safe. But within days, the FAA also grounded the plane.

It soon became clear that MCAS had brought down Ethiopian Airlines Flight 302 in a chilling repeat of the crash in Indonesia. Somehow, the single sensor protruding from the fuselage had been damaged, possibly by a bird strike. That caused the plane to think it was pitching up, and MCAS repeatedly pushed the nose down until the Max slammed into the ground. This time, however, there were no inexperienced pilots or faulty maintenance records to blame. Ethiopian Airlines had the best pilots in Africa, and nothing was amiss with the plane before it went down. Something was wrong with the Max itself.

In the weeks after the second crash, Boeing attempted a high-wire act—expressing sympathy for the victims but not admitting guilt, promising a MCAS software update without saying the Max was flawed. Muilenburg came off as robotic and wouldn't field questions, an early indication that he seemed to lack the requisite tools to handle a crisis of this magnitude. He appeared incapable of expressing genuine emotion when making public statements about the crashes and seemed eager to put the whole thing behind him. The hope, Boeing said initially, was to get the Max back in the air in a matter of weeks, a month or two at the most. Yet the more the public learned, the more damning the facts appeared to be—Boeing had known MCAS was a risk and let the Max keep flying. It had sold safety features as extras. The system was poorly designed, lacking the necessary redundancy.

By July, Boeing had slashed production of the Max, a sign that the grounding would be long and costly. And the problems kept coming. The Max simulators didn't work properly. The work of a subcontractor writing code for the MCAS software update was flawed. As the families of the victims of the Ethiopian crash learned more about the tragedy, they came to an inescapable conclusion. "The second crash was corporate manslaughter," said Zipporah Kuria, whose father died on ET302. "They knew what the issues were and they did nothing about them. If they had grounded the plane after the first crash, my dad would still be here."

In the months after the second crash, Boeing kept promising a fix. Even as family members testified before Congress and investigators interrogated the causes of the accidents, the company kept saying that it was just months away from that long-awaited MCAS update, and that the Max would be back in the air soon. But the months slid by, and by the end of 2019 the grounding of the Max had become the longest ever in commercial aviation. As Boeing fiddled with MCAS, more new problems with the Max arose. Airlines were furious. Pilots had lost faith in the company. Lawmakers in Washington were apoplectic. In mid-October, the Boeing board stripped Muilenburg of his title as chairman of the company. In his place, they elevated Dave Calhoun—the former GE executive who was a dark-horse candidate to succeed Welch—to chairman. Though Boeing said the move was simply a formality that would allow Muilenburg to focus on returning the Max to service, it was clear that Boeing now had a CEO-in-waiting. It would only be a matter of time before another GE loyalist was back in control.

Days after demoting Muilenburg and elevating Calhoun, the Boeing board fired Kevin McAllister, the former GE executive who was head of Boeing commercial airplanes. McAllister had mishandled the crisis internally and aggravated key airline customers. He was the first senior executive to be fired as a result of the Max crashes, more than a year after the first had occurred. Soon after that, Muilenburg spent two days testifying before Congress in a performance that would seal his fate.

Muilenburg began with a note of contrition, apologizing to the families of the victims—"We are sorry," he said. "Deeply and truly sorry." He was then ceaselessly berated by lawmakers. They presented damning new evidence that Boeing engineers had considered making pilots aware of MCAS, but then backtracked, and details about the company's efforts to get the FAA to remove mention of the new software from the training manual. "I would walk before I was to get on a 737 Max," said Senator Jon Tester, Democrat of Montana, adding, "You shouldn't be cutting corners, and I see corners being cut."

Muilenburg held on for another couple of months as the bad news kept piling up. The FAA made it clear that the Max would not fly again anytime soon. Boeing took the drastic step of completely shutting down production of the plane. And new whistleblowers came forward with damaging information about the company and its management. In September, days after the the *New York Times* published a scathing article about Muilenburg that included harsh quotes from the CEO of Southwest Airlines, the Boeing board fired Muilenburg. It was an ignominious end to his time atop Boeing, but Muilenburg, who did so much to coax the company's stock price higher with buybacks and dividends, didn't go home empty-handed. His exit package was worth $62.2 million. The company's chief financial officer, Greg Smith, would take over on an interim basis, and then Calhoun would begin as CEO in January. A Welch disciple was once again in charge of Boeing.

Before ET302 crashed, I had paid little attention to Boeing, and had only barely registered the Lion Air disaster. But on March 11, 2019, I walked into the newsroom of the *New York Times* and was quickly summoned by the business editor. Another Boeing plane had gone down, and the paper needed help covering the story. I wasn't an aviation reporter at the time, but I knew enough about covering big corporations, and started making calls. For the next year, I was one of the lead reporters on the Boeing story, along with my colleague Natalie Kitroeff. We traveled the country following leads, met with the families of the victims, attended congressional hearings, and burrowed our way inside the senior ranks of Boeing and the FAA. After we reported on the failings at the 787 Dreamliner plant in North Charleston, the head of the factory was fired. After we revealed how key customers were furious with McAllister, he was ousted. And the day after we published a major investigation into Muilenburg's mishandling of the crisis, the board called a meeting and replaced him with Calhoun. Yet in all that time, we were never granted an interview with Muilenburg himself. Once, I cornered him in the Grand Hyatt above Grand Central Terminal at an event hosted by the Economic Club of New York. But as soon I introduced myself and his handlers realized who I was, he was whisked away, and I couldn't ask a question. So it came as a surprise when, shortly after Calhoun took over, Natalie and I were invited to interview the new CEO in person. We would be the first print journalists to have the chance, and no topic would be off limits.

For the better part of a week, the Boeing public relations team went back and forth about where the interview would take place. It might be in the Seattle area, where the 737 was built. Or maybe Chicago, where corporate headquarters was. In the end, the company settled upon the Boeing Leadership Center outside St. Louis—the complex built around the château that Stonecipher had bought while he was running McDonnell Douglas, and which Boeing had turned into its own version of Crotonville. Calhoun, hoping to channel his GE roots, was now using the center as his makeshift office as he tried to revive the company.

We flew from New York to St. Louis on the first Monday of March 2020. The Covid-19 pandemic was worsening around the world, and although we didn't know it at the time, in a little over a week the country would grind to a halt. After landing, Boeing executives showed us around the company's fighter jet factory and a nearby innovation lab, before taking us to the Leadership Center. There, we got a tour of a campus designed in Crotonville's image, from the sloping grounds overlooking a river to the large cafeteria with soaring cathedral windows. In a lounge area, there were plaques glorifying Boeing's storied history and highlighting the work of various executives, with one prominent but outdated display celebrating the recently ousted Muilenburg. Finally, we sat down with Calhoun in a cramped, dimly lit conference room. As we made small talk, I asked why we were doing the interview at the Leadership Center. Calhoun didn't miss a beat.

"My forever mentor used his learning center as his headquarters," he said.

"And who was that?" I asked, knowing the answer.

"Jack Welch, ironically," Calhoun replied. "Ironically," Calhoun said, because the day before, on March 1, 2020, Welch had died at the age of eighty-four.

Calhoun didn't dwell on Welch, wanting to get down to business, but he added one more note about why we were here on the grounds of a French château refurbished to resemble a GE training facility for a company that peaked two decades ago. "This was built in its image," Calhoun said. "It was built by ex-GE people in the image of Crotonville under the notion that that's what it would be used for. So we're going to reinvigorate that every which way I can think of."

Natalie and I spent more than an hour questioning Calhoun on his leadership of Boeing, his decision to stand by Muilenburg for so long, and what he might do to revive the company's fortunes. Calhoun admitted that things inside the company were worse than he expected, even though he had been chairman of the board. "It's more than I imagined it would be, honestly," he said. "And it speaks to the weaknesses of our leadership." When we asked about Muilenburg's ouster, and why there wasn't a more orderly succession plan in place, Calhoun said: "We had a backup plan." He added, "I am the backup plan."

Calhoun, who had been paid huge sums of money during his career, and who, as a member of the board that had approved Muilenburg's compensation, criticized the former CEO for aggressively pushing Boeing to increase production of the Max. "I'll never be able to judge what motivated Dennis, whether it was a stock price that was going to continue to go up and up, or whether it was just beating the other guy," he said. He added later, "If anybody ran over the rainbow for the pot of gold on stock, it would have been him." Calhoun defended Boeing's culture, and said the mountain of incriminating emails that had recently been released were the result of a few bad apples. "I see a couple of people who wrote horrible emails," he told us.

Addressing the crashes, he tried to have it both ways. He acknowledged that the company made a "fatal mistake" by assuming pilots would immediately take all the right steps to manage an MCAS malfunction. But in the next breath, he suggested that pilots from Indonesia and Ethiopia, "where pilots don't have anywhere near the experience that they have here in the U.S.," were to blame as well. When we asked Calhoun whether he believed American pilots would have been able to handle a software malfunction, he asked to speak off the record. We said no. "Forget it," Calhoun then said. "You can guess the answer."

It was hardly the contrition we expected from the CEO of a company whose products had killed 346 people and whose business lay in tatters. Instead, Calhoun was defiant and accusatory, brimming with the same in-your-face bluster for which Welch was so well known. When we published our story a few days later, there was an uproar inside and outside Boeing. Calhoun sent an apologetic note to senior leaders at the company. "I am both embarrassed and regretful about the article," he wrote. "It suggests I broke my promise to former CEO Dennis Muilenburg, the executive team and our people that I would have their back when it counted most. I want to reassure you that my promise remains intact." And though he didn't say it in his note, sources told Natalie and me that when Calhoun tried to explain to confidants what had possessed him to give such an erratic performance, he said that he was upset and distracted by the death of his "forever mentor," Jack Welch.

Though Calhoun was on the board during the crucial years when the Max and MCAS were developed, he took no responsibility for it. Though he had supported the appointment of Muilenburg, he disavowed the former CEO. And despite all the evidence that Boeing had designed a fatally flawed airplane that claimed hundreds of lives, he continued to cast blame on the pilots. He was pugnacious and unrepentant, exhibiting the Type A bombast he had learned from Welch decades before. The parallels were impossible to ignore, even to the families of the victims.

One of the passengers on Ethiopian Airlines Flight 302 was Samya Stumo, a bright, idealistic twenty-four-year-old from Massachusetts. Samya's parents were Michael Stumo and Nadia Milleron, and Nadia's uncle was Ralph Nader, the longtime consumer rights advocate who for years had railed against the airline industry and the FAA. After the second crash, Nadia and Michael emerged as de facto organizers for the victims' families and dedicated themselves to holding Boeing accountable. Both grew well versed in the technical details of the Max and MCAS. Michael became an outspoken critic of Boeing's corporate culture, and Nadia confronted Muilenburg at a congressional hearing. Shortly after Calhoun took over, Stumo penned an op-ed for *USA Today* expressing his skepticism that the new CEO was fit for the job. The reason for his concern? "Calhoun comes from a background working under Jack Welch at General Electric," Stumo wrote, "when the company transitioned from making great products toward a finance-oriented approach."

There was no single reason that the 737 Max crashed twice in five months. The angle of attack sensors failed. MCAS was reliant on just one sensor. The pilots, overwhelmed, didn't perform every function correctly in the few seconds they had to avert disaster. Those errors, however, were merely the final slips of fate that unleashed an inevitable disaster. Ever since Boeing turned its back on engineering and set its sights on short-term profits, the company was careening toward a moment like this. All the decisions made by Stonecipher, McNerney, Muilenburg, McAllister, and Calhoun helped create a broken culture, which in turn produced a flawed airplane. Welchism had infected America's great aerospace company, and killed 346 people.

"A Donald Trump, a Jack Welch"

Over the decades, in ways large and small, direct and indirect, Jack Welch abetted the rise of Donald Trump, partnering with him on real estate deals, lending him credibility, and ultimately supporting his campaign and his presidency. Welch and Trump orbited each other as colleagues and friends, two megalomaniacs taking advantage of each other's wealth and credibility as it suited their own needs. The year after Welch hired Roger Ailes to head CNBC—setting in motion events that would lead to the creation of Fox News—Welch went into business with Trump. In 1994, the GE Pension Trust, which managed savings for the company's retirees, partnered with the real estate tycoon to redevelop a tower on the southwest corner of Central Park. In 2004, NBC—then still owned by GE—picked up *The Apprentice*, giving Trump a national platform and a new fortune.

Welch loved *The Apprentice*. "I knew it was going to be a good show when Suzy and I were watching it in bed with her two kids and they started shouting, 'You're fired! You're fired!'" Welch said. "It's a homerun." The show was a surreal simulacrum of his own life, allowing Welch to watch layoffs from the comfort of his own couch. For Trump, this was CEO cosplay, offering him a taste of the very real power Neutron Jack once wielded. And when Welch needed to peddle the Jack Welch Management Institute, he turned to Trump for a cameo on *The Apprentice*, followed by an appearance on the *Today* show.

Each had a bit of what the other one coveted. To Welch, who loved the media's razzmatazz even if he hated its scrutiny, Trump was the perfect celebrity—a bulletproof star who projected the aura of success 24/7, managing to dance around controversies and jump from one unlikely venture to the next, appearing to make money every step of the way. And for Trump, who was much less successful than the businessman he played on TV, Welch was the ultimate embodiment of the CEO, the commander of what had legitimately been the most valuable company in the world.

The two seemed to genuinely enjoy each other's company, too, palling around and attending New England Patriots games together. It was a mutual admiration society, as they talked each other up to anyone who would listen. In 2004, when Trump's latest book fetched a $5 million advance—$1 million more than the $4 million Welch and Wetlaufer got for *Winning*—the former CEO shrugged it off with a bit of self-deprecation. "Jack Welch is a peanut compared to Donald

Trump," Welch said. During the financial crisis, Trump suggested on Fox News that Welch be named the czar to oversee the recovery of the auto industry. Trump was a funhouse mirror reflection of Welch, and even Roger Stone, the cunning, corrupt political operative, saw the likeness. "It's our private sector that has our greatest minds, a Donald Trump, a Jack Welch, a Warren Buffet," Stone told Tucker Carlson in 2007. "These are the greatest negotiators—some of the greatest minds in our society."

During President Obama's second term, Welch's affinity for Trump became more consequential than he could have imagined. By appearing next to Trump for so long, Welch became one of many who lent the real estate huckster a veneer of legitimacy, and thus power. More than once, when Trump was asked who he would select for his cabinet, he floated Welch as a potential treasury secretary. Welch said he would decline the post if offered—just as he said he had declined offers to join the cabinets of Presidents Reagan and George H. W. Bush. By this time Welch was old, in poor health, and more cantankerous than ever. But Welch didn't hesitate to support Trump. "It's almost must-see TV whenever he shows up," Welch told CNN. Welch went on to tout Trump's business bona fides. "He sure gets things done," Welch said.

In 2016, as the campaign entered the final stretch, Welch said that Trump, as a free market Republican, was better than whatever the Democrats had to offer. "I know I got a better shot at jobs, less regulation," he said. And as the election neared, Welch appeared on CNBC to promote Trump once more. He liked that Trump was tough on unions and believed that he would shrink the federal workforce, Neutron Jack style. "I have a hope that a businessman like Trump can go into that vast bureaucracy, all through both defense and all over the government, and cut it," he said. Welch said the Environmental Protection Agency was "out of control," and that Trump was more likely to fix public education than Hillary Clinton, who he said was "beholden to the unions." He said the country was being "drowned in regulations" and parroted Trump's calls for a crackdown on immigration.

Trump welcomed the adulation and courted Welch's endorsement. Yet on the campaign trail, he railed against the world that Welch had helped create, positioning himself as a champion of the downtrodden working class. The reality television star was an unlikely savior, of course, a coiffured billionaire pretending to look out for the everyman. But Trump deftly homed in on the disillusionment festering in cities that had been abandoned by companies like GE. "Our workers' loyalty was repaid with betrayal," Trump said in one of the major economic speeches of his campaign. "Our politicians have aggressively pursued a policy of globalization—moving our jobs, our wealth and our factories to Mexico and overseas. . . . Globalization has made the financial elite who donate to politicians very wealthy. But it has left millions of our workers with nothing but poverty and heartache. . . . Our politicians took away from the people their means of making a living and supporting their families. Skilled craftsmen and tradespeople and factory workers have seen the jobs they loved shipped thousands of miles away. . . . This wave of globalization has wiped out our middle class." Trump's whole campaign, it seemed, was a rebuttal of Welchism.

Historians will spend years unpacking the complex mix of factors that led to Trump's election. Race, gender, nationalism, and the media all played a role. Yet it is also indisputable that many Trump voters were the kinds of men and women who had once worked in GE factories and had since fallen on hard times. The dismantling of American manufacturing, the hollowing out of the middle class, the replacement of factory jobs with service jobs—they all sowed deep discontent in a large segment of the electorate. Trump may not have had any intention of addressing their needs. But he picked up on their anger and used it as fuel for his campaign.

When it came time to identify the root cause of these problems, however, Trump missed the mark. While he pointed to "Washington," and Democrats in particular, as the villains, it was CEOs like Welch who actually deserved much of the blame. It was executives, not congressmen, who closed factories in Ohio and moved production to Mexico and set wages so low. It was men like Welch, Immelt, Nardelli, and McNerney who reversed the flow of wealth, sending it to their own bank accounts, and to bankers on Wall Street, instead of employees in Schenectady. GE was the first major American corporation to turn its back on the working class, setting in motion the slow erosion of prosperity across so many zip codes. And inasmuch as politicians were to blame, it was mostly Republicans who had championed free trade, free markets, weaker unions, and reduced regulation for so long. But during the 2016 election, the root causes of this discontent didn't seem to matter to much of the electorate. What mattered was that someone was acknowledging their despair. For forty-five years, working-class whites had steadily been losing ground. Here, finally, was someone who seemed to be as angry about that as they were. And then, with men like Welch cheering him on and tens of thousands of disaffected workers wearing MAGA hats at his rallies, Trump improbably won.

Shortly after he was inaugurated, Trump summoned Welch to the White House. "We had a hell of a meeting," Welch told Fox Business, speaking from the South Lawn. "I've been coming down here since 1980, and this was the first presidential meeting I've ever had where it was like talking to a peer." It was a telling aside. Of all the U.S presidents Welch had met, Trump was the one in whom he saw his own likeness.

Before long, Welch was claiming that the Democrats had "made up" the Trump campaign's ties with Russia and that Trump was a uniquely gifted president. "This guy was rolling up his sleeves and talking about the issues, and his depth of knowledge on every issue was amazing," Welch said after another meeting with the new president. It was a reprise of Welch the conspiracy theorist, only this time, instead of spouting nonsense about the Obama administration fabricating job numbers, Welch was glorifying Trump. The Manager of the Century had been conned by the huckster of the millennium.

A few months after Trump took office, Welch was raving about Trump on television. "I give him an A on policy. I give him an A on appointments," he said. "I love the people he's picked." Welch went on to praise Betsy DeVos, the education secretary who worked to starve public schools of funding, and Scott Pruitt, the Environmental

Protection Agency administrator who would resign in a morass of scandal. "I give him an A on the morale of the business community and the morale of the country, the spirit of the country," Welch said. It was the kind of ring-kissing that Trump reveled in, and it earned Welch a seat at the table.

Trump was largely dismissed by mainstream CEOs before he won. Almost none endorsed him during the campaign. Once in office, however, he quickly created a pair of advisory groups stuffed with big-name CEOs who were there, ostensibly, to give the president economic advice. The Strategic and Policy Forum, one of the two groups, was a Who's Who of CEOs, and included big names like Jamie Dimon of JPMorgan, Doug McMillon of Walmart, and Mary Barra of General Motors. It also included Welch. The group never served any practical function. When the CEOs gathered at the White House, it was mostly to serve as props for a presidential photo op. No strategy emanated from this assemblage of business minds, nor did any discernible policy. And in any case, the charade didn't last long.

On August 12, 2017, white nationalists marched on Charlottesville, Virginia. Carrying torches and swastika flags, wearing Trump campaign gear and Make America Great Again hats, they rioted in the streets, and one counterprotester was killed. In the aftermath of the violence, Trump took pains to emphasize that there were "very fine people" on "both sides." The president's equivocation created its own uniquely Trumpian news cycle, as Democrats excoriated the amoral commander in chief, and Republicans made excuses, or pretended not to have heard what Trump said. Yet the CEOs, of all people, found the nerve to act.

At first there was just one. The day after Trump's "both sides" remark, Ken Frazier, the chief executive of Merck, and a Black man whose grandfather was born into slavery, said he was stepping down from another one of the president's business advisory groups. "America's leaders must honor our fundamental values by clearly rejecting expressions of hatred, bigotry and group supremacy, which run counter to the American ideal that all people are created equal,"

Frazier said. The rebuke prompted Trump to lash out on Twitter: "Now that Ken Frazier of Merck Pharma has resigned from President's Manufacturing Council, he will have more time to LOWER RIPOFF DRUG PRICES!" But Frazier's remarks also appeared to give the other CEOs the courage, or at least the cover, to act. In a matter of days, the CEOs decided to disband the groups. The decision was nearly unanimous, save for a few men who wanted to stand by the president, believing that however appalling Trump's comments were, it wasn't enough to justify abandoning a president who so thoroughly supported their pro-business agenda. Among those in favor of soldiering on: Jim McNerney—the former Boeing CEO and runner-up to the top job at GE—and Welch himself.

It took a particular kind of loyalty to stand by Trump after his remarks in the wake of Charlottesville. Not necessarily a fealty to the man, though plenty of his acolytes in the West Wing found ways to justify their continued support of a president giving cover to white supremacists. In Welch's and McNerney's case, it was more likely a loyalty to Trump's wholehearted embrace of their economic priorities, namely lower taxes and less regulation. Were executives really going to let apparent sympathy for neo-Nazis get in the way of that? For most mainstream CEOs, the answer was obvious. They were done. Yet for McNerney and Welch, the calculus was not so clear. Trump, they understood, may have been morally compromised, but he was also one of their own.

The objections of Welch and McNerney were not enough to save Trump's business advisory councils, but that hardly mattered. While the president had swept into office promising to take on the corporate overlords and empower the working man, Trump, once in office, did the opposite. His major policy accomplishment, an overhaul of the tax code, was a boondoggle for companies and the wealthy, drastically reducing tax bills for multinational corporations and small-time real estate investors alike, while also encouraging offshoring and shifting profits abroad. He rolled back environmental regulations and worker protections, and prevented workers from gaining more bargaining power. Under Trump, workplace safety inspections dropped, companies had an easier time avoiding paying overtime, and pay for migrant farmworkers was lowered. It was Welchism playing out on a national scale. After so many years, Neutron Jack was no longer shaping just the business world. With his friend Donald Trump in the White House, his values were impacting all of American life as well.

EIGHT

Beyond Welchism

"A more responsible business model"

Identifying companies where Welchism has taken root is not particularly difficult these days. During his career and in retirement, Welch's influence was so pervasive that the GE way of doing business became the norm in corporate America, from Amazon to Boeing to Kraft Heinz, and beyond. Identifying companies that have deliberately resisted the temptation to follow his lead is a harder task. But they are out there. And as we look to the future, it is important to recognize those CEOs who are trying to chart a different course, allowing them to serve as reminders of what is possible when leaders look beyond the bottom line.

In 2009, a Dutchman named Paul Polman took over Unilever, the Anglo-Dutch consumer goods company. Initially, there was little reason to believe Polman was anything but another conventional executive who got ahead by boosting profits in a multinational corporation. Before joining Unilever, he had spent years at Procter & Gamble and served as chief financial officer at Nestlé. Yet Polman came to the job with a unique perspective. Before going into business, he had studied to be a Jesuit priest. He may well have finished his studies and become a man of the cloth, but the seminary where he was studying closed because too few students had enrolled. Instead, Polman went into business, and as he climbed the corporate ladder he brought some of the empathy he had cultivated in the church to the business world.

Unilever was in decline when Polman took over. The company was reeling in the wake of the financial crisis, and sales had fallen sharply. Polman still believed the company—which made everything from Dove soap to Ben & Jerry's ice cream—had a bright future and strong brands, but he also knew Unilever needed a hard reset. And to do that, he tried to return to the company's roots. Unilever was founded by Lord William Lever, a late-nineteenth-century British entrepreneur. Lever set up a factory in Port Sunlight, in southern England, where he began mass-producing soap, and built a company town where his employees enjoyed health care, benefits, and entertainment. "He built Port Sunlight before the factories were fully running to provide houses for his employees," Polman said. "He had the highest number of volunteers in World War I because he guaranteed the wages and the jobs, and he helped the wives when the men were gone. No smoking and no drinking in Port Sunlight made the life expectancy better. He fought for six-day work weeks. He introduced pensions in the U.K. He brought these values to the company, and he believed in shared prosperity."

Soon after taking over, Polman took his management team to Port Sunlight for a multiday retreat, where he tried to recapture the benevolent spirit that had animated Unilever a century before. Polman believed that a company like Unilever could prosper and take excellent care of its employees simultaneously. He believed that even though a big corporation used massive amounts of resources, it could still exert a positive influence on the natural world. So at Port Sunlight, in addition to the normal strategic planning, Polman had his executives reflect on Lord Lever and what had made Unilever great in the first place. Polman and his team emerged with an ambitious agenda: the company would aim to decouple its growth from its environmental impact. That is, even as the company continued to expand, it would endeavor to use fewer natural resources. "Going back to our roots gave me the permission to drive change," Polman said. "We needed to have a more responsible business model."

When Polman took over, he said, Unilever was playing the same kind of games with its earnings that GE and so many other companies had perfected—finding ways to smooth out quarters and keep Wall Street happy. "We were doing the same thing," Polman said. "We were more occupied by the quarters and would hold spending back and start it again a month later, or do other things that weren't in the best interest of the company. I wanted to get out of that. We needed to provide the environment for people to be successful. You cannot solve issues like poverty or climate change or food security with the myopic focus on quarterly reporting."

Polman needed to send a signal to the market that he was serious about change, and soon after the retreat, he announced that he would stop issuing quarterly guidance. He was putting Wall Street on notice, making it clear that he didn't intend to be measured by short-term results. Unilever stock dropped sharply, as investors offloaded shares of a company that no longer appeared to be focused on the bottom line. Yet in time, the shareholder base turned over, with new, more patient investors buying the stock, and within four months Unilever shares began to rise.

When Polman was asked why he stopped issuing quarterly guidance, he invoked Welch. "You have to get out of this rat race of quarterly reporting and quarterly behavior," Polman said. "Many companies manipulate their behaviors, their spending, to avoid missing expectations. Jack Welch, in his book *Jack: Straight from the Gut*, talks about hitting quarterly expectations over and over and missing it only twice by one penny, how wonderful that was." Polman noted that the former GE chief was only able to post such stellar returns thanks to his accounting games. "If he was that wonderful, he should have been in Las Vegas," he said. In the eyes of Polman, Welch was little more than a gambler.

Polman then crafted an ambitious agenda to reduce Unilever's carbon footprint, dampen the negative impacts of its work around the globe, and find areas where it could make a positive difference in people's lives. Polman got Unilever to reduce its use of palm oil, which devastates rain forests. He transitioned to organic crops, even for American cupboard staples like Hellmann's mayonnaise. And he began paying workers and suppliers more. Those efforts cost money, but they paid off. Unilever began to take market share from its competitors, consumers supported a company with a conscience, employees were motivated and engaged.

Shortly before he retired, Polman was presented with a Faustian bargain. Kraft Heinz, the food giant run by the Welch imitators at 3G Capital, made an unsolicited takeover offer for Unilever. The proposed deal, valued at $143 billion, would likely have made Polman phenomenally rich. Unilever shareholders, too, would have realized an instant gain on their holdings. And Unilever was just the kind of target 3G could feast upon. With its vast operations around the globe, there were countless costs to cut, endless pennies to pinch. A merger would have made Kraft Heinz one of the biggest food companies on earth, fulfilling the Welchian mandate to be number one or number two in the industry. A takeover would have been deeply symbolic, too—the most Welchian company around swallowing up one of the few corporations seeking to chart a new course.

But the Brazilians had misjudged their prey. Polman, who had spent a decade forging a reputation as a crusader in sustainability and good governance circles, rejected the offer outright. Beyond the price being too low, Unilever made it clear that it had little regard for 3G's approach. Polman and the Brazilians had diametrically opposed views of how to run a business, and Polman wasn't about to sell Unilever to the would-be Welches of Kraft Heinz and 3G Capital. "It was a purely financial transaction that was attractive on paper, but was really two conflicting economic systems," Polman said. "Unilever is a company that works for the long term and focuses on the billions of people that we serve. Kraft Heinz is clearly focused on a few billionaires that do extremely well, but the company is on the bottom of the human rights indexes or on the efforts to get out of deforestation. Kraft Heinz is built on the concept of cutting costs." It was a decisive rebuke. Polman held his ground with the support of his board. Kraft Heinz made a hasty retreat. And for a moment at least, the Welchian way of doing business had met its match in the form of a former seminary student who was running his business with more in mind than just shareholder returns and his own stock options.

In the years after Polman rejected the offer, Kraft Heinz stock plunged. A lack of investment in new products, a disaffected workforce, and a culture of playing fast and loose with finances had caught up with the company. Unilever, meanwhile, saw its stock price continue to rise, outperforming peers and sending Polman, who retired in 2019, out on a high. At every turn, he had done just about the opposite of what Welch would have done. His success proved that there was another way to do business, offering further evidence that Welchism was not a winning strategy. And a couple years after Unilever rebuffed Kraft Heinz, reflecting on the deal, Polman couldn't help but gloat. "Since then, their share price is down 70 percent, and they now face legal issues around reporting," he said. "Our share price is up about 50 percent. Some people think greed is good. But over and over it's proven that ultimately generosity is better."

Polman was an outlier when he took over Unilever, one of the few CEOs willing to question the status quo and set ambitious targets to reduce the harm his company did to the world. Yet today Polman is one of many. Over the past decade, he has been joined by a diverse array of CEOs who have found different ways to push back against Welchism, an effort that extends from the European headquarter of Unilever to the techno-utopian campuses of Silicon Valley. For example at PayPal, the online payments platform that was spun out of eBay into a public company in 2015, CEO Dan Schulman is changing his company's relationship with its workers, starting with how much he pays them.

When Schulman took over PayPal in 2014, he embraced the

idealistic language of Silicon Valley, trumpeting a corporate mission statement that suggested technology could solve all the world's problems. "Our mission as a company is to try and democratize the management and movement of money, which basically means that managing and moving money should be a right for all citizens, not just a privilege for the affluent," Schulman said. "It's a very inclusive statement, and the reason we have that as our mission is that so much of the world lives outside the financial system, and they struggle to make ends meet at the end of every single month." Schulman was quick to point out this is not just a problem in developing economies. "By the way, that's like two thirds of adults in the United States," he said—about 185 million people.

Schulman assumed that most all of PayPal's employees were well off. After all, the company was worth more than $100 billion, and Silicon Valley behemoths are known for their generous compensation. But in 2017, he learned that many of PayPal's lowest-paid employees were having a hard time making ends meet. The company had set up a $5 million fund to help workers who were experiencing unexpected financial crises. As soon as the fund was announced, it was overwhelmed with applications. "We found urgent requests for help were increasingly the result of everyday events, like an unexpectedly steep medical bill, a student loan payment, or a car breaking down," Schulman said.

The next year, PayPal decided to survey its low-paid and entry-level employees, a group that included many men and women working in call centers, and which accounted for about half the company's workforce. Schulman went into the exercise with high hopes. "Honestly I was doing it because I thought the results that would come back were going to be really good, because PayPal is a tech company, and we pay at or above market rates everywhere around the world because we want to attract really great employees," he said.

That was not the case. Two thirds of respondents said they were running short on cash between paychecks. "We got the survey results back and I was actually shocked to see that our hourly workers—like our call center employees, our entry-level employees—were just like the rest of the market, struggling to make ends meet." Schulman was stunned. "What it told me is that for about half our employees, the market wasn't working. Capitalism wasn't working." At one of the most profitable companies in the world, more than 10,000 employees were barely making enough to survive. "What we found out is that employees were making trade-offs, like do I get health care or do I put food on the table?" he said. "That's ridiculous."

Schulman resolved to do something, but he knew it wouldn't be enough to just hand out some bonuses and hope for the best. Instead, he looked for data that would tell him whether or not whatever interventions PayPal devised were making a difference. He wanted a way to measure "the financial health of our employees" that went beyond basic metrics like the minimum wage, the purchasing power of which varies by zip code. Over the course of a few months, PayPal worked with academics and nonprofit groups to create a new metric: "net disposable income," or NDI. That, Schulman explained, amounted to "how much money do you have after you pay all of your taxes and your essential living expenses, like housing and food and that kind of thing."

PayPal and its partners estimated that an NDI of 20 percent was about what was needed for a family to meet its needs—basics like rent and food, plus things like medical expenses, school supplies, and clothes—and still be able to save. With the new metric in hand, Schulman's team revisited the survey data. The results were grim. About half of PayPal employees had an NDI of 4 percent, leaving them with just a small fraction of their paycheck after paying for basic necessities. It was a bleak statistic, but now Schulman had a target. The goal would be to get all PayPal employees to at least an NDI of 20 percent. There wasn't one silver bullet that would easily accomplish that. Instead, PayPal created a four-part financial wellness program for its lower-paid employees that was unique among big companies.

First, PayPal raised the wages for those employees with low NDIs. The company already paid above minimum wage everywhere it had offices, but that clearly wasn't enough. So it upped hourly compensation for its call center workers.

It then gave every employee, even entry-level ones, an opportunity to own stock in the company. That was hardly a token gesture. Given the disproportionate amount of value that is created through the appreciation of public company stock, it could be a meaningful way for workers to accumulate real wealth. And sure enough, PayPal stock doubled in the year after the program was introduced.

Next, PayPal rolled out a comprehensive financial literacy program for its employees, offering pointers on saving, investing, and managing money. All of that was above and beyond what most big companies were doing, but Schulman then took one more critical step.

One surprising finding from financial wellness survey was just how much health care was costing PayPal employees. Each month, workers at one of the country's richest corporations had to choose between medical care and textbooks, between prescriptions and gas for the car. Health care costs were consuming a meaningful part of their NDI. So Schulman lowered health care costs for the company's lowest-paid employees by 60 percent.

It was the most impactful of PayPal's interventions. "I think if we had just done health care, it would have been a gigantic relief for our employees," Schulman said. Several months after the program was implemented, PayPal surveyed its employees again. This time, many of the targeted employees had net disposable income of more than 20 percent, with the lowest coming in at 16 percent.

The financial wellness program at PayPal cost tens of millions of dollars, money that didn't go out the door in buybacks or dividends. "It was a significant material investment in our employees," Schulman said. But he likened it to investments in other parts of the business, be it advertising or infrastructure. "I believe very strongly that the only sustainable competitive advantage that a company has is the skill set and the passion of their employees," he said.

Schulman insists that the expense was worth it. In the months after the program began, customer satisfaction ticked up, employees were more engaged, and PayPal's stock continued to soar. Whereas Welch and so many of his followers saw labor as a cost to be minimized, Schulman saw his work force for what it was—PayPal's greatest asset. "Over the medium and long term, that investment will pay back to shareholders," Schulman said. "This whole idea that profit and purpose are at odds with each other is ridiculous. I mean, if you ever have any chance of moving from being a good company to a great company, you have to have the very best employees, that love what they're doing, that are passionate about what they're doing. Everything else will emanate from there."

Schulman and Polman are part of a new generation of corporate leaders rewriting the rules that for too long have told CEOs how to run their companies. Espousing what they call "stakeholder capitalism," these executives are attempting to uproot habits that are by now deeply ingrained in the corporate world. Rather than resort to layoffs as a knee-jerk reaction to adversity, they are looking to invest in their employees. Rather than exploiting communities for cheap labor, they seek to support the areas where they maintain factories and offices. And rather than run their businesses with the sole goal of maximizing shareholder value, they consider investors as one constituency among many, while also taking into account the needs of workers, governments, customers, suppliers, and the environment. It is, in other words, the antithesis of Welchism.

"Where the fiduciary duty is starting to move"

Stakeholder capitalism is, in many ways, a nod to the Golden Age of Capitalism, a return to the collectivist spirit that prevailed before Welch arrived. And it is hardly a new invention. Indeed, even as Welchism was ascendant, a few lonely voices in the business world continued to call for a more holistic approach. Klaus Schwab, a German academic and the founder of the World Economic Forum, which for fifty years has gathered politicians and executives for an invitation-only retreat in Davos, Switzerland, has been advocating for the approach for decades.

In 1971, as Schwab began his annual gatherings, he sought a way to articulate his theory of business and society. Picking up on the work of Adolf A. Berle Jr. and Gardiner C. Means, who wrote *The Modern Corporation and Private Property* in 1932, Schwab argued that companies should not put shareholders first, but instead needed to heed their influence on workers, the environment, and society at large. For most of the past four decades, Schwab's stakeholder theory took a backseat to the ideas promulgated by Welch and his cronies. But in recent years, as the negative externalities kept piling up, Schwab's thinking has resurfaced as an alternative framework for how CEOs might approach their duties.

One of the earliest signs that the stakeholder movement was finally gaining traction was the emergence of the B Corp movement. Organized by a handful of idealistic capitalists in 2006, the B Corp movement created a framework to measure a company's overall impact on employees, the environment, and society. Companies could apply for certification, and if they were deemed sufficiently virtuous, emblazon their products with the B Corp logo. The effort was largely theatrics. It was nonbinding, hard to measure, and almost impossible to achieve for big corporations. And still, it caught on as a few aspirational companies looked for new ways to set themselves apart from the pack. Patagonia, Seventh Generation, and others signed on, and even some larger companies, like Danone, the French dairy maker, and Natura, a big Brazilian cosmetics maker, managed to earn the B Corp seal of approval.

What began as a marketing effort ultimately resulted in some regulatory changes, too. Thanks in part to the B Corp movement, there is now a new way for companies to incorporate themselves in the United States: the public benefit corporation. While most for-profit companies are organized as so-called C Corporations, with bylaws that simply state directors and executives must do what's in "the best interest of the corporation" without actually defining what that means, the charters of public benefit corporations are unambiguous. Included in their bylaws are explicit commitments to have a positive influence on society, and to take care of workers, the environment, and communities. Maryland became the first state to allow public benefit corporations in 2010, and a decade later almost every state has passed laws that enable companies to choose this path. Already, some well-known companies, including Kickstarter and Patagonia, have done so.

By writing a more expansive set of priorities into their governing documents, executives are at once codifying their values and rebuking the notion that they are obliged to maximize its short-term profits. As Patagonia founder Yvon Chouinard said when his company made the transition to public benefit corporation, "Benefit Corporation legislation creates the legal framework to enable mission-driven companies like Patagonia to stay mission-driven through succession, capital raises, and even changes in ownership, by institutionalizing the values, culture, processes, and high standards put in place by founding entrepreneurs."

There are other ways in which shareholder primacy appears to be losing its grip on the marketplace, too. In recent years, a handful of major investors, including the largest asset manager in the world, BlackRock, have begun encouraging companies to look beyond profits as a way of measuring their success. For years, BlackRock thrived on unqualified profit maximization. Fatter quarterly margins at the companies BlackRock invested in meant higher returns for the asset manager itself, and BlackRock's portfolio managers pressed companies to boost returns by any means necessary. But starting in 2014, Larry Fink, BlackRock's CEO, began embracing the rhetoric of stakeholder capitalism.

"It concerns us that, in the wake of the financial crisis, many companies have shied away from investing in the future growth of their companies," Fink wrote in an open letter to corporate America that year. "Too many companies have cut capital expenditure and even increased debt to boost dividends and increase share buybacks." No longer would it be enough for companies to make profits, contended Fink, who continued developing his argument in subsequent annual letters. Instead, if corporations wanted the support of BlackRock, they would need to make a positive contribution to the world around them. "Society is demanding that companies, both public and private, serve a social purpose," Fink wrote in 2018. "To prosper over time, every company must not only deliver financial performance, but also show how it makes a positive contribution to society. Companies must benefit all of their stakeholders, including shareholders, employees, customers, and the communities in which they operate."

Even the Business Roundtable, after decades of adhering to Welch's priorities, finally came around. The Business Roundtable had last updated its definition of the purpose of a corporation in 1997. That missive codified Welchism as the dominant worldview of the day, declaring that "the paramount duty of management and of boards of directors is to the corporation's stockholders." It was a pledge of allegiance to the free market dogma, reaffirming corporate America's belief that shareholders came first. And even as the dot-com bubble burst and the financial crisis roiled global markets, the country's most influential CEOs didn't think to reevaluate their stated mission.

Then in August 2019, the Business Roundtable abruptly embraced the notion of stakeholder capitalism. With Trump in the White House, mounting populist anger over income inequality, and a rising crop of progressive politicians calling for new regulations, the country's corporate leaders—including the CEOs of Amazon, Apple, Bank of America, JPMorgan, and Walmart—issued a monumental about-face. "While each of our individual companies serves its own corporate purpose, we share a fundamental commitment to all of our stakeholders," the statement read, enumerating the ways in which companies should behave fairly and ethically with customers, employees, suppliers, communities, and investors. "We commit to deliver value to all of them, for the future success of our companies, our communities and our country." The new statement was heralded as a breakthrough, proof positive that CEOs were finally getting serious about looking beyond the bottom line.

Real change will require more than rhetoric, however. To uproot Welchism and create a more just economy, there are urgent changes that CEOs, board members, policymakers, and even consumers can make right now.

Offer Better Pay and Benefits

For starters, companies should commit to taking exceptional care of their workers. That begins with compensation. Paying workers a living wage—one that allows them to meet their basic needs while also saving for the future—should be a given. We need to move beyond a world where employees of profitable multinational corporations qualify for food stamps, and that can only happen when employers commit to offering their workers a living wage. Numerous studies have demonstrated that raising wages for workers does not lead to unemployment or inflation. To the contrary, research has shown that raising the minimum wage has the effect of increasing productivity, improving morale, and generally helping the companies that take better care of their employees.

Companies should also use a greater share of their profits to subsidize benefits such as health care and child care for their lowest-paid workers. We've seen what happened at PayPal when health care costs were lowered—morale went up, workers were able to save more, and the corporate profits kept flowing. Imagine the benefit if more big companies followed Schulman's lead.

Share Profits, and Equity

Simply taking home a paycheck—even a living wage—isn't enough to truly advance in today's economy, however. For that reason, companies should make a habit of distributing profits to their workers. This can sometimes take the form of simple profit-sharing plans. Delta Air Lines, a public company, has routinely set aside meaningful chunks of its corporate profits to distribute to frontline workers in the form of annual bonuses.

Other major companies operate as cooperatives. REI, the outdoor retailer, is privately held and offers a share of its profits to employees. Another way workers can share in the profits is by receiving stock or options. Real wealth in today's economy is created through investing, not earning, and everyday employees should be able to share in the upside when their company's stock price rises. Here, too, there is a large body of research demonstrating that profit-sharing plans improve worker morale and boost productivity, leading to even stronger companies.

Upskill Workers

Companies should also take a more active role in making sure their workers are well prepared to meet the demands of a rapidly changing technological landscape. Had Welch invested in his workers, giving them new skills and advanced training, he may well have been able to put them to productive use, rather than firing them while pursuing cheap labor overseas. Likewise, Amazon and other mass employers would do well to create new pathways for employees, giving them the chance to learn more valuable skills, assume more senior roles, and see their compensation increase over time. Beyond creating a more dynamic workforce that is prepared to adapt to market changes and technological advancements, upskilling leaves workers better prepared in the event that they move on from their employer, or if layoffs are necessary.

Put Workers on Boards

If companies are serious about serving stakeholders beyond their Wall Street investors, they can codify those commitments by including a broader range of perspectives—including those of workers—on their boards. This has happened in the past, albeit briefly. In the 1970s Chrysler welcomed onto its board the head of its biggest union, the United Auto Workers, who promptly voted against an enormous pay package for CEO Lee Iacocca.

Chrysler's experiment didn't last. But today worker representation on boards, an arrangement known as "co-determination," is thriving in Europe. In Germany, for example, workers are entitled to elect half the members of supervisory boards—the equivalent of U.S. boards. German workers also get to select representatives for so-called work councils, which deal with the nitty-gritty of running a large workforce, such as overtime and layoffs. The idea is gaining traction in the United States. At several major companies, including Microsoft and Walmart, minority shareholders have proposed giving workers spots on corporate boards. Democratic lawmakers have gone further, introducing legislation that would grant workers the right to elect 40 percent of board seats at their companies. These are first steps in a journey that could give employees a deserved seat at the boardroom table.

Think Long Term

The relentless pressure created by quarterly earnings reports is impossible for most public companies to ignore. It warps executive behavior in the worst way, incentivizing short-term decision-making and disincentivizing investments that will create value years down the road. But time and again, we have seen that the corporations that create the most wealth in the long run are those that develop the capacity to think beyond the next ninety days.

One way companies can to do this is by explicitly rejecting the tyranny of the markets, as Paul Polman did at Unilever, and as some big tech companies have done with dual-class share structures and a patient approach that sometimes results in years of meager profits.

Companies should also embrace a more judicious approach to mergers and acquisitions, looking for takeover targets that they can grow and expand, rather than strip for parts and mine for cash. This won't just make for more disciplined decision-making, it would be a more prudent use of capital. In the twenty years after Welch retired, GE paid its financial advisers—the investment banks and white-shoe law firms that encourage it to do deals—a whopping $7.2 billion in fees, money that could have been put to good use elsewhere.

Magnanimous CEOs will only get us so far, however. Forty years of Welchism has made it clear that the pressures of the markets, the allure of enormous executive compensation packages, and a half century of bad habits are too powerful for most CEOs to resist. Instead of simply hoping and wishing that executives will change their ways, achieving the kinds of systemic reforms necessary for the creation of a truly equitable economy will require strong actions from policy-makers in Washington. Here's how they can start.

Raise the Minimum Wage

As we've seen over the past half century, companies can't be counted on to pay their workers fair wages, let alone ones that keep up with inflation. For that reason, the federal government must step in and raise the minimum wage, which would be more than three times its current rate if it had kept pace with inflation over the past half century. It's a simple step that is long overdue and would make an immediate impact in the lives of millions.

Raise Taxes

Many wealthy Americans enjoy lower tax rates than their working-class neighbors, and many corporations and individuals exploit loopholes to pay virtually no taxes at all. While tax reform is arduous and complex, it's a necessary corrective after decades when conservative economic policies have whittled down the tax base, leaving federal and local governments underfunded, and thereby contributing to a cascade of self-reinforcing social ills, from poor public education to an unskilled labor pool to families with insufficient savings to take care of their basic needs in a medical emergency.

Broadly, we should impose higher taxes on capital gains—things like real estate transactions and stock sales—and lower taxes on labor or earned wages. A wealth tax on the very richest Americans could also be effective. By one estimate, an annual 2 percent levy on those with a net worth between $50 million and $1 billion, and a 6 percent tax on net worth exceeding $1 billion, would raise about $3.7 trillion over ten years.

Corporate taxes should also go up, but not all of them. Payroll taxes—which can serve as a perverse disincentive for companies to hire additional workers—should be eased, while taxes on profits—including those recorded overseas—should go up. And critically, return-of-capital programs—namely buybacks and dividends—should be more stringently taxed.

Finally, municipalities should stop luring companies to invest in their cities with tax breaks. This would have avoided, for example, Boeing's defection from Seattle to Chicago, and GE's own move, in 2016, from Fairfield, Connecticut, to Boston, which was sweetened with $87 million in tax breaks. Such incentives rarely deliver the promised value for local governments, as the GE move made clear. Just three years after moving to Boston and promising to plow money into a new corporate headquarters that would employ 800 executives, GE scrapped its plans for a new twelve-story building on the waterfront, sold the land, and said it would only be employing 250 people in Boston, after all.

Strengthen Antitrust Policies

While it's too late to prevent many of the mergers that have consolidated industries from telecommunications to airlines to food, the promise of stricter antitrust action may help prevent future deals that further concentrate market share and ultimately create a less dynamic economy. By taking a longer-term view when considering the consequences of market concentration, antitrust regulators will have a better chance at intervening in potentially harmful deals. And by thinking more broadly about the ways in which consumers are harmed—considering the potential for lost jobs and lower wages, instead of just sticker prices, for example—regulators are likely to have a broader view of which deals merit their attention.

Cap Executive Compensation

The SEC has begun requiring companies to disclose the ratio between their CEO and the median worker salary at their company. A good next step would be mandating that executive pay packages not exceed a certain threshold. There is no conceivable reason why a CEO should make 300, or 1,000 times what an average worker makes in a year. Such caps on executive pay would not prevent company founders from growing wealthy if they are able to retain equity in a company as it grows more valuable, but they would put an end to some of the most egregious drivers of income inequality—and ultimately require that CEOs get paid less, or that workers get paid more.

These polices aren't just ethical and just, they're also good for business. Study after study shows that when wages are higher, the economy is stronger for all; that when the government is well funded, democracy thrives; that when companies exist in a dynamic, competitive landscape, jobs are more abundant and consumers benefit; and that when wealth is shared with workers instead of hoarded by executives, everyone wins. Anecdotal evidence abounds as well. Whether it was Paul Polman at Unilever eschewing quarterly earnings targets and investing for the long term, or Dan Schulman at PayPal doubling down on his employees' financial well-being, it is increasingly clear that when big companies take good care of all stakeholders, they thrive. "If you want to maximize your shareholder return, it leads you automatically to a more responsible ESG, multi-stakeholder type business model," Polman said, referring to the environmental, social, and governance movement that is trying to make corporations better actors. "That's what the numbers keep telling us, and that's also where the fiduciary duty is starting to move to."

"Jack set the path"

Jack Welch died on March 1, 2020. His funeral was held in St. Patrick's Cathedral in New York. Ken Langone, the Home Depot founder and former GE director was there. So was Larry "the Knife" Bossidy, the former GE executive who went on to run AlliedSignal and Honeywell. Matt Lauer, the former NBC host who had interviewed Welch on 9/11, turned up. Barry Diller, the billionaire media mogul, was an honorary pallbearer, as was Patriots coach Bill Belichick.

The grief was real. Welch was loved by many, and maintained extensive networks of friends and associates until his final days. Suzy offered a heartfelt lament for her husband, calling attention to his vast influence and their many endeavors. "More than anything else—leader, business icon, management genius—more than those things, although they are all true too—Jack was a lifeforce made of love," she said in a statement.

David Zaslav, the Discovery Communications CEO who orchestrated the megadeal with AT&T to create his own empire, remembered Welch as an almost godlike figure. "Jack set the path. He saw the whole world. He was above the whole world," Zaslav said. "What he created at GE became the way companies now operate."

Jamie Dimon, the chairman and CEO of JPMorgan, and one of the most enduring and respected business leaders of his generation, portrayed Welch as a paragon of morality. "He stood tall and always did the right thing for his company and his country," Dimon said. "He really set the standard as a CEO, not just in his performance running the company and as a legendary leader, but in his deep integrity, big heart and strategic vision."

None of the tributes paused to consider the thousands who lost their jobs on Welch's watch. There was no mention of the downsizing, the bad deals, or the manipulated earnings. By glossing over the unsavory parts of his legacy, his allies helped perpetuate the myth of his sainthood. One admirer, however, wouldn't let the world forget who Welch really was. Upon learning of his death, President Trump tweeted a tribute to his old friend and collaborator. Trump missed the mark, however, invoking as a badge of honor the nickname that Welch had always despised. "There was no corporate leader like 'Neutron' Jack," Trump tweeted. "He was my friend and supporter. We made wonderful deals together."

The funeral, held just as the Covid-19 pandemic was taking hold in the United States, was the last time such a collection of business luminaries would gather for more than a year. Within a matter of weeks, much of the global economy ground to a halt. Travel all but stopped. Restaurants were shuttered. Offices emptied out. Factories closed. Global supply chains sputtered. The stock market plunged and the mass layoffs began. Unemployment spiked to 15 percent in the United States. The ripple effects were endless.

The pandemic provided a test case for companies that had boasted about stakeholder values and shared sacrifice, giving them an opportunity to recapture the spirit of the Golden Age of Capitalism and make good on the recently updated commitments of the Business Roundtable. Few rose to the challenge. Rather, within weeks of Covid taking hold, it became clear that in the face of a once-in-a-lifetime crisis, most corporations would continue putting shareholders and executives first. Despite all the good intentions and talk of stakeholders, despite the promise of more regulation and even some good actors like Polman and Schulman, little had changed. Welch had died, but Welchism lived on.

At company after company, the profits kept flowing, but workers were left behind. Berkshire Hathaway, the diversified conglomerate run by Warren Buffett, raked in $42.5 billion in profits in 2020. During this same time, Berkshire Hathaway laid off 13,000 employees, many of them factory workers. It didn't matter that Buffett's conglomerate was awash in cash, or that workers who lost their incomes and health insurance in the middle of a pandemic faced existential risks to their health and livelihoods. Berkshire Hathaway evidently determined that the downsizing was the most rational move in an economy where the pursuit of shareholder value takes precedence over everything else.

Amazon, meanwhile, went on a hiring spree during the pandemic. With much of the world stuck at home, online shopping was booming, and Amazon brought on more than 100,000 workers to meet the surging demand. Amazon's stock price practically doubled in 2020, and founder Jeff Bezos became the first person in history to be worth $200 billion, using his money, in part, to pursue his dream of colonizing Mars via a base on the moon. On a single day, his net worth increased by $13 billion. But Amazon, one of the world's most valuable companies, would not be sharing much of its record profits with its new "team members." The starting salary for most of those entry-level jobs was $15 an hour, a figure that, while higher than the federal minimum wage, was not enough to live comfortably on in most American cities. As Bezos was accumulating wealth at a rate of $13.4 million an hour, his newest employees were joining a company that has long been accused of mistreating workers, skimping on benefits, and suppressing organized labor.

Even white-collar workers were in jeopardy during the pandemic. Many of the technology companies that benefited from the rise of remote work also felt the need to downsize at a time of record unemployment, casting millions of people into a historically bad job market. Microsoft, Oracle, Comcast, and AT&T all enjoyed rapid rises in their sales, profits, and stock prices during the pandemic, and all of them laid off office workers in 2020. Sometimes, the layoffs came after the CEOs publicly vowed not to let anyone go amidst the crisis. And often, the same CEOs who authorized those layoffs were rewarded with pay days of $20 million and more.

At Norwegian Cruise Line, which lost $4 billion during the first year of the pandemic and furloughed 20 percent of its staff, the CEO, Frank Del Rio, got $36.4 million in 2020. At Hilton, which laid off thousands of workers and lost nearly $1 billion, the CEO, Chris Nassetta, got $55.9 million. Overall, companies in the S&P 500 stock index paid their chief executives an average of 264 times as much as median employees during the first year of the pandemic. Indeed, CEO pay was actually up 16 percent in 2020, while average worker compensation rose less than 2 percent. One study showed that companies that signed the Business Roundtable statement were actually more likely to announce layoffs in the first months of the pandemic than companies that didn't sign the statement, and that the companies that pledged to serve all stakeholders actually distributed more of their profits to shareholders than those who didn't publicly pledge to look out for the common good. That is, there was inverse correlation between virtue signaling and actual virtuousness.

"Since the pandemic's inception," the study said, the Business Roundtable statement "has failed to deliver fundamental shifts in corporate purpose in a moment of grave crisis when enlightened purpose should be paramount." Marriott International, one of the statement's signatories, furloughed most of its American workers, even as it continued to pay a dividend and raised executive pay. Macy's, another Business Roundtable company, furloughed most of its workers while continuing its dividend payments. As the litany of hollow corporate commitments piled up, Senator Elizabeth Warren sent a letter to the leaders of the Business Roundtable excoriating them for their hypocrisy, her office issuing a press release that minced no words, "Business Roundtable: Your 2019 Commitment to 'Promote an Economy that Serves all Americans' Was an Empty Publicity Stunt."

Years of spending on buybacks and dividends had left many companies unprepared for a sharp downturn. Boeing, which was still trying to recover from the 737 Max disaster, had to lay off 30,000 employees, shutter production lines, and take a $12 billion loss. (It still managed to pay Calhoun, the CEO, $21.1 million.) The major airlines, which together had spent billions on buybacks in the years preceding the pandemic, had inadequate cash reserves when a crisis hit. As a result, they needed a $50 billion bailout from Washington to survive.

At GE, the pandemic only spelled more trouble. John Flannery had been fired a year before Covid hit, and Larry Culp had taken over, the third CEO in as many years. But while Culp arrived with a reputation as a turnaround artist and the full confidence of the board, there was little indication that he had a viable plan, and he was initially unable to reverse the slide in GE's stock. In his first full year as CEO, shares fell another 8 percent. With the pandemic, demand for jet engines, one of the company's last lucrative divisions, disappeared as air travel came to a standstill. Power plant sales shriveled up, too. Overall, GE's revenues fell sharply. Hoping to preserve cash, GE turned to layoffs, firing tens of thousands of workers across every part of the company. In the three years after Immelt was ousted, GE had shed some 140,000 jobs, or nearly 45 percent of its workforce. It was the Neutron Jack years all over again, with the GE workforce being gutted. Despite these challenges, the board restructured Culp's contract with a gargantuan new pay package. Thanks to a new multiyear contract and what the board called a "Leadership Performance Share Award," he was in line to receive GE stock that could be worth as much as $233 million.

As GE struggled to survive the pandemic, it was also forced to confront unsavory episodes from its past. In 2019, GE finally agreed to settle with the Justice Department for its dealings during the subprime mortgage crisis and pay a fine of $1.5 billion. "We are pleased to put this matter behind us," the company said in a statement. A decade had passed, and the bad loans issued by WMC, which were then bundled into mortgage-backed securities that poisoned the entire financial system, were still haunting the company.

Then in December of 2020, the SEC fined GE $200 million for misleading investors about the source of profits in its power business in 2016 and 2017, and for misleading investors about the riskiness of GE Capital from 2015 to 2017. It was classic earnings manipulation, and it had continued long after Welch's departure and deep into Immelt's tenure. "Investors are entitled to an accurate picture of a company's material operating results," said Stephanie Avakian, director of the SEC's enforcement division. "GE's repeated disclosure failures across multiple businesses materially misled investors about how it was generating reported earnings and cash growth as well as latent risks in its insurance business." GE did not admit or deny culpability, stating only that "no corrections or revisions to our financial statements are required."

Culp finally caught a few breaks a year into the pandemic. He sold GE's aircraft leasing business—the last vestiges of GE Capital, in a move as symbolic as it was strategic. With the disposal, GE Capital was completely disbanded at last. "Today marks GE's transformation to a more focused, simpler, and stronger industrial company," Culp said on the day of the deal. Some four decades after Welch set his sights far beyond GE's traditional manufacturing business, the company had come full circle. All of Welch's empire building had amounted to little in the end.

As the economy bounced back, GE's battered businesses began to recover, and investors finally saw the glimmer of what GE had once been so many decades ago: a reliable manufacturer of indispensable industrial products. But almost as soon as Culp had GE back on solid ground, he pulled one last Welchian move. In the waning days of 2021, GE finally announced that it would break itself up, once and for all. The days of the conglomerate were over. Culp would spin off the power division and the health care division as new public companies, leaving General Electric—a company that practically invented the modern American economy as we know it—as nothing more than a supplier of airplane engines.

It was a definitive repudiation of Welch's vision. The GE that he had built into the most valuable company on earth decades before— with its vast array of industrial divisions, its black box financial unit, and its imperialistic ambitions—no longer had a place among the great American companies. Instead, fittingly, it was being taken apart piece by piece, as executives and investment bankers tried to figure out how to make the most of what was left of the house that Jack built.

From his home office in South Carolina, Jeff Immelt looked on, smarting at what he saw as his run of historic bad luck. Immelt had enjoyed sixteen years as one of the most powerful CEOs in the world, running GE like a small nation-state and earning money like an oligarch. His end, when it came, was ignominious. GE was in tatters, his reputation was damaged, his relations with Welch were at a low. In the few years since his ousting, he had tried to remain relevant, attempting to fashion himself as an elder statesman in Silicon Valley. He made a public push to become the new CEO of Uber after founder Travis Kalanick was ousted following a series of scandals. He joined the faculty at the Stanford Graduate School of Business, where he taught a class about how he'd led GE through so many crises. He joined a venture capital firm, offering advice to entrepreneurs trying to get their companies off the ground. And early in 2021, he published a book, *Hot Seat*.

Shortly before the book was published, I spoke with Immelt for two hours, reviewing his tenure at GE, how he viewed the Welch legacy, and what he was up to then. He enjoyed counseling start-ups, and said he was able to give young executives a visceral sense of what it is like to struggle. "I'm the guy in the boardroom who knows what really shitty days look like," he said. "For entrepreneurs, it's lonely. So having somebody that isn't sitting there looking at a spreadsheet, but can kind of just say, 'Hey, I know how you're feeling. Here's two or three things I'd be thinking about.'—it turns out that that's pretty valuable."

Immelt was still stewing about all those shitty days. He acknowledged that under Welch, GE effectively stopped innovating. "Jack didn't engender a profound respect for technology, a profound respect for engineers," he said. And he conceded that the campaign against loyalty had eroded the middle class, breaking the social contract between employer and worker. "CEOs like me grew up in the era of wage arbitrage, where we felt like we could put jobs anywhere we wanted to and have people still love us," Immelt said. "Those days are long over."

He tried to make the case that he was a champion of bringing jobs back from Mexico to the United States, and indeed, he did some of that on his watch at GE. But by and large, Immelt, like Welch, treated labor like a cost, not an asset, and the results were predictable. "Over time, I became cognizant that there was a reason why American society didn't trust business," he said. "And it had a lot to do with wage arbitrage, outsourcing—things that really had a negative impact on the high-end industrial worker that was so essential. In a town like Erie, Pennsylvania, people don't go from working at GE, making $36 an hour, to working at factory X making $30 an hour. They go from earning $36 an hour to earning $15 an hour. And that gap is a hugely negative impact. I get that."

As for GE's relentless earnings management, Immelt owned the fact that it was an addiction he'd had a hard time breaking. "The incredible strategic vein that Jack hit in the late '80s and through most of the '90s was that you could take industrial cash flow, lever it 8 to 1, and build a financial services business whose earnings were valued like a high-tech industrial company," he said. "And that became so seductive to the company. The accounting stuff and pressure, I don't really want to go there. But I do think that strategic thing just became really seductive over that period of time. No question about it."

Immelt knew he had a chance to reset GE after 9/11, and regretted not acting with a sense of urgency. "I thought I had the luxury of time," he admitted. "I thought that we could do this a little bit at a time, and do it over a period of five or eight years." But again, he said, the pressure to continue that unbeaten run of earnings was impossible to resist. "You're with the most admired company, with the most admired team, right after a crisis like 9/11," he said. "Standing up and saying, 'Hey, the place is broken'—I had no foundation for that." And so he did just the opposite, allowing GE Capital to grow even larger and more unwieldy, letting outsourcing and offshoring continue apace, pursuing more ill-fated mergers and acquisitions, and spending more than ever on buybacks and dividends.

Overall, however, Immelt was defiant. He believed he had been doomed to failure by the impossibly high expectations set by Welch. He trumpeted his accomplishments and dismissed the notion that he had overpaid for deals or failed to hear bad news. He felt terrible that GE stock had fallen so precipitously, wiping out the investments of so many millions of retirees and pensioners. And he acknowledged that the Welch playbook was finally past its expiration date. "If you're a company today and you're studying management stuff that worked in the '90s, you're in the wrong neighborhood," he said. "Something bad is about to happen."

For the half century after the Great Depression, capitalism in America was a well-oiled machine that produced economic growth for many corporations, many families, Wall Street firms, and the nation as a whole. Technological breakthroughs—including many engineered by GE—took us to the moon, modernized our lives, and turbocharged the economy. Thousands of companies became major employers, and the profits they generated were distributed widely—to investors, yes, but also to workers and the IRS, and back into the company in the form of capital expenditures and R&D. It was working well right up until 1981, when Jack Welch broke it.

Welch wasn't the only one responsible, of course. Milton Friedman and other free market thinkers laid the groundwork for his revolution. Corporate raiders figured out how to leverage small ownership stakes to effect dramatic changes, precipitating waves of layoffs and mergers. Other CEOs, including Roberto Goizueta at Coca-Cola, Lee Iacocca at Chrysler, and Lou Gerstner at IBM, all had a hand in changing what was deemed acceptable behavior by big business. And Welch's many acolytes took his most brutal techniques and ran with them.

Yet more than anyone else, it was Welch himself who created the schism between the Golden Age of Capitalism and the unequal, unsustainable era of shareholder primacy in which we now live. He was the first CEO to take a healthy company and treat it like a turnaround job, preemptively laying off tens of thousands of workers and kick-starting the era of mass downsizing, outsourcing, and offshoring. He was the first to use dealmaking to expand the business into any industry possible, setting in motion decades of consolidation that concentrated industries and made the economy less dynamic. He was the first who brought to his job a singular focus on quarterly earnings, and employed financialization, earnings smoothing, buybacks, and everything else in his power to see that GE's stock price continued to rise.

For all this, Welch was revered. During his two decades leading GE, he set the standard against which all other CEOs were measured. With his brutal tactics endowing him with a vast personal fortune, and the legendary GE company conferring the whole enterprise with unassailable credibility, Welch redefined what it meant to be a successful CEO. Achievement was measured not by jobs created, but by jobs cut. Value creation was measured not over the course of years, but in discrete, predictable ninety-day cycles. The quantity of a company's profits became more important than the quality of its products. Welch set the bar against which other CEOs were measured soon after he took over, and even now, with stakeholder capitalism on the rise, many executives continue to model his behavior. Years after his death, Welch still looms over the corporate world as the Manager of the Century, living rent-free in the minds of CEOs around the world.

Friedrich Hayek, one of the chief progenitors of the intellectual revolution that laid the groundwork for Welchism, noted that new ideas usually require "a generation or even more" to gain traction. Hayek, speaking years before Welch would make real what he could only imagine at the time, went on to acknowledge the hopelessness one can feel at the beginning of an ambitious project, when "our present thinking seems too powerless to influence events." It can be easy to feel the same way now, when the hegemony of Welch and all he stood for still seems so absolute. With so many companies and so much of the economy yet under his spell, it can seem like we are all still living in the world Welch created, too. Many of our biggest companies still prioritize short-term gains, devalue workers, fudge the numbers, and heap unjustifiable rewards upon CEOs. The products and services we consume help perpetuate an economic system that continues to distribute wealth in deeply inequitable ways. Executives that make a show of doing the right thing often turn out to be greenwashing, and signs of durable, systemic change are few and far between.

Yet history has shown us that transformation is possible. The highly unequal Gilded Age gave way to the Golden Age of Capitalism, and a similar transition is within reach today. For the first time in decades, there is real reason for hope. The negative externalities of the Jack Welch way of doing business are now simply too glaring to ignore, the consequences of unfettered profit maximization take too great a toll on the common good. Decades of data have made it clear that short-termism and shareholder primacy simply don't work. In the long run, companies that pursue downsizing, dealmaking, and financialization run themselves into the ground. Executives are beginning to understand that history may not judge them by their quarterly performance, but by their broader impact on society.

Closing the book on Welchism will require more than good-hearted CEOs and selfless policymakers. If we are to stop being a society that rewards job destroyers and punishes the unemployed, we will need to renounce the toxic myths that allowed our current system to become so horribly imbalanced in the first place. There is no law that dictates corporations must maximize shareholder value, and after a half century fever dream, the public, policymakers, and even some CEOs seem to be accepting as much. We will need to articulate a new set of shared goals designed to promote broad economic prosperity, not widespread inequality. Stakeholder capitalism is a useful first step, but will only matter if the companies making bold pledges follow through with equally bold actions.

To create a new economy we will need a new framework for success. This will require celebrating leaders who prioritize long-term growth over short-term gains, and putting an end, once and for all, to the bankrupt practice of making men like Welch our heroes. We will need to raise pay, improve benefits, and share wealth with our workers. And perhaps most difficult of all, we will need to uproot the legacy of a tough kid from the Boston suburbs who rose to become the most powerful CEO in the world. These efforts will not be easy. But if successful, they have the potential to create something with truly enduring value: a world beyond Welchism.

AFTERWORD

October 22, 2022

David Gelles

Not long after I turned in the final draft of this book, in early 2022, something strange began happening to the American economy. For decades, workers had been losing ground, watching their relative pay decline even as productivity soared. As corporate profits ballooned, buybacks rained down on shareholders, and executives took home ever-larger pay packages thanks to Welchism, the men and women toiling in factories and stores and restaurants saw their fortunes steadily decline.

Then, as the world shuddered back to life after a year of pandemic-induced shock, workers suddenly had momentum. With so many Americans still on the sidelines—some were taking care of children or loved ones, some were living off generous federal stimulus—there suddenly weren't enough workers. The unemployment rate, which had spiked to nearly 16 percent in April 2020, snapped back to below 4 percent. Hardly a year after the darkest days of Covid, companies couldn't hire fast enough. And with employers competing with one another for labor, they started paying more. Restaurant workers got raises. Retail associates got bonuses. Wages were up across the board. Companies seemed to recall that their workers were an asset— something worth investing in—not just a cost to be minimized.

There were other signs that the economy was regaining some of its pre-Welch robustness, too. The labor movement was enjoying a renaissance. At companies including Starbucks, Amazon, and Trader Joe's, workers were joining unions. And after decades of relentless offshoring, factory jobs came back to the United States in droves, rebounding to levels higher even than before the pandemic. Manufacturing—the kind of work that Welch himself dismissed as "making things . . . pounding and grinding it out to make a nickel"— was back in vogue. Altogether, it seemed that the worst effects of Welchism were subsiding, and perhaps corporate America was prepared to make good on some of that idealistic stakeholder capitalism rhetoric as it moved past Covid.

If only. Within months, the stock market went topsy-turvy yet again. First, Russia invaded Ukraine, roiling global markets. Then, American investors got spooked by rising inflation. The result was predictable: big companies, worried about their stock price, looked for ways to boost short-term earnings, leading to new rounds of mass layoffs. Enormously profitable companies, including tech behemoths like Microsoft and Meta, unleashed waves of downsizing reminiscent of the Neutron Jack years. Elon Musk said he had a "super bad feeling" about the economy and said he would cut 10 percent of Tesla's salaried employees, evoking the specter of Welchian stack ranking. Musk then bought Twitter for $44 billion, loaded up with debt, and fired half its workforce in a bid to slash costs, eliciting a Bloomberg headline that read: "Neutron Elon: Why Twitter's Boss Is More Like Jack Welch Than You Think." Little, it seemed, had really changed. While companies might appear to be growing more generous with their workers in the best of times, most resorted to their usual defensive postures at the first sign of trouble. It was all further confirmation that undoing Jack Welch's legacy would be a lengthy project.

This book tells what is essentially an eighty-year story—beginning with the postwar boom, progressing through the Golden Age of Capitalism, and slouching through the stagflation of the 1970s before Welch shows up. It then chronicles his twenty years as CEO of GE, and the more than two decades since he retired, as his way of doing business became the status quo for the corporate world. The rise of this insidious ideology took decades, and that time frame should be instructive as we think about unwinding Welch's influence.

The work to create a new narrative for the American economy—if that is even possible—will be similarly multigenerational. Just as the intellectual underpinnings for shareholder primacy percolated for more than a decade before Welch seized on them and put them into action, all the recent talk of stakeholder capitalism may be just that—talk—for a long time to come. And even if more big companies do start to serve the best interests of all their constituents, rather than just investors, I suspect it will be harder to walk away from the profits-first mentality than it was to embrace it in the first place. After all, the forces that conspire to perpetuate Welchism are deeply entrenched and enormously powerful. Expectations for short-term profits, investors who only care about their own returns, and executives who often stand to gain by shirking their own workers make the prospect of durable change elusive at best.

But there is reason for hope. In addition to wage gains for American workers and the resurgence of the labor movement, we can discern other signs that change is arriving on the margins. When Democrats muscled through their major climate change legislation in the summer of 2022, known as the Inflation Reduction Act, they included in it a 1 percent tax on stock buybacks, one of the very proposals I called for in the last chapter of this book. A few months after that, Yvon Chouinard, the founder of Patagonia, announced he was giving away his company in an act of stunning selflessness and estate-planning ingenuity. Rather than sell Patagonia or take it public or leave it to his children, Chouinard and his family donated all the shares of the company to a set of newly established trusts and nonprofit organizations that would ensure it gave away all its profits to fight the climate crisis and preserve the environment. It was a reminder that businesses can in fact do well by doing good, and a revolutionary act of philanthropy—proof positive that there was another way for billionaires to manage their fortunes.

More than any developments in the news, what truly gave me hope that the days of Welchism might finally be ending was the response to this book. People were eager to have a conversation about what was wrong with our economy, who was responsible for the carnage, and how to fix it. And it wasn't just critics of capitalism who wanted to take part. I was asked to speak about the book at major corporate law firms that profit from relentless dealmaking, at public relations firms that earn their coin burnishing the reputations of amoral CEOs, at private equity firms lousy with GE alumni, and at top business schools where Welch is still seen as a hero—including at the Stanford Graduate School of Business, where I strolled past Jeff Immelt's empty office.

To be sure, some Welch loyalists disputed my account of the man they still believed to be the Manager of the Century, arguing that he was a model executive who had done much good for the business world. Notably, not long after the book was published, Immelt took to LinkedIn with a blog post titled "Jack Was Pretty Damn Good." But as I quickly pointed out in my response, Immelt himself had been one of Welch's harshest critics as GE fell apart. Beyond that, the tangible impacts of Welchism—as measured by everything from worker wages to mergers and acquisitions, to corporate concentration, to outsourcing and offshoring, to executive compensation—are indisputable at this point.

Yet even as so many sought a future beyond Welch, dispiriting reminders of his enduring influence were easy to find, starting with a pair of his protégés who still used his playbook. At Warner Bros. Discovery, David Zaslav instituted sweeping layoffs as he aimed to cut costs and improve profitability. At Boeing, Dave Calhoun remained CEO even after the company accepted sole responsibility for the 737 Max crashes, and its struggles continued. And, in an ironic coda at the end of 2022, GE announced it was selling Crotonville, the management training center that Welch turned into a temple to himself and an incubator for his disciples.

No longer would aspiring CEOs learn the cold-eyed tactics of profit maximization in the Pit, the amphitheater named after the North Salem playground where Welch grew up. No longer would the GE CEO have his own in-house business school where he could indoctrinate a new generation of corporate leaders with the Welchian dogma that companies should maximize profits at all costs. Instead, fittingly, Crotonville would be sold to the highest bidder, and a new owner would be given the opportunity to take one of Welch's most treasured possessions and craft a new narrative.

ACKNOWLEDGMENTS

There is one name on the spine of this book, but it required a devoted and talented ensemble to bring *The Man Who Broke Capitalism* to life. My wife, Alison, is my most dedicated supporter and friend, providing me with the love, encouragement, patience, and space I needed to do this work during years turned upside down by a pandemic. Thank you, hon. Our children, Franny and Clark, offered me necessary perspective and comedic relief, never letting me forget what is most important in life. My parents are both writers, and I'm proud to follow in their footsteps. I'm especially grateful to my dad, George Gelles, whose invaluable copy edits on a late draft of this manuscript made this a better book, and who has pushed me to become a sharper reader and writer for decades now. My mom, Bonnie Pitman, shows each day what it means to live with purpose and joy.

I'm fortunate to work with some of the best in the book business. My editor, Eamon Dolan, publishes books that change people's minds, and is supported by an ace team of assistants, copy editors, lawyers, and publicists at Simon & Schuster. My agent, Binky Urban, is a national treasure, and I'm lucky to work with her. Natalie Kitroeff, Scott Berinato, and Anand Giridharadas were instrumental in setting this project in motion. And many of my colleagues at the *New York Times* lent their support for this project along the way—especially Ellen Pollock and Rebecca Blumenstein.

I offer thanks to the many reporters who diligently covered the rise and fall of GE, Welch, and his acolytes for many decades before I came to the story. Over the years, writers like Geoff Colvin and Stratford Sherman at *Fortune* provided invaluable snapshots of Welch and GE in their prime. Thomas F. O'Boyle's *At Any Cost* was an early and comprehensive look at Welch's misdeeds. And most recently, *Lights Out* by Tedd Mann and Thomas Gryta was an excellent chronicle of Immelt's years at the company. This book wouldn't have been possible without their efforts.

Finally, a thanks to the many sources—from CEOs, to academics, to former factory workers—who helped shape my thinking about this book, where business leadership has gone awry over the years, and what a more just economy might look like.

NOTES

Introduction

5   *GE made nearly 1,000 acquisitions*: Matt Murray, "Why Jack Welch's Leadership Matters to Businesses World-Wide," *Wall Street Journal*, September 5, 2001, https://www.wsj.com/articles/why-jack-welchs-leadership-matters-to-businesses-world-wide-11583165675.

7   *landing him on Forbes's list*. "Welch Walks Away From Perks," *Forbes*, September 16, 2002, https://www.forbes.com/2002/09/16/0917welch.html.

7   *"Manager of the Century"*: Geoff Colvin, "The Ultimate Manager," *Fortune*, November 22, 1999, https://archive.fortune.com/magazines/fortune/fortune_archive/1999/11/22/269126/index.htm.

10   *American manufacturing jobs peaked*: Katelynn Harris, "Forty years of falling manufacturing employment," U.S. Bureau of Labor Statistics, November 2020, https://www.bls.gov/opub/btn/volume-9/forty-years-of-falling-manufacturing-employment.htm.

10   *American companies spent less than $50 billion*: Liyu Zeng, "Examining Share Repurchasing and the S&P Buyback Indices in the U.S. Market," S&P Dow Jones Indices, April 2016.

11   *In 1980 the average pay*: Lawrence Mishel and Julia Wolfe, "CEO compensation has grown 940% since 1978," Economic Policy Institute, August 14, 2019, https://www.epi.org/publication/ceo-compensation-2018/.

Chapter One: The Most Valuable Company in the World

17   *"Why would we want anything more?"*: Evan Osnos, "How Greenwich Republicans Learned to Love Trump," *New Yorker*, May 3, 2020, https://www.newyorker.com/magazine/2020/05/11/how-greenwich-republicans-learned-to-love-trump.

18 *"replaced a legend with a live wire"*: John R. Emshwiller, "Reginald Jones Plans April 1 Retirement from GE; John Welch Will Succeed Him," *Wall Street Journal*, December 22, 1980.

19 *"The process was like nothing"*: Jack Welch, John A. Byrne, *Jack: Straight from the Gut.* (New York, Warner Books, 2001), 139.

19 *"U.S. business today finds itself"*: Jack Welch and Reginald Jones, *General Electric Annual Report* (Fairfield, Conn., 1980), 4.

19 *half of GE's earnings*: Noel M. Tichy, Stratford Sherman, *Control Your Destiny or Someone Else Will*, (New York: HarperCollins, 1994), 35.

19 *"One of the narratives"*: Louis Hyman, in discussion with the author, 2020.

20 *reported an annual profit*: "'80 G.E. Profits Rose 7%, Westinghouse's 21.7%," *Washington Post*, January 23, 1981.

20 *"What we have to sell"*: Welch, Byrne, *Jack: Straight from the Gut*, 84.

20 *"I'm not sure he knew"*: Welch, Byrne, *Jack: Straight from the Gut*, xiii.

21 *"Jack, I give you"*: Ranjay Gulati, in discussion with the author, 2020.

23 *"devise ways and means"*: Osnos, "Why would we want anything more?"

23 *In 1929, Forbes observed*: B. C. Forbes, "The Latest Perk," *Forbes*, June 1, 1929.

23 *"in the balanced best interests"*: General Electric Annual Report, (Fairfield, Conn., 1953).

23 *"Maximizing employment security"*: Steven Greenhouse, *The Big Squeeze: Tough Times for the American Worker* (New York: Alfred A. Knopf, 2008), 78.

25 *From 1948 to 1979*: Christopher Ingraham, "The race for shareholder profits has left workers in the dust, according to new research," *Washington Post*, February 25, 2019, https://www.washingtonpost.com/us-policy/2019/02/25/race-shareholder-profits-has-left-workers-dust-according-new-research/.

26 *"business tries to strike"*: Kurt Andersen, *Evil Geniuses: The Unmaking of America* (New York: Random House Publishing Group, 2020), 52. http://citeseerx.ist.psu.edu/viewdoc/download?doi=10.1.1.458.458&rep=rep1&type=pdf#page=19.

27 *"with my nose pressed up"*: Welch, Byrne, *Jack: Straight from the Gut*, 11.

27 *"I wonder why my mother didn't"*: Christopher M. Byron, *Testosterone Inc: Tales of CEOs Gone Wild* (Hoboken: John Wiley & Sons, 2004), 6.

27 *"He hated losing"*: Joseph L. Bower and Jay Dial, "Jack Welch: General Electric's Revolutionary," *Harvard Business School Case*, (October 1993), 3.

27 *"Between the stutter and being smaller"*: Nicholas Heymann, in discussion with the author, 2021.

28 *"Someone told me they loved me"*: Ken Auletta, *Three Blind Mice: How the TV Networks Lost Their Way* (New York: Random House, 1991), 97.

31 *"What the fuck"*: Byron, *Testosterone Inc.*, 111.

32 *"Everybody was shocked"*: Ken Langone, in discussion with the author, 2020.

35 *"What the hell difference"*: Tichy, Sherman, *Control Your Destiny or Someone Else Will*, 72.

38 *"They said essentially you're"*: Roger Martin, in discussion with the author, 2021.

39 *"Jack sort of invented it"*: Gary Sheffer, in discussion with the author, 2021.

40 *"A CEO's primary social responsibility"*: Welch, Byrne, *Jack: Straight from the Gut*, 382.

Chapter Two: Neutron Jack

41 *"We all came to the party"*: Thomas C. Hayes, "G.E. Names Welch, 45, Chairman," *New York Times*, December 20, 1980, https://timesmachine.nytimes.com//1980/12/20/111325190.pdf.

42 *"Civility was no longer"*: Scott Malone, "Author says Welch's tough talk strengthened GE," Reuters, January 25, 2008, https://www.reuters.com/article/us-books-welch-idUSN2447486620080126.

43 *"inescapable"*: Tichy, Sherman, *Control Your Destiny or Someone Else Will*, 91.

43 *"Like many other large companies"*: Noel Tichy and Ram Charan, "Speed, Simplicity, Self-Confidence: An Interview with Jack Welch," *Harvard Business Review* (September–October 1989), https://hbr.org/1989/09/speed-simplicity-self-confidence-an-interview-with-jack-welch.

43 the *"Campaign Against Loyalty"*: Thomas F. O'Boyle, *At Any Cost: Jack Welch, General Electric, and the Pursuit of Profit* (New York: Vintage Books, 1999), 75.

44 *"It was a Jack Welch idea"*: Dennis Rocheleau, in discussion with the author, 2021.

44 *"Some think it's cruel"*: Welch, Byrne, *Jack: Straight from the Gut*, 161.

45 *"Jack loved the approval"*: Bill Lane, *Jacked Up: The Inside Story of How Jack Welch Talked GE Into Becoming the World's Greatest Company* (New York: McGraw-Hill, 2008), 57.

45 *"Don't own a cafeteria"*: Welch, Byrne, *Jack: Straight from the Gut*, 397.

46 *"The idea of who belongs"*: Louis Hyman, in discussion with the author, 2020.

48 *"If this is the best business"*: Tichy, Sherman, *Control Your Destiny Or Someone Else Will*, 238.

48 *"the buzz around the water cooler"*: Welch, Byrne, *Jack: Straight from the Gut*, 120.

48 *"Get that bozo"*: Lane, *Jacked Up*, 28.

49 *"Working for him is like"*: O'Boyle, *At Any Cost*, 83.

50 *"A lot of people initially"*: Scott Tong, "This is how shareholders got to be first in line for profits," *Insider*, Jun 14, 2016, https://www.businessinsider.com/the-story-of-shareholder-value-2016-6.

50 *"The model Jack had"*: Beth Comstock, in discussion with the author, 2020.

51 *"one dynamite company"*: Eric Berg, "G.E. Says Merger May Take a Year," *New York Times*, December 13, 1985, https://www.nytimes.com/1985/12/13/business/ge-says-merger-may-take-a-year.html.

52 *"We didn't need to"*: Bower and Dial, "Jack Welch: General Electric's Revolutionary."

53 *"You're killing all the stocks"*: O'Boyle, *At Any Cost*, 131.

53 *"Okay, how much"*: Gabriel Sherman, *The Loudest Voice in the Room: How the Brilliant, Bombastic Roger Ailes Built Fox News—and Divided a Country* (New York: Random House Publishing Group, 2014), 250.

54 *"We thought Kidder would"*: Welch, Byrne, *Jack: Straight from the Gut*, 218.

55 *"Having this reprehensible scheme"*: Stratford Sherman, "GE's Costly Lesson on

Wall Street," *Fortune*, May 9, 1988, https://money.cnn.com/magazines/fortune/fortune_archive/1988/05/09/70515/index.htm.

56   *"We screwed up"*: Rocheleau, interview.

57   *Of the companies*: Andrei Shleifer and Robert W. Vishny, "The Takeover Wave of the 1980s," *Science New Series*, Vol. 249, No. 4970 (August 17, 1990): 745–749, https://www.jstor.org/stable/2878074.

57   *"There's no commitment"*: Janet Lowe, *Jack Welch Speaks: Wit and Wisdom from the World's Greatest Business Leader* (New York: Wiley, 2008), 21.

58   *"Since I had been involved"*: Welch, Byrne, *Jack: Straight from the Gut*, 233.

58   *It became the world's largest*: John Curran, "GE Capital: Jack Welch's Secret Weapon," *Fortune*, November 10, 1997, https://archive.fortune.com/magazines/fortune/fortune_archive/1997/11/10/233789/index.htm.

60   *"Every planning meeting"*: Byron, *Testosterone Inc.*, 118.

60   *"GE was unique"*: Tom Rogers, in discussion with the author, 2020.

61   *GE Capital would take*: Rob Walker, "Overvalued: Why Jack Welch Isn't God," *New Republic*, June 11, 2001 http://www.robwalker.net/contents/mm_welch.html.

61   *"There was very little"*: Comstock, interview.

61   *"Offsetting the gain"*: Jon Birger, "Glowing Numbers," *Money Magazine*, November 1, 2000, https://money.cnn.com/magazines/moneymag/moneymag_archive/2000/11/01/290856/index.htm.

62   *As a result, GE could*: David Kocieniewski, "G.E.'s Strategies Let It Avoid Taxes Altogether," *New York Times*, March 24, 2011, https://www.nytimes.com/2011/03/25/business/economy/25tax.html.

62   *"Of course we're buying"*: Randall Smith, Steven Lipin, and Amal Naj, "Managing Profits: How General Electric Damps Fluctuations in Its Annual Earnings," *Wall Street Journal*, November 3, 1994.

63   *"We did what we were"*: Steve Kerr, in discussion with the author, 2021.

65   *"eating your own mother"*: O'Boyle, *At Any Cost*, 129.

66   *"That left very little"*: William Lazonick, "Profits Without Prosperity," *Harvard Business Review* (September 2014), https://hbr.org/2014/09/profits-without-prosperity.

67   *"GE is exceptionally good"*: Birger, "Glowing Numbers."

Chapter Three: That's Why They Got Hired

68   *"from the time I get up"*: Rick Wartzman, *The End of Loyalty: The Rise and Fall of Good Jobs in America* (United States: Public Affairs, 2017), 263.

68   *"The best thing"*: "Conversation with Jack Welch," *Wall Street Journal*, September 5, 2001, https://www.wsj.com/articles/SB999668999302595475.

71   *"Most CEOs are ridiculously overpaid"*: Harrison Smith, "Albert J. Dunlap, corporate turnaround specialist accused of accounting fraud, dies at 81," *Washington Post*, January 28, 2019, https://www.washingtonpost.com/local/obituaries/albert-j-dunlap-corporate-turnaround-specialist-accused-of-accounting-fraud-dies-at-81/2019/01/28/652d3a34-230f-11e9-90cd-dedb0c92dc17_story.html.

71   *"orchestrated a fraudulent scheme"*: Floyd Norris, "S.E.C. Accuses Former Sun-

beam Official of Fraud," *New York Times*, May 16, 2001, https://www.nytimes.com /2001/05/16/business/sec-accuses-former-sunbeam-official-of-fraud.html.

72 *"He was the most unpleasant"*: Byron, *Testosterone Inc.*, 19.

72 *"Myself, Jack Welch"*: Art Levy, "Icon: Al Dunlap," *Florida Trend*, June 1, 2008, https://www.floridatrend.com/article/7446/icon-albert-dunlap.

72 *"We have relationships"*: "Management Changes News Conference," *Ford Motor Company*, 2001.

74 *"General Electric is entitled now"*: Geoff Colvin, "What the Hell Happened at GE?", *Fortune*, May 24, 2018, https://fortune.com/longform/ge-decline-what-the-hell -happened/.

74 *"a bellwether of American"*: Christopher A. Bartlett and Meg Wozny, "GE's Two-Decade Transformation: Jack Welch's Leadership," Harvard Business School Case 399–150, (April 1999), https://www.hbs.edu/faculty/Pages/item.aspx?num=67.

74 *In 1956 alone*: Christopher A. Bartlett and Andrew N. McLean, "GE's Talent Machine: The Making of a CEO," Harvard Business School Case 304–049 (October 2003), https://www.hbs.edu/faculty/Pages/item.aspx?num=30482.

74 *"When a company needs a loan"*: Ellen Florian Kratz, "Get Me a CEO from GE!," *Fortune*, April 18, 2005, https://archive.fortune.com/magazines/fortune/fortune _archive/2005/04/18/8257015/index.htm.

75 *On Welch's orders*. Jeff Madrick, *Age of Greed: The Triumph of Finance and the Decline of America, 1970 to the Present* (New York: Vintage Books, 2012).

76 *One evening in 1985*: Tichy, Sherman, *Control Your Destiny or Someone Else Will*, 3.

78 *"GE was the place"*: Bill George, in discussion with the author, 2020.

78 *"That's why they got"*: William Conatay, in discussion with the author, 2020.

78 *"This organization needs"*: Thomas A. Stewart, "Allied-Signal's Turnaround Blitz, *Fortune*, November 30, 1992, https://money.cnn.com/magazines/fortune/fortune _archive/1992/11/30/77194/index.htm.

78 *"Do you deserve your pay?"*: Shawn Tully, "So Mr. Bossidy, We Know You Can Cut. Now Show Us How to Grow," *Fortune*, August 21, 1995, https://archive.fortune .com/magazines/fortune/fortune_archive/1995/08/21/205386/index.htm.

80 *"His strategy is to cut"*: Amy Barrett, "At Honeywell, It's Larry the Knife," *Bloomberg*, November 16, 2001, https://www.bloomberg.com/news/articles/2001-11 -25/at-honeywell-its-larry-the-knife#skip-to-main-content.

80 *"There are so many costs"*: David Cay Johnston, *Perfectly Legal: The Covert Campaign to Rig Our Tax System to Benefit the Super Rich—and Cheat Everybody Else* (New York: Penguin Publishing Group, 2005), 43.

81 *Soon, the employees*: Barbara Nagy and Dan Haar, "Retooling Stanley," *Hartford Courant*, April 9, 1999, https://www.courant.com/news/connecticut/hc-xpm -1999-04-09-9904090011-story.html.

81 *"New Britain built itself"*: Barbara Nagy, "'Mistakes Made,' Stanley Chairman Concedes," *Hartford Courant*, April 29, 1999, https://www.courant.com/news /connecticut/hc-xpm-1999-04-29-9904290065-story.html.

82 *"During this time of war"*: Dan Neal, "Stanley Move to Bermuda Lacks Integrity," *Morning Call*, May 19, 2002.

83 *"The company that doesn't"*: John Tagliabue, "Bringing Good Things to Fiat?," *New York Times*, September 12, 1999, https://www.nytimes.com/1999/09/12/business /bringing-good-things-to-fiat.html.

83 *"I want to maximize"*: Alan Friedman, "'I Wish I Had Been Luckier,' He Says of His Timing : Fresco, Recruited From GE, Battles the Many Ills of Fiat," *New York Times*, July 16, 1999, https://www.nytimes.com/1999/07/16/business/worldbusi ness/IHT-i-wish-i-had-been-luckier-he-says-of-his-timing.html.

84 *"Another Welch disciple"*: George, interview.

85 *"I'm not a communist"*: Tom Tiller, in discussion with the author, 2021.

87 *"There was a little surprise"*: Jerry Useem, "The Long-Forgotten Flight That Sent Boeing Off Course," *Atlantic*, November 20, 2019, https://www.theatlantic.com /ideas/archive/2019/11/how-boeing-lost-its-bearings/602188.

89 *"a culture of financial bullshit"*: Maureen Tkacik, "Crash Course," *New Republic*, September 18, 2019, https://newrepublic.com/article/154944/boeing-737--inves tigation-indonesia-lion-air-ethiopian-airlines-managerial-revolution.

89 *"What you had at"*: Sarah Moore and Leon Grunberg, *Emerging from Turbulence: Boeing and Stories of the American Workplace Today* (Lanham, MD: Rowman & Littlefield Publishers, 2015), 36.

89 *"If in fact there's"*: Useem, "The Long-Forgotten Flight That Sent Boeing Off Course."

90 *"When people say"*: Patricia Callahan, "So why does Harry Stonecipher think he can turn around Boeing?," *Chicago Tribune*, February 29, 2004, https://www.chicago tribune.com/chi-0402290256feb29-story.html.

91 *"that publications about him"*: Cornelia Hegele and Alfred Kieser, "Control the Construction of Your Legend or Someone Else Will: An Analysis of Texts on Jack Welch," *Journal of Management Inquiry*, 2001; 10(4): 298–309.

92 *"pay this man more"*: Lane, *Jacked Up*, 131

92 *"Jack was the rock star"*: Lynn Forrester de Rothschild, in discussion with the author, 2021.

94 *"Any honest Democrat"*: Lawrence Summers, "The Great Liberator," *New York Times*, November 19, 2006, https://www.nytimes.com/2006/11/19/opinion/19 summers.html.

94 *During the 1990s*: Julie Hatch and Angela Clinton, "Job growth in the 1990s: a retrospect," *Bureau of Labor Statistics Monthly Labor Review*, December 2000, https://www.bls.gov/opub/mlr/2000/12/art1full.pdf.

95 *"We have just seen"*: John McCarron, "The Midnight Ride of Felix Rohatyn," *Chicago Tribune*, Feb. 24, 1991, https://www.chicagotribune.com/news/ct-xpm -1991-02-24-9101170790-story.html.

95 *"Increasingly, I have become concerned"*: Arthur Levitt, "The 'Numbers Game,'" September 28, 1998, New York University Center for Law and Business, https:// www.sec.gov/news/speech/speecharchive/1998/spch220.txt.

96 *"Hate bureaucracy"*: Jack Welch, "Jack Welch final GE mgt meeting," Tri Suseno, https://www.youtube.com/watch?v=zwt74Sg96oE.

Chapter Four: The GE Glow

100 *"any credibility at all"*: William M. Carley, "GE Taps Trains Chief For Its Power Division," *Wall Street Journal*, May 6, 1996, https://www.wsj.com/articles/SB83 1345560369963500.

101 *"It's our new global language"*: "Illuminating Changes," *Inside Business*, September 1997.

102 *Under pressure from Welch*: Thomas Gryta and Ted Mann, *Lights Out: Pride, Delusion, and the Fall of General Electric* (Boston: Houghton Mifflin Harcourt, 2021), 28–29.

103 *"One of the"*: David Gelles, "Jeff Immelt Oversaw the Downfall of G.E. Now He'd Like You to Read His Book.," *New York Times*, February 5, 2021, https://www.ny times.com/2021/02/05/business/jeff-immelt-gen-eral-electric-corner-office.html, and Immelt, interview.

104 *"All three exceeded"*: Welch, Byrne, *Jack: Straight from the Gut*, 407.

104 *At a party at Crotonville*: Langone, interview.

104 *"GE has very bright people"*: George Anders, "General Electric Alumni Find It Harder to Shine," *Wall Street Journal*, May 15, 2003, https://www.wsj.com/articles /SB105294834598802700.

105 *"We got out"*: George Anders, "General Electric Alumni Find It Harder to Shine," *Wall Street Journal*, May 15, 2003, https://www.wsj.com/articles/SB10529 4834598802700.

106 *"take some time off"*: Sumner Lemon, "Intuit CEO to Step Down in December," *Computerworld*, August 23, 2007, https://www.computerworld.com/article /2540458/intuit-ceo-to-step-down-in-december.html.

106 *"A lot of GE leaders"*: George, interview.

106 *"They wouldn't know"*: Rotman, interview.

107 *"Boards get overenthusiastic"*: Claudia Deutsch, "The GE way isn't for everyone," *New York Times*, January 4, 2007, https://www.nytimes.com/2007/01/04/business /worldbusiness/04iht-ge.4102488.html.

108 *"I don't know"*: Langone, interview.

109 *"Bob wanted to prove"*: Jennifer Waters, "Nardelli's arrogance led to downfall at Home Depot," *Marketwatch*, January 3, 2007, https://www.marketwatch .com/story/nardellis-arrogance-led-to-downfall-analysts.

109 *"One of Bob's problems"*: Langone, interview.

111 *"Bankruptcy is not something"*: Heidi Moore, "Live-Blogging the Big Three Bailout Hearings," *Wall Street Journal*, December 4, 2008, https://www.wsj.com/articles /BL-DLB-3934.

112 *"The DNA of this"*: Andrew Haeg, "3M at 100 - on the right path for growth?," *Minnesota Public Radio*, June 10, 2002, http://news.minnesota.publicradio.org /features/200206/03_haega_3Mhistory/.

112 *"This was like"*: Andrew Haeg, "A leaner 3M," Minnesota Public Radio, April 22, 2002, http://news.minnesota.publicradio.org/features/200204/22_haega_3mup date/.

113 *"Invention is by its very"*: Brian Hindo, "At 3M, A Struggle Between Efficiency And Creativity," *Businessweek*, June 11, 2007, http://sjbae.pbworks.com/w/file /fetch/44897769/At%203M%20a%20struggle%20between%20efficiency%20 and%20creativity.pdf.

114 *"My second day"*: Gryta and Mann, *Lights Out*, 46.

114 *"Hey, give us a break"*: Jeff Immelt, in discussion with the author, 2021.

114 "It's hard to capture": Immelt, interview.

115 *"Despite a global"*: "GE Reports Record Fourth Quarter and Full-Year Results," GE.com, January 17, 2002, https://www.ge.com/news/press-releases/ge-reports -record-fourth-quarter-and-full-year-results-2001-earnings-grow-11-141.

115 *"honesty remains in doubt"*: William H. Gross, "Buffetting Corporate America," Pimco, March 1, 2002, https://www.pimco.com/en-us/insights/economic-and -market-commentary/investment-outlook/buffetting-corporate-america/.

116 *"GE has been shrouded"*: Gryta and Mann, *Lights Out*, 59

116 *"So much was depending"*: Tiller, interview.

117 *"a bizarre combination"*: William Powers, "High, Low Jack," *Atlantic*, October 1, 2002, https://www.theatlantic.com/politics/archive/2002/10/high-low-jack/37 7387/.

118 *"For some of the true"*: Suzy Welch, "Suzy Welch," *What's Her Story With Sam & Amy*, December 4, 2020, https://podcasts.apple.com/us/podcast/suzy-welch/id15 29348933?i=1000503380613.

119 *"for the remainder of his life"*: Geraldine Fabrikant, "G.E. Expenses For Ex-Chief Cited in Filing," *New York Times*, September 6, 2002, https://www.nytimes. com/2002/09/06/business/ge-expenses-for-ex-chief-cited-in-filing.html.

119 *"I think it was wrong"*: John Crudele, "Scandals' Chilling Effect on Business," *New York Post*, November 12, 2002, https://nypost.com/2002/11/12/scandals-chilling -effect-on-business/.

120 *"responsible for the market's nosedive"*: Powers, "High, Low Jack."

121 *"I felt I had the"*: Tina Brown, "The dish on Liz Smith," *Salon*, February 7, 2003, https://www.salon.com/2003/02/06/smith_20/.

124 *"one of the most"*: "Waste Management Founder and Five Other Former Top Of- ficers Sued for Massive Fraud," SEC.gov, March 26, 2002, https://www.sec.gov /news/press/2002-44.txt.

Chapter Five: Rotten Apples

124 *"combination of what Jack Welch"*: Anthony Bianco, "The Rise and Fall of Den- nis Kozlowski," *Businessweek*, December 23, 2002, https://www.bloomberg.com /news/articles/2002-12-22/the-rise-and-fall-of-dennis-kozlowski.

126 *"Before Enron, neither analysts"*: Jeff Immelt, *Hot Seat: What I Learned Leading a Great American Company* (New York: Simon & Schuster, 2021), 29.

126 *"It seemed to the public"*: Welch, Byrne, *Jack: Straight from the Gut*, 441.

128 *"If a certain group"*: Dominic Gates, "McNerney: Boeing will squeeze suppliers and cut jobs," *Seattle Times*, May 24, 2013, https://www.seattletimes.com/business/mc nerney-boeing-will-squeeze-suppliers-and-cut-jobs.

128 *"the Jack Welch style"*: Rami Grunbaum, "Boeing's McNerney apologizes for remark about 'cowering' workers," *Seattle Times*, July 25, 2014, https://www.seattletimes.com /business/boeingrsquos-mcnerney-apologizes-for-remark-about-lsquocowering rsquo-workers/?_ga=2.111030272.401898431.1600046199-449720823.1599165414.

130 *"I've told my wife"*: Natalie Kitroeff and David Gelles, "Claims of Shoddy Production Draw Scrutiny to a Second Boeing Jet," *New York Times*, April 20, 2019, https://www.nytimes.com/2019/04/20/business/boeing-dreamliner-production -problems.html.

132 *"Without her ignition"*: Sheelah Kolhatkar and Diane Brady, "Jack Welch's Unretirement," *Businessweek*, November 21, 2012, https://www.bloomberg.com/news /articles/2012-11-21/jack-welchs-unretirement.

133 *"We used to say"*: Abby Goodnough, "Executive Who Saved G.E. Is to Train School Principals," *New York Times*, January 14, 2003, https://www.nytimes .com/2003/01/14/nyregion/executive-who-saved-ge-is-to-train-school-princi pals.html.

133 *"Children are not products"*: Mary Hoffman, "Jack Welch is My Daddy," Parent advocates.org, March 8, 2005, https://nycrubberroomreporter.blogspot.com/2015 /11/re-post-of-mary-hoffmans-article-on.html.

133 *"It takes specific things"*: Alex Zimmerman, "New York City closes the door on Mayor Bloomberg's boot camp for principals, marking end of an era," Chalkbeat, August 31, 2017, https://ny.chalkbeat.org/2017/8/31/21100934/new-york-city -closes-the-door-on-mayor-bloomberg-s-boot-camp-for-principals-marking -end-of-an-era.

134 *"Suzy was the ball bearing"*: Sheelah Kolhatkar and Diane Brady, "Jack Welch's Unretirement."

135 *"Donald has been extremely helpful"*: Jack Welch, "Jack Welch and Donald Trump on the Today Show," Jack Welch MBA program, November 12, 2010, https:// www.youtube.com/watch?v=crP1Hv_W1kA.

135 *"I love Jack Welch"*: Muath Bin Hussain, in discussion with the author, 2020.

135 *"His agenda is"*: Sheelah Kolhatkar and Diane Brady, "Jack Welch's Unretirement," *Businessweek*, November 21, 2012, https://www.bloom-berg.com/news /articles/2012-11-21/jack-welchs-unretirement.

138 *"When you tried"*: Aaron Dignan, in discussion with the author, 2020.

139 *"He had the same status"*: Eric Reis, in discussion with the author, 2020.

139 *"Ecomagination fooled many"*: Paul Polman, in discussion with the author, 2020.

Chapter Six: Bad Trades

142 *Had GE looked closely*: Michael Hudson, "Fraud and Folly," Center for Public Integrity, January 6, 2012, https://publicintegrity.org/inequality-poverty-opportu nity/fraud-and-folly-the-untold-story-of-general-electrics-subprime-debacle/.

143 *"I wish we'd never gotten"*: Immelt, *Hot Seat*, 122.

143 *The consultants believed*: DealBook, "With GE Capital, McKinsey Missed the Financial Crisis," *New York Times*, December 6, 2010, https://dealbook.nytimes .com/2010/12/06/with-ge-capital-mckinsey-missed-the-financial-crisis/.

144 *"I was on the train"*: Nelson D. Schwartz and Claudia H. Deutsch, "G.E.'s Shortfall Calls Credibility Into Question," *New York Times*, April 17, 2008, https://www .nytimes.com/2008/04/17/business/17electric.html.

145 *On the afternoon of:* Geoff Colvin and Katie Benner, "GE under siege," *Fortune*, October 15, 2008, https://archive.fortune.com/2008/10/09/news/companies/colvin _ge.fortune/index.htm.

146 *"He said, 'The biggest'"*: Langone, interview.

146 *"Here's the screw-up"*: Natalie Erlich, "Jack Welch: GE CEO Immelt Has 'Credibility Issue,'" CNBC.com, April 16, 2008, https://www.cnbc.com/2008/04/16/jack -welch-ge-ceo-immelt-has-credibility-issue.html.

146 *"Following you has"*: Immelt, *Hot Seat*, 125.

147 *"Not only could anyone"*: Steve Clemons, "Financial Times: The Worst of Times?," *Washington Note*, February 18, 2009, https://washingtonnote.com/the_best_of _tim/.

147 *"The motivation was to"*: Marie Leone and Tim Reason, "GE Settles Accounting Fraud Charges," *CFO*, August 4, 2009, https://www.cfo.com/accounting -tax/2009/08/ge-settles-accounting-fraud-charges/.

148 *"GE bent the accounting rules"*: "SEC Charges General Electric With Accounting Fraud," SEC.gov, August 4, 2009, https://www.sec.gov/news/press/2009/2009 -178.htm.

151 *"On the face of it"*: Francesco Guerrera, "Welch condemns share price focus," *Financial Times*, March 12, 2009, https://www.ft.com/content/294ff1f2-0f27-11de-ba 10-0000779fd2ac.

151 *Not long after:* Larry Kudlow, "An Interview with Jack Welch," *National Review*, March 17, 2009, https://www.nationalreview.com/kudlows-money-politics/inter view-jack-welch-larry-kudlow/.

152 *One of his posts:* Jack Welch, "'Rank-and-Yank'? That's Not How It's Done," LinkedIn.com, December 2, 2013, https://www.linkedin.com/pulse/20131202152255-86541065--rank -and-yank-that-s-not-how-it-s-done.

152 *"Forbes has run headlines"*: Steve Denning, "The Dumbest Idea In The World: Maximizing Shareholder Value," *Forbes*, November 28, 2011, https://www.forbes .com/sites/stevedenning/2011/11/28/maximizing-shareholder-value-the-dumb est-idea-in-the-world.

156 *"You don't want to"*: Dominic Gates and Mike Baker, "The inside story of MCAS: How Boeing's 737 MAX system gained power and lost safeguards," *Seattle Times*, June 22, 2019, https://www.seattletimes.com/seattle-news/times-watchdog/the -inside-story-of-mcas-how-boeings-737-max-system-gained-power-and-lost -safeguards/.

156 *"The timeline was extremely"*: David Gelles, Natalie Kitroeff, Jack Nicas, and Rebecca R. Ruiz, "Boeing Was 'Go, Go, Go' to Beat Airbus With the 737 Max," *New York Times*, March 23, 2019, https://www.nytimes.com/2019/03/23/business /boeing-737-max-crash.html.

156 *"This airplane is designed by clowns"*: David Gelles, "'I Honestly Don't Trust Many People at Boeing': A Broken Culture Exposed," *New York Times*, January 10, 2020,

https://www.nytimes.com/2020/01/10/business/boeing-737-employees-mes
sages.html.

156 *"Frankly right now all"*: David Gelles, "Boeing 737 Max Factory Was Plagued With
Problems, Whistle-Blower Says," *New York Times*, December 9, 2019, https://
www.nytimes.com/2019/12/09/business/boeing-737-max-whistleblower.html.

157 *"That liberal asshole!"*: Lane, *Jacked Up*, 130–131.

158 *"You've lost your mind"*: Simone Foxman, "Twitter laughs at Jack Welch's suggestion that the US jobs report was manipulated," Quartz.com, October 5, 2012,
https://qz.com/12540/twitter-laughs-at-jack-welchs-suggestion-that-the-us-jobs
-report-was-manipulated/.

158 *"100 percent correct"*: Javier David, "Jack Welch '100%' Right, Jobs Data Are
Wrong: Trump," CNBC, October 9, 2012, https://www.cnbc.com/id/49343981.

159 *"In order for the employment"*: Sheelah Kolhatkar and Diane Brady, "Jack Welch's
Unretirement."

159 *"did not find any evidence"*: Ben Casselman, "The Jobs Numbers Are Wrong, But
Don't Blame Obama's 'Chicago Guys,'" FiveThirtyEight, May 1, 2014, https://
fivethirtyeight.com/features/the-jobs-numbers-are-wrong-but-dont-blame
-obamas-chicago-guys/.

159 *He called climate change*: Peter Sasso, "Former General Electric CEO Jack Welch:
Global Warming Skeptic," mrc *NewsBusters*, July 3, 2008, https://www.news
busters.org/blogs/nb/peter-sasso/2008/07/03/former-general-electric-ceo-jack
-welch-global-warming-skeptic.

160 *"While some of America's"*: Gryta and Mann, *Lights Out*, 137

162 *"General Electric was created"*: Bernie Sanders meets with the Daily News Editorial
Board, *New York Daily News*, April 1, 2016, https://www.nydailynews.com/opin
ion/transcript-bernie-sanders-meets-news-editorial-board-article-1.2588306

162 *"GE has been in business"*: Jeffrey Immelt, April 6, 2016, *Washington Post*, https://
www.washingtonpost.com/opinions/ge-ceo-bernie-sanders-says-were-destro
ying-the-moral-fabric-of-america-hes-wrong/2016/04/06/8499bc8c-fc23-11e5
-80e4-c381214de1a3_story.html.

163 *"the imperial CEO"*: James Stewart, "Metaphor for G.E.'s Ills: A Corporate Jet
With No Passengers," *New York Times*, November 2, 2017, https://www.nytimes
.com/2017/11/02/business/ge-corporate-jets.html.

163 *"Jeff brought his best"*: Lauren Thomas, "General Electric's Jeff Immelt is stepping
down; John Flannery named chairman and CEO," CNBC, June 12, 2017, https://
www.cnbc.com/2017/06/12/general-electrics-immelt-is-stepping-down-john
-flannery-named-chairman-and-ceo.html.

164 *"There is very bad blood"*: Brian Schwartz and Charlie Gasparino, "GE CEO feud:
Welch vs. Immelt," FoxBusiness.com, January 10, 2018, https://www.foxbusiness
.com/markets/ge-ceo-feud-welch-vs-immelt.

165 *"GE no longer qualifies"*: Michael Wursthorn and Thomas Gryta, "GE Drops Out
of the Dow After More Than a Century," *Wall Street Journal*, June 19, 2018 https://
www.wsj.com/articles/walgreens-to-replace-ge-in-dow-industrials-1529443336

Chapter Seven: Negative Externalities

169 *"The research evidence has"*: "How Layoffs Hurt Companies," *Knowledge@Wharton*, April 12, 2016, https://knowledge.wharton.upenn.edu/article/how-layoffs-cost -companies/.

171 *"This caused people to"*: Bob Sutton, "Dysfunctional Internal Competition at Microsoft: We've seen the enemy, and it is us!," *Work Matters*, July 6, 2012, https://bobsutton.typepad.com/my_weblog/2012/07/dysfunctional-internal -competition-at-microsoft-weve-seen-the-enemy-and-it-is-us.html.

171 *"We met those expectations"*: Reeves Wiedeman, *Billion Dollar Loser: The Epic Rise and Spectacular Fall of Adam Neumann and Wework* (New York: Little Brown, 2021), 207.

172 *"our nature as humans"*: Jodi Kantor, Karen Weise and Grace Ashford, "The Amazon That Customers Don't See," *New York Times*, June 15, 2021, https://www.ny times.com/interactive/2021/06/15/us/amazon-workers.html.

172 *"We're not treated as human beings"*: Patrice Taddonio, "'You're Just Dispos-able': New Accounts from Former Amazon Employees Raise Questions About Working Conditions," *Frontline*, February 14, 2020, https://www.pbs.org/wgbh /frontline/article/youre-just-disposable-new-accounts-from-former-amazon -employees-raise-questions-about-working-conditions/.

174 *"The people we hire here"*: "Amazon Chief's Message to Employees," *New York Times*, August 17, 2015, https://www.nytimes.com/2015/08/18/business/amazon -chiefs-message-to-employees.html.

177 *Companies in highly concentrated industries also spend*: Tom Orlik, Justin Jimenez and Cedric Sam, "World-Dominating Superstar Firms Get Bigger, Techier, and More Chinese," Bloomberg, May 21, 2021, https://www.bloomberg.com /graphics/2021-biggest-global-companies-growth-trends/

178 *"We'd read everything about Jack"*: Francisco S. Homem de Mello, *The 3G Way: An Introduction to the Management Style of the Trio Who's Taken Over Some of the Most Important Icons of American Capitalism*, (Brazil: Ajax Books, 2014), 124.

178 *"We're a copycat, really"*: Daniel Roberts, "Here's what happens when 3G Capi-tal buys your company," *Fortune*, March 25, 2015, https://fortune.com/2015/03 /25/3g-capital-heinz-kraft-buffett/.

179 *"Yes, there will"*: Homem de Mello, *The 3G Way*, 42.

179 *Those who remained*: Jennifer Reingold, "Squeezing Heinz," *Fortune*, October 10, 2013, https://fortune.com/2013/10/10/squeezing-heinz/.

180 *"3G is a perfect partner"*: Rob Mckenzie, "3G boss Jorge Paulo Lemann cut his teeth on Wimbledon lesson," *National News*, April 3, 2015, https://www.the nationalnews.com/business/3g-boss-jorge-paulo-lemann-cut-his-teeth-on -wimbledon-lesson-1.47000.

182 *"It was all in the name"*: Khadeeja Safdar and Aruna Viswanatha, "Inside Under Armour's Sales Scramble: 'Pulling Forward Every Quarter,'" *Wall Street Journal*, November 14, 2019, https://www.wsj.com/articles/inside-under-armours-sales -scramble-pulling-forward-every-quarter-11573777489.

183 *A 2019 study found*: Aimee Picchi, "Almost half of all Americans work in low-wage jobs," CBS News, December 2, 2019, https://www.cbsnews.com/news/minimum-wage-2019-almost-half-of-all-americans-work-in-low-wage-jobs/.

189 *"The second crash"*: Zipporah Kuria, in discussion with the author, 2019.

190 *"I would walk before"*: Natalie Kitroeff and David Gelles, "Boeing C.E.O. Knew About Pilot's Warnings Before Second Crash," *New York Times*, October 29, 2019, https://www.nytimes.com/2019/10/29/business/boeing-ceo-hearing.html.

192 *"My forever mentor"*: Dave Calhoun, in discussion with the author, 2020.

192 *"It's more than I imagined"*: Natalie Kitroeff and David Gelles, "'It's More Than I Imagined': Boeing's New C.E.O. Confronts Its Challenges," *New York Times*, March 5, 2020, https://www.nytimes.com/2020/03/05/business/boeing-david-calhoun.html.

194 *Stumo penned an op-ed*: A Boeing 737 Max crash killed my daughter. Boeing's board and CEO don't inspire optimism," *USA Today*, Michael Stumo. January 17, 2020. https://www.usatoday.com/story/opinion/2020/01/17/boeing-david-calhoun-airline-safety-culture-lawsuit-ceo-column/4479056002/.

195 *"I knew it was going"*: Keith Naughton, "The World According to Trump," *Newsweek*, February 29, 2004, https://www.newsweek.com/world-according-trump-131529.

196 *"Jack Welch is a peanut"*: Keith Kelly, "Welch Book Deal Trumped," *New York Post*, February 6, 2004, https://nypost.com/2004/02/06/welch-book-deal-trumped-the-donald-1m-ups-jacks-4m-harper-contract/.

196 *"It's almost must-see TV"*: Jack Welch, "Welch: 'No' to Serving as Trump Treasury Secretary," CNN, October 3, 2015, https://www.cnn.com/videos/tv/2015/10/03/exp-smr-welch.cnn.

196 *"I know I got a better shot"*: Jack Welch, "Why I back Donald Trump: Jack Welch," CNBC, September 20, 2016, https://www.cnbc.com/video/2016/09/20/why-i-back-donald-trump-jack-welch.html.

198 *"We had a hell of a meeting"*: Jack Welch, "Jack Welch: We had a 'hell of a meeting' with Trump," Fox Business, February 3, 2017, https://www.youtube.com/watch?v=hYl1qphvE3E.

198 *"I give him an A"*: Jack Welch, "Jack Welch: I Give Trump a D- on Management and Bureaucracy," CNBC, May 17, 2017, https://www.youtube.com/watch?v=G5nd_FIdJ3g.

Chapter Eight: Beyond Welchism

204 *"He built Port Sunlight"*: David Gelles, "He Ran an Empire of Soap and Mayonnaise. Now He Wants to Reinvent Capitalism," *New York Times*, August 29, 2019, https://www.nytimes.com/2019/08/29/business/paul-polman-unilever-corner-office.html.

206 *"It was a purely financial"*: David Gelles, "He Ran an Empire of Soap and Mayonnaise. Now He Wants to Reinvent Capitalism," *New York Times*, August 29, 2019, https://www.nytimes.com/2019/08/29/business/paul-polman-unilever-corner-office.html.

208 *"Our mission as"*: Dan Schulman, in discussion with the author, 2021.

213 *"Benefit Corporation legislation"*: Elissa Loughman, "Benefit Corporation Update: Patagonia Passes B Impact Assessment, Improves Score to 116," Patagonia .com, https://www.patagonia.com/stories/benefit-corporation-update-patagonia -passes-b-impact-assessment-improves-score-to-116/story-17871.html.

213 *"It concerns us that"*: Lazonick, *Profits Without Prosperity*.

213 *"Society is demanding"*: Larry Fink, "A Sense of Purpose," Harvard Law School Forum on Corporate Governance, January 17, 2018, https://corpgov.law.harvard .edu/2018/01/17/a-sense-of-purpose/.

216 In the 1970s Chrysler: Susan Holmberg, "Workers on Corporate Boards? Germany's Had Them for Decades," *New York Times*, January 6, 2019, https://www .nytimes.com/2019/01/06/opinion/warren-workers-boards.html.

220 *"If you want to maximize"*: Deonna Anderson, "Paul Polman: 'Businesses cannot succeed in societies that fail,'" *GreenBiz*, July 22, 2020, https://www.greenbiz.com /article/paul-polman-businesses-cannot-succeed-societies-fail.

221 *"More than anything else"*: Marty Steinberg, "Jack Welch, former chairman and CEO of GE, dies at 84," CNBC, March 2, 2020, https://www.cnbc.com/2020/03/02 /jack-welch-obit-ge.html.

221 *"Jack set the path"*: Jill Goldsmith, "Jack Welch Dies: Legendary General Electric CEO Was 84," *Yahoo News*, March 2, 2020, https://www.yahoo.com/now/jack -welch-dies-legendary-general-144744535.html.

221 *"He stood tall"*: Reuters Staff, "Trump, business leaders comment on Jack Welch's death," Reuters, March 2, 2020, https://www.reuters.com/article/people-jack welch/quote-box-trump-business-leaders-comment-on-jack-welchs-death -idUSL4N2AV4GM.

222 During this same time: Douglas MacMillan, Peter Whoriskey and Jonathan O'Connell, graphics by Chris Alcantara, "America's biggest companies are flourishing during the pandemic and putting thousands of people out of work," *Washington Post*, December 16, 2020, https://www.washingtonpost.com/graphics /2020/business/50-biggest-companies-coronavirus-layoffs/.

223 *"At Norwegian Cruise Line"*: David Gelles, "C.E.O. Pay Remains Stratospheric, Even at Companies Battered by Pandemic," *New York Times*, April 24, 2021, https://www.nytimes.com/2021/04/24/business/ceos-pandemic-compensation .html.

223 *"One study showed"*: Jerry Useem, "Beware of Corporate Promises," August 6, 2020, https://www.theatlantic.com/ideas/archive/2020/08/companies-stand-solidarity -are-licensing-themselves-discriminate/614947/.

224 *"Business Roundtable: Your 2019 Commitment"*: "Senator Warren to Business Roundtable: Your 2019 Commitment to 'Promote an Economy that Serves all Americans' Was an Empty Publicity Stunt," Elizabeth Warren, September 17, 2020, https://www.warren.senate.gov/newsroom/press-releases/senator-warren -to-business-roundtable-your-2019-commitment-to-promote-an-economy -that-serves-all-americans-was-an-empty-publicity-stunt.

227 *"I'm the guy"*: David Gelles, "Jeff Immelt Oversaw the Downfall of G.E. Now He'd

Like You to Read His Book.," *New York Times*, February 5, 2021, https://www
.nytimes.com/2021/02/05/business/jeff-immelt-general-electric-corner-office
.html, and Immelt, interview.

230 *"a generation or even more"*: Rutger Bregman, "The neoliberal era is ending.
What comes next?," *The Correspondent*, May 14, 2020, https://thecorrespon
dent.com/466/the-neoliberal-era-is-ending-what-comes-next/61655148676
-a00ee89a.

INDEX

in JW vision for GE, 2–3, 4–8, 20,
33–35, 52, 68, 151–52
stakeholder capitalism vs., 36, 37,
151–52, 203–20, 231
Welchism and, 8–9, *see also* Welchism
Sharer, Kevin, 106
Sheffer, Gary, 39–40
Siegel, Marty, 54–55
60 Minutes (CBS TV program), 42, 131
Six Sigma, 101, 112–13, 127
Skilling, Jeffrey, 124
Sloan, Alfred, 25
Smith, Greg, 190
Smith, Kyle, 89
Sonnenfeld, Jeffrey, 164
Sorscher, Stan, 89
Southwest Airlines, 190
S&P Dow Jones Indices, 165
Spencer Stuart, 78
Spitzer, Eliot, 109–10, 125–26
Sprint, 169
SPX, 77, 105
stack ranking:
Amazon and, 171–74
at Ford, 171
at Microsoft, 171
by 3G Capital, 179
at 3M, 112, 171
Vitality Curve at GE, 4, 44–45, 96–97,
152, 171, 172, 174
at WeWork, 171
stagflation, 18, 25, 33
stakeholder capitalism, 203–20, 231
activism and, 149–52
B Corp movement / public benefit
corporations in, 212–13
at BlackRock, 213–14
Business Roundtable and, 26, 214,
222–24
at Chrysler, 216
at Delta Air Lines, 215
employee board representation,
216–17
employee compensation, 207–11,
215–16, 220
executive compensation in, 217–18,
219–20
GE as once-model corporate citizen, 4,
16, 20, 21–26, 42–43, 74, 165
long-term view in, 217–18
minimum wage and, 93, 183, 209, 215,
218, 223

nature of, 12–13
need for, 12–13
at PayPal, 207–11, 215, 220
at REI, 215–16
shareholder capitalism vs., 36, 37,
151–52, 203–20, 231
strengthening antitrust policies, 219
sustainability and good governance
in, 205–7
taxation in, 23, 218–19
at Unilever, 203–7, 211, 217, 220
upskilling workers, 216
World Economic Forum and, 211–12
see also Golden Age of Capitalism
Stanley, Frederick T., 80
Stanley Works, 77, 83–84, 110
Starbucks, 170
Stephanopoulos, George, 157
Stephenson, Randall, 175
Stiglitz, Joseph, 132
stock buybacks, *see* financialization
(generally); financialization at GE
stock market performance, *see*
shareholder capitalism
Stone, Roger, 196
Stonecipher, Harry, 87–90, 127, 128–29,
187, 191, 194
Stumo, Michael, 194
Stumo, Samya, 194
subprime mortgage crisis, 8, 137–38,
141–45, 148–49, 150, 165, 225
Success magazine, 91, 132
Summers, Larry, 93–94
Sunbeam Products, 71–72
Sundstrand, 87
Swope, Gerard, 22–23, 43
Symantec, 77, 105–6

Taco Bell, 170
TaskRabbit, 170
taxation:
"active financing" exception, 62–63
corporate headquarters in Bermuda,
81–82
decline in U.S. corporate taxes, 63
in GE dealmaking, 51, 61, 62–63
in stakeholder capitalism, 23, 218–19
tax breaks for corporate expansion /
relocations, 88–89, 173, 219
tax reduction efforts, 10, 63, 81–82,
88–89, 162, 185, 200–201
Trump and, 200–201